ON FREUD'S
"SCREEN MEMORIES"

CONTEMPORARY FREUD
Turning Points and Critical Issues

Series Editor: Gennaro Saragnano

IPA Publications Committee
Gennaro Saragnano (Rome), Chair; Leticia Glocer Fiorini (Buenos Aires), Consultant; Samuel Arbiser (Buenos Aires); Paulo Cesar Sandler (São Paulo); Christian Seulin (Lyon); Mary Kay O'Neil (Montreal); Gail S Reed (New York); Catalina Bronstein (London); Rhoda Bawdekar (London), ex-officio as Publications Officer; Paul Crake (London), IPA Executive Director (ex officio)

On Freud's "Analysis Terminable and Interminable"
edited by Joseph Sandler

On Freud's "On Narcissism: An Introduction"
edited by Joseph Sandler, Ethel Spector Person, Peter Fonagy

On Freud's "Observations on Transference-Love"
edited by Ethel Spector Person, Aiban Hagelin, Peter Fonagy

On Freud's "Creative Writers and Day-Dreaming"
edited by Ethel Spector Person, Peter Fonagy, Sérvulo Augusto Figueira

On Freud's "A Child Is Being Beaten"
edited by Ethel Spector Person

On Freud's "Group Psychology and the Analysis of the Ego"
edited by Ethel Spector Person

On Freud's "Mourning and Melancholia"
edited by Leticia Glocer Fiorini, Thierry Bokanowski, Sergio Lewkowicz

On Freud's "The Future of an Illusion"
edited by Mary Kay O'Neil and Salman Akhtar

On Freud's "Splitting of the Ego in the Process of Defence"
edited by Thierry Bokanowski and Sergio Lewkowicz

On Freud's "Femininity"
edited by Leticia Glocer Fiorini and Graciela Abelin-Sas

On Freud's "Constructions in Analysis"
edited by Thierry Bokanowski and Sergio Lewkowicz

On Freud's "Beyond the Pleasure Principle"
edited by Salman Akhtar and Mary Kay O'Neil

On Freud's "Negation"
edited by Mary Kay O'Neil and Salman Akhtar

On Freud's "On Beginning the Treatment"
edited by Christian Seulin and Gennaro Saragnano

On Freud's "Inhibitions, Symptoms and Anxiety"
edited by Samuel Arbiser and Jorge Schneider

On Freud's "The Unconscious"
edited by Salman Akhtar and Mary Kay O'Neil

ON FREUD'S "SCREEN MEMORIES"

Edited by
Gail S. Reed and Howard B. Levine

Series Editor
Gennaro Saragnano

CONTEMPORARY FREUD
Turning Points and Critical Issues

LONDON AND NEW YORK

First published 2015 by Karnac Books Ltd.

Published 2018 by Routledge
2 Park Square, Milton Park, Abingdon, Oxon OX14 4RN
711 Third Avenue, New York, NY 10017, USA

Routledge is an imprint of the Taylor & Francis Group, an informa business

Copyright © 2015 to Gail S. Reed and Howard B. Levine for the edited collection, and to the individual authors for their contributions.

The rights of the contributors to be identified as the authors of this work have been asserted in accordance with §77 and 78 of the Copyright Design and Patents Act 1988.

All rights reserved. No part of this book may be reprinted or reproduced or utilised in any form or by any electronic, mechanical, or other means, now known or hereafter invented, including photocopying and recording, or in any information storage or retrieval system, without permission in writing from the publishers.

Notice:
Product or corporate names may be trademarks or registered trademarks, and are used only for identification and explanation without intent to infringe.

British Library Cataloguing in Publication Data

A C.I.P. for this book is available from the British Library

ISBN 9781782200550 (pbk)

Edited, designed and produced by The Studio Publishing Services Ltd
www.publishingservicesuk.co.uk
e-mail: studio@publishingservicesuk.co.uk

CONTENTS

CONTEMPORARY FREUD
    IPA Publications Committee   vii

ACKNOWLEDGEMENTS   ix

EDITORS AND CONTRIBUTORS   x

PART I
"Screen memories" (1899a)
    Sigmund Freud   1

PART II
Discussion of "Screen memories"   25

1   Screen memories: a reintroduction
    Gail S. Reed and Howard B. Levine   27

2   The screen memory and the act of remembering
    Lucy LaFarge   36

3	Screen memories: the faculty of memory and the importance of the patient's history *Franco De Masi*	58
4	The screen and behind it: manifest and latent themes in Freud's *Über Deckerinnerungen* *Rivka R. Eifermann*	80
5	The waning of screen memories: from the Age of Neuroses to an Autistoid Age *Jorge L. Ahumada*	104
6	"Screen memories" revisited *Shlomith Cohen*	118
7	Reading Freud's semiotic passion *John P. Muller*	135
8	Phyllis Greenacre: screen memories and reconstruction *Nellie Thompson*	150
9	Screen memories today: a neuropsychoanalytic essay of definition *Florence Guignard*	172
10	Some final thoughts on memory and screen memory *Howard B. Levine and Gail S. Reed*	185
REFERENCES		192
INDEX		205

CONTEMPORARY FREUD

IPA Publications Committee

This significant series was founded by Robert Wallerstein and subsequently edited by Joseph Sandler, Ethel Spector Person, Peter Fonagy, and lately by Leticia Glocer Fiorini. Its important contributions have always greatly interested psychoanalysts of different latitudes. It is therefore my great honour, as the new Chair of the Publications Committee of the International Psychoanalytical Association, to continue the tradition of this most successful series.

The objective of this series is to approach Freud's work from a present and contemporary point of view. On the one hand, this means highlighting the fundamental contributions of his work that constitute the axes of psychoanalytic theory and practice. On the other, it implies the possibility of getting to know and spreading the ideas of present psychoanalysts about Freud's *oeuvre*, both where they coincide and where they differ.

This series considers at least two lines of development: a contemporary reading of Freud that reclaims his contributions, and a clarification of the logical and epistemic perspectives from which he is read today.

Freud's theory has branched out, and this has led to a theoretical, technical, and clinical pluralism that has to be worked through. It has therefore become necessary to avoid a snug and uncritical coexistence of concepts in order to consider systems of increasing complexities that take into account both the convergences and the divergences of the categories at play.

Consequently, this project has involved an additional task—that is, gathering psychoanalysts from different geographical regions representing, in addition, different theoretical stances, in order to be able to show their polyphony. This also means an extra effort for the reader that has to do with distinguishing and discriminating, establishing relations or contradictions that each reader will have to eventually work through.

Being able to listen to other theoretical viewpoints is also a way of exercising our listening capacities in the clinical field. This means that the listening should support a space of freedom that would allow us to hear what is new and original.

In this spirit we have brought together authors deeply rooted in the Freudian tradition and others who have developed theories that had not been explicitly taken into account in Freud's work.

"Screen Memories" is one of Freud's first and most original articles. Written in 1899, it is part of the result of his own pioneering work of self-analysis, which would soon culminate with the "*Traumdeutung*", and contains the seminal idea that memories, when referred to one's infancy, are subject to processes of concealment and retranscription in order to keep unconscious material that would generate anxiety in the subject. In this new and important volume, edited by Gail S. Reed and Howard B. Levine, Freud's concept of "screen memories" has been revisited in depth by the editors and by eight highly distinguished psychoanalysts, from different geographical areas and from different theoretical frames, who have written about the relevant clinical complexities it uncovers, and have put them in the light of contemporary psychoanalytic theory and practice, thus perfectly fulfilling the aim of this book series. Special thanks are therefore due to all the contributors to this volume which enriches the Contemporary Freud series.

Gennaro Saragnano
Series Editor
Chair, IPA Publications Committee

ACKNOWLEDGEMENTS

To our eight contributors, for struggling creatively with screen memories.

EDITORS AND CONTRIBUTORS

Jorge L. Ahumada is a training analyst at the Argentine Psychoanalytic Association, a Distinguished Fellow of the British Psychoanalytical Society. He was Mary S. Sigourney Awardee for 1996 and has authored *The Logics of the Mind* (Karnac) and *Insight. Essays on Psychoanalytic Knowing* (Routledge).

Shlomith Cohen is a training psychoanalyst for children and adults at the Israel Psychoanalytic Society. She served as the head of its scientific committee. She has contributed theoretically and clinically to the creation of a therapeutic model for children at high risk for abuse and neglect in their families.

Franco De Masi is a training analyst of the Italian Psychoanalytical Society. His main interests have been focused on the theoretical and technical psychoanalytical issues related to severely ill or psychotic patients. Among his books are: *Sadomasochistic Perversion. The Object and Theories* (Karnac, 2003), *Making Death Thinkable. A Psychoanalytical Contribution to the Problem of the Transience of Life* (FAB, 2004), *Vulnerabilty to Psychosis* (Karnac, 2009).

Rivka Eifermann is Professor Emeritus, Psychology Department, the Hebrew University of Jerusalem. She is a training, teaching, and supervising analyst of the Israel Psychoanalytic Society, past president of the Society, and former head of its training committee. Her psychoanalytic publications are mainly in the areas of self-analysis, psychoanalytic listening, and teaching psychoanalysis.

Florence Guignard, while studying to become a psychoanalyst, studied and taught in Geneva in the fields of clinical psychology and research. She then spent forty-three years in Paris as a training analyst of the Paris Society. In 1994, she created the European Society for Child Analysis (SEPEA). A Member of the COCAP/IPA since its creation, she was its Chair from 2010 to 2013. She was the Head of the team of translation of the *International Journal of Psychoanalysis* into French: *L'année Psychanalytique Internationale*. She has written more than 250 papers and several books, among the latter: *Au Vif de l'Infantile*, *Epître à l'objet*, and *Mère et fille, entre partage et clivage*.

Lucy LaFarge, MD is a training and supervising analyst at the Columbia University Psychoanalytic Center and clinical professor of psychiatry at Weil Cornell Medical College. Currently editor for North America of the *International Journal of Psychoanalysis*, she has published papers on psychoanalytic listening and technique, narcissism, revenge, forgiveness, and deception.

Howard B. Levine is a member of the faculty at the Psychoanalytic Institute of New England East (PINE), a member of the faculty and supervising analyst at the Massachusetts Institute for Psychoanalysis (MIP), and is in private practice in Brookline, Massachusetts. He is a founding member of the Group for the Study of Psychoanalytic Process (GSPP) and The Boston Group for Psychoanalytic Studies, Inc. (BGPS). Dr Levine has served on the editorial boards of the *International Journal of Psychoanalysis*, the *Journal of the American Psychoanalytic Association*, and *Psychoanalytic Inquiry*, and currently serves as North American Representative on the Board of the IPA. He is editor of *Adult Analysis and Childhood Sexual Abuse* (Analytic Press, 1990), co-editor of *The Psychology of the Nuclear Threat* (Analytic Press, 1986), *Growth and Turbulence in the Container/Contained*

(Routledge, 2013), and *Unrepresented States and the Construction of Meaning* (Karnac, 2013). He has authored numerous articles, book chapters, and reviews on various subjects related to psychoanalytic process and technique, intersubjectivity, comparative psychoanalytic studies, the treatment of primitive personality disorders, and the consequences and treatment of early trauma and childhood sexual abuse.

John P. Muller, PhD, is a faculty member and supervising psychoanalyst on the staff at the Austen Riggs Center, a psychiatric hospital in Stockbridge, Massachusetts. He has published widely on Lacan, Peirce, and semiotics.

Gail S. Reed, PhD, LP practices psychoanalysis in New York City. She is the president and a founding member of the Group for the Study of the Psychoanalytic Process (GSPP), and a training analyst and founding member of the Berkshire Psychoanalytic Institute. She is also a training analyst of the Contemporary Freudian Society (IPA) and NPAP. She is a co-editor with Dominique Scarfone and Howard Levine of *Unrepresented States and the Construction of Meaning* (Karnac, 2013) and author of *Transference Neurosis and Psychoanalytic Experience* (Yale University Press, 1994) and *Clinical Understanding* (Aronson, 1996). In addition to publishing over thirty articles, she is currently an associate editor of JAPA and on the Editorial Board of the *Psychoanalytic Quarterly* and other publications.

Nellie Thompson, PhD is an historian and member of the New York Psychoanalytic Society and Institute. Her research interests include the role of women in the psychoanalytic movement and the contributions of émigré analysts to psychoanalysis in America.

PART I

"Screen memories" (1899a)

Sigmund Freud

EDITOR'S NOTE

ÜBER DECKERINNERUNGEN

(a) GERMAN EDITIONS:
1899   *Mschr. Psychiat. Neurol.*, **6** (3), 215–30. (September.)
1925   *G.S.*, **1**, 465–88.
1952   *G.W.*, **1**, 531–54.

(b) ENGLISH TRANSLATION:
         'Screen Memories'
1950   *C.P.*, **5**, 47–69. (Tr. James Strachey.)

The present translation is a slightly revised reprint of that published in 1950.

An unpublished letter of Freud's to Fliess of May 25, 1899, tells him that on that date this paper was sent in to the editor of the periodical in which it appeared later in the year. He adds that he was immensely pleased by it during its production, which he takes as a bad omen for its future fate.

The concept of 'screen memories' was here introduced by Freud for the first time. It was no doubt brought into focus by his consideration of the particular instance which occupies the major part of the paper and which had been alluded to in a letter to Fliess of January 3, 1899 (Letter 101). Nevertheless the topic was closely related to several others which had been occupying his mind for many months previously—in fact ever since he had embarked on his self-analysis in the summer of 1897—problems concerning the operation of memory and its distortions, the importance and *raison d'être* of phantasies, the amnesia covering our early years, and, behind all this, infantile sexuality. Readers of the Fliess letters will find many approaches to the present discussion. See, for instance, the remarks on phantasies in Draft M of May 25, 1897 and in Letter 66 of July 7, 1897. The screen memories analysed by Freud at the end of

Chapter IV of the 1907 edition of *The Psychopathology of Everyday Life* (1901*b*) go back to this same summer of 1897.

It is a curious thing that the type of screen memory mainly considered in the present paper—one in which an early memory is used as a screen for a later event—almost disappears from later literature. What has since come to be regarded as the regular type—one in which an early event is screened by a later memory—is only barely alluded to here, though it was already the one almost exclusively dealt with by Freud only two years later, in the chapter of *The Psychopathology of Everyday Life* just mentioned. (See also footnote, p. 322.)

The intrinsic interest of this paper has been rather undeservedly overshadowed by an extraneous fact. It was not difficult to guess that the incident described in it was in fact an autobiographical one, and this became a certainty after the appearance of the Fliess correspondence. Many of the details, however, can be traced in Freud's published writings. Thus the children in the screen memory were in fact his nephew John and his niece Pauline, who appear at several points in *The Interpretation of Dreams* (1900*a*). (Cf., for instance, *Standard Ed.*, **5**, 424–5, 483 and 486.) These were the children of his much older half-brother, who is mentioned in Chapter X of *The Psychopathology of Everyday Life* (1901*b*), ibid., **6**, 227. This brother, after the break-up of the family at Freiberg when Freud was three, had settled in Manchester, where Freud visited him at the age of nineteen—not twenty, as is implied here (p. 314)—a visit alluded to in the same passage in *The Psychopathology of Everyday Life* and also in *The Interpretation of Dreams* (ibid., **5**, 519). His age at the time of his first return to Freiberg was also a year less than is represented here. He was sixteen, as he tells us in 'Letter to the Burgomaster of Příbor' (1931*e*), ibid., **21**, 259. We learn from this source too that the family with whom he stayed was named Fluss, and it was one of the daughters of this family, Gisela, who was the central figure of the present anecdote. The episode is fully described in the first volume of Ernest Jones's biography (1953, 27–9 and 35–7).[1]

[1] The name of Gisela Fluss makes an unexpected and quite unimportant appearance in Freud's notes on the 'Rat Man' analysis (1955*a*), *Standard Ed.*, **10**, 280.

SCREEN MEMORIES

In the course of my psycho-analytic treatment of cases of hysteria, obsessional neurosis, etc., I have often had to deal with fragmentary recollections which have remained in the patient's memory from the earliest years of his childhood. As I have shown elsewhere,[1] great pathogenic importance must be attributed to the impressions of that time of life. But the subject of childhood memories is in any case bound to be of psychological interest, for they bring into striking relief a fundamental difference between the psychical functioning of children and of adults. No one calls in question the fact that the experiences of the earliest years of our childhood leave ineradicable traces in the depths of our minds. If, however, we seek in our *memories* to ascertain what were the impressions that were destined to influence us to the end of our lives, the outcome is either nothing at all or a relatively small number of isolated recollections which are often of dubious or enigmatic importance. It is only from the sixth or seventh year onwards—in many cases only after the tenth year—that our lives can be reproduced in memory as a connected chain of events. From that time on, however, there is also a direct relation between the psychical significance of an experience and its retention in the memory. Whatever seems important on account of its immediate or directly subsequent effects is recollected; whatever is judged to be inessential is forgotten. If I can remember an event for a long time after its occurrence, I regard the fact of having retained it in my memory as evidence of its having made a deep impression on me at the time. I feel surprised at forgetting something important; and I feel even more surprised, perhaps, at remembering something apparently indifferent.

It is only in certain pathological mental conditions that the relation holding in normal adults between the psychical significance of an event and its retention in memory once more ceases to apply. For instance, a hysteric habitually shows amnesia for some or all of the experiences which led to the onset

[1] [Cf., for instance, 'The Aetiology of Hysteria' (1896), p. 202 f. above.]

of his illness and which from that very fact have become important to him and, apart from that fact, may have been important on their own account. The analogy between pathological amnesia of this kind and the normal amnesia affecting our early years seems to me to give a valuable hint at the intimate connection that exists between the psychical content of neuroses and our infantile life.

We are so much accustomed to this lack of memory of the impressions of childhood that we are apt to overlook the problem underlying it and are inclined to explain it as a self-evident consequence of the rudimentary character of the mental activities of children. Actually, however, a normally developed child of three or four already exhibits an enormous amount of highly organized mental functioning in the comparisons and inferences which he makes and in the expression of his feelings; and there is no obvious reason why amnesia should overtake these psychical acts, which carry no less weight than those of a later age.

Before dealing with the psychological problems attaching to the earliest memories of childhood, it would of course be essential to make a collection of material by circularizing a fairly large number of normal adults and discovering what kind of recollections they are able to produce from these early years. A first step in this direction was taken in 1895 by V. and C. Henri, who sent round a paper of questions drawn up by them. The highly suggestive results of their questionnaire, which brought in replies from 123 persons, were published by the two authors in 1897. I have no intention at present of discussing the subject as a whole, and I shall therefore content myself with emphasizing the few points which will enable me to introduce the notion of what I have termed 'screen memories'.

The age to which the content of the earliest memories of childhood is usually referred back is the period between the ages of two and four. (This is the case with 88 persons in the series observed by the Henris.) There are some, however, whose memory reaches back further—even to the time before the completion of their first year; and, on the other hand, there are some whose earliest recollections go back only to their sixth, seventh, or even eighth year. There is nothing at the moment to show what else is related to these individual differences; but it

SCREEN MEMORIES

is to be noticed, say the Henris, that a person whose earliest recollection goes back to a very tender age—to the first year of his life, perhaps—will also have at his disposal further detached memories from the following years, and that he will be able to reproduce his experiences as a continuous chain from an earlier point of time—from about his fifth year—than is possible for other people, whose first recollection dates from a later time. Thus not only the date of the appearance of the first recollection but the whole function of memory may, in the case of some people, be advanced or retarded.

Quite special interest attaches to the question of what is the usual *content* of these earliest memories of childhood. The psychology of adults would necessarily lead us to expect that those experiences would be selected as worth remembering which had aroused some powerful emotion or which, owing to their consequences, had been recognized as important soon after their occurrence. And some indeed of the observations collected by the Henris appear to fulfil this expectation. They report that the most frequent content of the first memories of childhood are on the one hand occasions of fear, shame, physical pain, etc., and on the other hand important events such as illnesses, deaths, fires, births of brothers and sisters, etc. We might therefore be inclined to assume that the principle governing the choice of memories is the same in the case of children as in that of adults. It is intelligible—though the fact deserves to be explicitly mentioned—that the memories retained from childhood should necessarily show evidence of the difference between what attracts the interest of a child and of an adult. This easily explains why, for instance, one woman reports that she remembers a number of accidents that occurred to her dolls when she was two years old but has no recollection of the serious and tragic events she might have observed at the same period.

Now, however, we are met by a fact that is diametrically opposed to our expectations and cannot fail to astonish us. We hear that there are some people whose earliest recollections of childhood are concerned with everyday and indifferent events which could not produce any emotional effect even in children, but which are recollected (*too* clearly, one is inclined to say)[1] in

[1] [Cf. footnote 1, p. 291 above. The point appears again below on pp. 312 and 313.]

every detail, while approximately contemporary events, even if, on the evidence of their parents, they moved them intensely at the time, have not been retained in their memory. Thus the Henris mention a professor of philology whose earliest memory, dating back to between the ages of three and four, showed him a table laid for a meal and on it a basin of ice. At the same period there occurred the death of his grandmother which, according to his parents, was a severe blow to the child. But the professor of philology, as he now is, has no recollection of this bereavement; all that he remembers of those days is the basin of ice. Another man reports that his earliest memory is an episode upon a walk in which he broke off a branch from a tree. He thinks he can still identify the spot where this happened. There were several other people present, and one of them helped him.

The Henris describe such cases as rare. In my experience, based for the most part, it is true, on neurotics, they are quite frequent. One of the subjects of the Henris' investigation made an attempt at explaining the occurrence of these mnemic images, whose innocence makes them so mysterious, and his explanation seems to me very much to the point. He thinks that in such cases the relevant scene may perhaps have been only *incompletely* retained in the memory, and that that may be why it seems so unenlightening: the parts that have been forgotten probably contained everything that made the experience noteworthy. I am able to confirm the truth of this view, though I should prefer to speak of these elements of the experience being *omitted* rather than forgotten. I have often succeeded, by means of psycho-analytic treatment, in uncovering the missing portions of a childhood experience and in thus proving that when the impression, of which no more than a torso was retained in the memory, had been restored to completeness, it did in fact agree with the presumption that it is the most important things that are recollected. This, however, provides no explanation of the remarkable choice which memory has made among the elements of the experience. We must first enquire why it should be that precisely what is important is suppressed and what is indifferent retained; and we shall not find an explanation of this until we have investigated the mechanism of these processes more deeply. We shall then form a notion that two psychical forces are concerned in bringing about memories of this sort.

One of these forces takes the importance of the experience as a motive for seeking to remember it, while the other—a resistance—tries to prevent any such preference from being shown. These two opposing forces do not cancel each other out, nor does one of them (whether with or without loss to itself) overpower the other. Instead, a compromise is brought about, somewhat on the analogy of the resultant in a parallelogram of forces. And the compromise is this. What is recorded as a mnemic image is not the relevant experience itself—in this respect the resistance gets its way; what is recorded is another psychical element closely associated with the objectionable one—and in this respect the *first* principle shows its strength, the principle which endeavours to fix important impressions by establishing reproducible mnemic images. The result of the conflict is therefore that, instead of the mnemic image which would have been justified by the original event, another is produced which has been to some degree associatively *displaced* from the former one. And since the elements of the experience which aroused objection were precisely the important ones, the substituted memory will necessarily lack those important elements and will in consequence most probably strike us as trivial. It will seem incomprehensible to us because we are inclined to look for the reason for its retention in its own content, whereas in fact that retention is due to the relation holding between its own content and a different one which has been suppressed. There is a common saying among us about shams, that they are not made of gold themselves but have lain beside something that *is* made of gold.[1] The same simile might well be applied to some of the experiences of childhood which have been retained in the memory.

There are numerous possible types of case in which one psychical content is substituted for another, and these come about in a variety of psychological constellations. One of the simplest of these cases is obviously that occurring in the childhood memories with which we are here concerned—the case, that is, where the essential elements of an experience are represented in memory by the inessential elements of the same experience. It is a case of displacement on to something associated by continuity; or, looking at the process as a whole, a case

[1] [The simile reappears in Chapter VII of Freud's book on jokes (1905c), *Standard Ed.*, **8**, 184.]

of repression accompanied by the substitution of something in the neighbourhood (whether in space or time). I have elsewhere[1] had occasion to describe a very similar instance of substitution which occurred in the analysis of a patient suffering from paranoia. The woman in question hallucinated voices, which used to repeat long passages from Otto Ludwig's novel *Die Heiterethei* to her. But the passages they chose were the most trifling and irrelevant in the book. The analysis showed, however, that there were other passages in the same work which had stirred up the most distressing thoughts in the patient. The distressing affect was a motive for putting up a defence against them, but the motives in favour of pursuing them further were not to be suppressed. The result was a compromise by which the innocent passages emerged in the patient's memory with pathological strength and clarity. The process which we here see at work—conflict, repression, substitution involving a compromise—returns in all psychoneurotic symptoms and gives us the key to understanding their formation. Thus it is not without importance if we are able to show the same process operating in the mental life of normal individuals, and the fact that what it influences in normal people is precisely their choice of childhood memories seems to afford one more indication of the intimate relations which have already been insisted upon between the mental life of children and the psychical material of the neuroses.

The processes of normal and pathological defence and the displacements in which they result are clearly of great importance. But to the best of my knowledge no study whatever has hitherto been made of them by psychologists; and it remains to be ascertained in what strata of psychical activity and under what conditions they come into operation. The reason for this neglect may well be that our mental life, so far as it is the object of our *conscious* internal perception, shows nothing of these processes, apart from instances which we classify as 'faulty reasoning' and some mental operations which aim at producing a comic effect. The assertion that a psychical intensity[2] can be displaced from one presentation (which is then abandoned) on to another (which thenceforward plays the psychological part of the

---

[1] 'Further Remarks on the Neuro-Psychoses of Defence' (1896*b*). [See above, p. 181.]   [2] [Cf. p. 67 above.]

former one) is as bewildering to us as certain features of Greek mythology—as, for instance, when the gods are said to clothe someone with beauty as though it were with a veil, whereas *we* think only of a face transfigured by a change of expression.

Further investigation of these indifferent childhood memories has taught me that they can originate in other ways as well and that an unsuspected wealth of meaning lies concealed behind eir apparent innocence. But on this point I shall not content myself with a mere assertion but shall give a detailed report of one particular instance which seems to me the most instructive out of a considerable number of similar ones. Its value is certainly increased by the fact that it relates to someone who is not at all or only very slightly neurotic.

The subject of this observation is a man of university education, aged thirty-eight.[1] Though his own profession lies in a very different field, he has taken an interest in psychological questions ever since I was able to relieve him of a slight phobia by means of psycho-analysis. Last year he drew my attention to his childhood memories, which had already played some part in his analysis. After studying the investigation made by V. and C. Henri, he gave me the following summarized account of his own experience.

'I have at my disposal a fair number of early memories of childhood which I can date with great certainty. For at the age of three I left the small place where I was born and moved to a large town; and all these memories of mine relate to my birthplace and therefore date from my second and third years. They are mostly short scenes, but they are very well preserved and furnished with every detail of sense-perception, in complete contrast to my memories of adult years, which are entirely lacking in the visual element. From my third year onwards my recollections grow scantier and less clear; there are gaps in them which must cover more than a year; and it is not, I believe, until my sixth or seventh year that the stream of my memories becomes continuous. My memories up to the time of my leaving

[1] [There can be no doubt that what follows is autobiographical material only thinly disguised. See Editor's Note, p. 302 above. At the date at which this paper was sent in for publication in May 1899, Freud was in fact just forty-three years old.]

my first place of residence fall into three groups. The first group consists of scenes which my parents have repeatedly since described to me. As regards these, I feel uncertain whether I have had the mnemic image from the beginning or whether I only construed it after hearing one of these descriptions. I may remark, however, that there are also events of which I have no mnemic image in spite of their having been frequently retailed by my parents. I attach more importance to the second group. It comprises scenes which have not (so far as I know) been described to me and some of which, indeed, *could* not have been described to me, as I have not met the other participants in them (my nurse and playmates) since their occurrence. I shall come to the third group presently. As regards the content of these scenes and their consequent claim to being recollected, I should like to say that I am not entirely at sea. I cannot maintain, indeed, that what I have retained are memories of the most important events of the period, or what I should to-day judge to be the most important. I have no knowledge of the birth of a sister, who is two and a half years younger than I am; my departure, my first sight of the railway and the long carriage-drive before it—none of these has left a trace in my memory. On the other hand, I can remember two small occurrences during the railway-journey; these, as you will recollect, came up in the analysis of my phobia. But what should have made most impression on me was an injury to my face which caused a considerable loss of blood and for which I had to have some stitches put in by a surgeon. I can still feel the scar resulting from this accident, but I know of no recollection which points to it, either directly or indirectly.[1] It is true that I may perhaps have been under two years old at the time.

'It follows from this that I feel no surprise at the pictures and scenes of these first two groups. No doubt they are displaced memories from which the essential element has for the most part been omitted. But in a few of them it is at least hinted at, and in others it is easy for me to complete them by following certain pointers. By doing so I can establish a sound connec-

---

[1] [This accident is referred to twice in *The Interpretation of Dreams* (1900*a*), *Standard Ed.*, **4**, 17 and footnote, and **5**, 560; also, indirectly, in a letter to Fliess of October 15, 1897 (Freud 1950*a*, Letter 71) and near the beginning of Lecture XIII of the *Introductory Lectures* (1916–17).]

tion between the separate fragments of memories and arrive at a clear understanding of what the childish interest was that recommended these particular occurrences to my memory. This does not apply, however, to the content of the third group, which I have not so far discussed. There I am met by material—one rather long scene and several smaller pictures—with which I can make no headway at all. The scene appears to me fairly indifferent and I cannot understand why it should have become fixed in my memory. Let me describe it to you. I see a rectangular, rather steeply sloping piece of meadow-land, green and thickly grown; in the green there are a great number of yellow flowers—evidently common dandelions. At the top end of the meadow there is a cottage and in front of the cottage door two women are standing chatting busily, a peasant-woman with a handkerchief on her head and a children's nurse. Three children are playing in the grass. One of them is myself (between the age of two and three); the two others are my boy cousin, who is a year older than me, and his sister, who is almost exactly the same age as I am. We are picking the yellow flowers and each of us is holding a bunch of flowers we have already picked. The little girl has the best bunch; and, as though by mutual agreement, we—the two boys—fall on her and snatch away her flowers. She runs up the meadow in tears and as a consolation the peasant-woman gives her a big piece of black bread. Hardly have we seen this than we throw the flowers away, hurry to the cottage and ask to be given some bread too. And we are in fact given some; the peasant-woman cuts the loaf with a long knife. In my memory the bread tastes quite delicious—and at that point the scene breaks off.

'Now what is there in this occurrence to justify the expenditure of memory which it has occasioned me? I have racked my brains in vain over it. Does the emphasis lie on our disagreeable behaviour to the little girl? Did the yellow colour of the dandelions—a flower which I am, of course, far from admiring to-day—so greatly please me? Or, as a result of my careering round the grass, did the bread taste so much nicer than usual that it made an unforgettable impression on me? Nor can I find any connection between this scene and the interest which (as I was able to discover without any difficulty) bound together the other scenes from my childhood. Altogether, there seems to me something not quite right about this scene. The yellow of the flowers is a disproportionately prominent element in the situation as a whole, and the nice taste of the bread seems to me exaggerated in an almost hallucinatory fashion. I cannot help being reminded of some pictures that I once saw in a burlesque exhibition. Certain portions of these pictures, and of course the most inappropriate ones, instead of being painted, were built up in three dimensions—for instance, the ladies' bustles. Well, can you point out any way of finding an explanation or interpretation of this redundant memory of my childhood?'

I thought it advisable to ask him since when he had been occupied with this recollection: whether he was of opinion that it had recurred to his memory periodically since his childhood, or whether it had perhaps emerged at some later time on some occasion that could be recalled. This question was all that it was necessary for me to contribute to the solution of the problem; the rest was found by my collaborator himself, who was no novice at jobs of this kind.

'I have not yet considered that point,' he replied. 'Now that you have raised the question, it seems to me almost a certainty that this childhood memory never occurred to me at all in my earlier years. But I can also recall the occasion which led to my recovering this and many other recollections of my earliest childhood. When I was seventeen and at my secondary school, I returned for the first time to my birthplace for the holidays, to stay with a family who had been our friends ever since that remote date. I know quite well what a wealth of impressions overwhelmed me at that time. But I see now that I shall have to tell you a whole big piece of my history: it belongs here, and you have brought it upon yourself by your question. So listen. I was the child of people who were originally well-to-do and who, I fancy, lived comfortably enough in that little corner of the provinces. When I was about three, the branch of industry in which my father was concerned met with a catastrophe. He lost all his means and we were forced to leave the place and move to a large town. Long and difficult years followed, of which, as it seems to me, nothing was worth remembering. I never felt really comfortable in the town. I believe now that I was never free from a longing for the beautiful woods near our home, in which (as one of my memories from those days tells me) I used to run off from my father, almost before I had learnt to walk. Those holidays, when I was seventeen, were my first holidays in the country, and, as I have said, I stayed with a family with whom we were friends and who had risen greatly in the world since our move. I could compare the comfort reigning there with our own style of living at home in the town. But it is no use evading the subject any longer: I must admit that there was something else that excited me powerfully. I was seventeen, and in the family where I was staying there was a daughter of fifteen, with whom I immediately fell in love. It was my first calf-love and sufficiently intense, but I kept it completely secret. After a few days the girl went off to her school (from which she too was home for the holidays) and it was this separation after such a short acquaintance that brought my longings to a really high pitch. I passed many hours in solitary walks through the lovely woods that I had found once more and spent my time building castles in the air. These, strangely enough, were not concerned with the future but sought to improve the past. If only the smash had not occurred! If only I had stopped at home and grown up in the country and grown as strong as the young men in the house, the brothers of my love! And then if only I had followed my father's profession and if I had finally married her—for I should have known her intimately all those years! I had not the slightest doubt, of course, that in the circumstances created by my imagination I should have loved her just as passionately as I really seemed to then. A strange thing. For when I see her now from time to time—she happens to have married someone here—she is quite exceptionally indifferent to me. Yet I can remember quite well for what a long time afterwards I was affected by the yellow colour of the dress she was wearing when we first met, whenever I saw the same colour anywhere else.'

That sounds very much like your parenthetical remark to the effect that you are no longer fond of the common dandelion. Do you not suspect that there may be a connection between the yellow of the girl's dress and the ultra-clear yellow of the flowers in your childhood scene?[1] [Cf. footnote 1, p. 291.]

[1] [This was Freud's regular method of reporting conversations—his interlocutor's remarks in inverted commas and his own without any. Cf., for instance, the dialogue in *The Question of Lay Analysis* (1926*e*).]

'Possibly. But it was not the same yellow. The dress was more of a yellowish brown, more like the colour of wallflowers. However, I can at least let you have an intermediate idea which may serve your purpose. At a later date, while I was in the Alps, I saw how certain flowers which have light colouring in the lowlands take on darker shades at high altitudes. Unless I am greatly mistaken, there is frequently to be found in mountainous regions a flower which is very similar to the dandelion but which is dark yellow and would exactly agree in colour with the dress of the girl I was so fond of. But I have not finished yet. I now come to a second occasion which stirred up in me the impressions of my childhood and which dates from a time not far distant from the first. I was seventeen when I revisited my birthplace. Three years later during my holidays I visited my uncle and met once again the children who had been my first playmates, the same two cousins, the boy a year older than I am and the girl of the same age as myself, who appear in the childhood scene with the dandelions. This family had left my birthplace at the same time as we did and had become prosperous in a far-distant city.'

And did you once more fall in love—with your cousin this time—and indulge in a new set of phantasies?

'No, this time things turned out differently. By then I was at the University and I was a slave to my books. I had nothing left over for my cousin. So far as I know I had no similar phantasies on that occasion. But I believe that my father and my uncle had concocted a plan by which I was to exchange the abstruse subject of my studies for one of more practical value, settle down, after my studies were completed, in the place where my uncle lived, and marry my cousin. No doubt when they saw how absorbed I was in my own intentions the plan was dropped; but I fancy I must certainly have been aware of its existence. It was not until later, when I was a newly-fledged man of science and hard pressed by the exigencies of life and when I had to wait so long before finding a post here, that I must sometimes have reflected that my father had meant well in planning this marriage for me, to make good the loss in which the original catastrophe had involved my whole existence.'

Then I am inclined to believe that the childhood scene we are considering emerged at this time, when you were struggling for your daily bread—provided, that is, that you can confirm my idea that it was during this same period that you first made the acquaintance of the Alps.

'Yes, that is so: mountaineering was the one enjoyment that I allowed myself at that time. But I still cannot grasp your point.'

I am coming to it at once. The element on which you put most stress in your childhood scene was the fact of the country-made bread tasting so delicious. It seems clear that this idea, which amounted almost to a hallucination, corresponded to your phantasy of the comfortable life you would have led if you had stayed at home and married this girl [in the yellow dress]—or, in symbolic language, of how sweet the bread would have tasted for which you had to struggle so hard in your later years. The yellow of the flowers, too, points to the same girl. But there are also elements in the childhood scene which can only be related to the *second* phantasy—of being married to your cousin. Throwing away the flowers in exchange for bread strikes me as not a bad disguise for the scheme your father had for you: you were to give up your unpractical ideals and take on a 'bread-and-butter' occupation, were you not?

'It seems then that I amalgamated the two sets of phantasies of how my life could have been more comfortable—the "yellow" and the "country-made bread" from the one and the throwing-away of the flowers and the actual people concerned from the other.'

Yes. You projected the two phantasies on to one another and made a childhood memory of them. The element about the alpine flowers is as it were a stamp giving the date of manufacture. I can assure you that people often construct such things unconsciously—almost like works of fiction.

'But if that is so, there was *no* childhood memory, but only a phantasy put back into childhood. A feeling tells me, though, that the scene is genuine. How does that fit in?'

There is in general no guarantee of the data produced by our memory. But I am ready to agree with you that the scene is genuine. If so, you selected it from innumerable others of a similar or another kind because, on account of its content (which in itself was indifferent) it was well adapted to represent the two phantasies, which were important enough to you.

recollection of this kind, whose value lies in the fact that it represents in the memory impressions and thoughts of a later date whose content is connected with its own by symbolic or similar links, may appropriately be called a '*screen memory*'. In any case you will cease to feel any surprise that this scene should so often recur to your mind. It can no longer be regarded as an innocent one since, as we have discovered, it is calculated to illustrate the most momentous turning-points in your life, the influence of the two most powerful motive forces—hunger and love.[1]

'Yes, it represented hunger well enough. But what about love?'

In the yellow of the flowers, I mean. But I cannot deny that in this childhood scene of yours love is represented far less prominently than I should have expected from my previous experience.

'No. You are mistaken. The essence of it is its representation of love. Now I understand for the first time. Think for a moment! Taking flowers away from a girl means to deflower her. What a contrast between the boldness of this phantasy and my bashfulness on the first occasion and my indifference on the second.'

I can assure you that youthful bashfulness habitually has as its complement bold phantasies of that sort.

'But in that case the phantasy that has transformed itself into these childhood memories would not be a conscious one that I can remember, but an unconscious one?'

Unconscious thoughts which are a prolongation of conscious ones. You think to yourself 'If I had married so-and-so', and behind the thought there is an impulse to form a picture of what the 'being married' really is.

'I can go on with it now myself. The most seductive part of the whole subject for a young scapegrace is the picture of the marriage night. (What does he care about what comes afterwards?) But that picture cannot venture out into the light of day: the dominating mood of diffidence and of respect towards the girl keeps it suppressed. So it remains unconscious—'

And slips away into a childhood memory. You are quite

[1] [An allusion to a favourite line of Freuds' from Schiller' 'Die Weltweisen'.

right. It is precisely the coarsely sensual element in the phantasy which explains why it does not develop into a *conscious* phantasy but must be content to find its way allusively and under a flowery disguise into a childhood scene.

'But why precisely, into a *childhood* scene, I should like to know?'

For the sake of its innocence, perhaps. Can you imagine a greater contrast to these designs for gross sexual aggression than childish pranks? However, there are more general grounds that have a decisive influence in bringing about the slipping away of repressed thoughts and wishes into childhood memories: for you will find the same thing invariably happening in hysterical patients. It seems, moreover, as though the recollection of the remote past is in itself facilitated by some pleasurable motive: *forsan et haec olim meminisse juvabit*.[1]

'If that is so, I have lost all faith in the genuineness of the dandelion scene. This is how I look at it: On the two occasions in question, and with the support of very comprehensible realistic motives, the thought occurred to me: "If you had married this or that girl, your life would have become much pleasanter." The sensual current in my mind took hold of the thought which is contained in the protasis[2] and repeated it in images of a kind capable of giving that same sensual current satisfaction. This second version of the thought remained unconscious on account of its incompatibility with the dominant sexual disposition; but this very fact of its remaining unconscious enabled it to persist in my mind long after changes in the real situation had quite got rid of the conscious version. In accordance, as you say, with a general law, the clause that had remained unconscious sought to transform itself into a childhood scene which, on account of its innocence, would be able to become conscious. With this end in view it had to undergo a fresh transformation, or rather two fresh transformations. One of these removed the objectionable element from the protasis by expressing it figuratively; the second forced the apodosis into a shape capable of visual representation—using for the purpose

---

[1] ['Some day, perhaps, it will be a joy to remember even these things.' Virgil, *Aeneid*, I, 203.]

[2] [A protasis is a conditional clause and an apodosis (see below) is a consequential one.]

the intermediary ideas of "bread" and "bread-and-butter occupations". I see that by producing a phantasy like this I was providing, as it were, a fulfilment of the two suppressed wishes—for deflowering a girl and for material comfort. But now that I have given such a complete account of the motives that led to my producing the dandelion phantasy, I cannot help concluding that what I am dealing with is something that never happened at all but has been unjustifiably smuggled in among my childhood memories.'

I see that I must take up the defence of its genuineness. You are going too far. You have accepted my assertion that every suppressed phantasy of this kind tends to slip away into a childhood scene. But suppose now that this cannot occur unless there is a memory-trace the content of which offers the phantasy a point of contact—comes, as it were, half way to meet it. Once a point of contact of this kind has been found—in the present instance it was the deflowering, the taking away of the flowers—the remaining content of the phantasy is remodelled with the help of every legitimate intermediate idea—take the bread as an example—till it can find further points of contact with the content of the childhood scene. It is very possible that in the course of this process the childhood scene itself also undergoes changes; I regard it as certain that falsifications of memory may be brought about in this way too. In your case the childhood scene seems only to have had some of its lines engraved more deeply: think of the over-emphasis on the yellow and the exaggerated niceness of the bread. But the raw material was utilizable. If that had not been so, it would not have been possible for this particular memory, rather than any others, to make its way forward into consciousness. No such scene would have occurred to you as a childhood memory, or perhaps some other one would have—for you know how easily our ingenuity can build connecting bridges from any one point to any other. And apart from your own subjective feeling which I am not inclined to under-estimate, there is another thing that speaks in favour of the genuineness of your dandelion memory. It contains elements which have not been solved by what you have told me and which do not in fact fit in with the sense required by the phantasy. For instance, your boy cousin helping you to rob the little girl of her flowers—can you make any sense of the

SCREEN MEMORIES

idea of being helped in deflowering someone? or of the peasant-woman and the nurse in front of the cottage?

'Not that I can see.'

So the phantasy does not coincide completely with the childhood scene. It is only based on it at certain points. That argues in favour of the childhood memory being genuine.

'Do you think an interpretation like this of an apparently innocent childhood memory is often applicable?'

Very often, in my experience. Shall we amuse ourselves by seeing whether the two examples given by the Henris can be interpreted as screen memories concealing subsequent experiences and wishes? I mean the memory of a table laid for a meal with a basin of ice on it, which was supposed to have some connection with the death of the subject's grandmother, and the other memory, of a child breaking off a branch from a tree while he was on a walk and of his being helped to do it by someone.

He reflected for a little and then answered: 'I can make nothing of the first one. It is most probably a case of displacement at work; but the intermediate steps are beyond guessing. As for the second case, I should be prepared to give an interpretation, if only the person concerned had not been a Frenchman.'

I cannot follow you there. What difference would that make?

'A great deal of difference, since what provides the intermediate step between a screen memory and what it conceals is likely to be a verbal expression. In German "to pull one out" is a very common vulgar term for masturbation.[1] The scene would then be putting back into early childhood a seduction to masturbation—someone was helping him to do it—which in fact occurred at a later period. But even so, it does not fit, for in the childhood scene there were a number of other people present.'

Whereas his seduction to masturbate must have occurred in solitude and secrecy. It is just that contrast that inclines me to accept your view: it serves once again to make the scene innocent. Do you know what it means when in a dream we see 'a lot of strangers', as happens so often in dreams of nakedness in which we feel so terribly embarrassed? Nothing more nor less

[1] [Cf. *The Interpretation of Dreams* (1900a), Standard Ed., 5, 348, footnote 2.]

than secrecy, which there again is expressed by its opposite.[1] However, our interpretation remains a jest, since we have no idea whether a Frenchman would recognize an allusion to masturbation in the words *casser une branche d'un arbre* or in some suitably emended phrase.

This analysis, which I have reproduced as accurately as possible, will, I hope, have to some extent clarified the concept of a 'screen memory' as one which owes its value as a memory not to its own content but to the relation existing between that content and some other, that has been suppressed. Different classes of screen memories can be distinguished according to the nature of that relation. We have found examples of two of these classes among what are described as the earliest memories of childhood—that is, if we include under the heading of screen memories the incomplete childhood scenes which are innocent by very reason of their incompleteness. It is to be anticipated that screen memories will also be formed from residues of memories relating to later life as well. Anyone who bears in mind their distinctive feature—namely that they are extremely well remembered but that their content is completely indifferent—will easily recall a number of examples of the sort from his own memory. Some of these screen memories dealing with events later in life owe their importance to a connection with experiences in early youth which have remained suppressed. The connection, that is, is the reverse of the one in the case which I have analysed, where a childhood memory was accounted for by later experiences. A screen memory may be described as 'retrogressive' or as having 'pushed forward' according as the one chronological relation or the other holds between the screen and the thing screened-off.[2] From another point of view, we can distinguish positive screen memories from negative ones (or refractory memories) whose content stands in a contrary relation to the suppressed material. The whole subject deserves a more thorough examination; but I must content myself with pointing out what complicated processes—processes, incidentally, which are altogether analogous to the for-

[1] [Cf. ibid., **4**, 245–6.]
[2] [I.e. according to whether the displacement has been in a backward or forward direction.]

mation of hysterical symptoms—are involved in the building up of our store of memories.

Our earliest childhood memories will always be a subject of special interest because the problem mentioned at the beginning of this paper (of how it comes about that the impressions which are of most significance for our whole future usually leave no mnemic images behind) leads us to reflect upon the origin of conscious memories in general. We shall no doubt be inclined at first to separate off the screen memories which are the subject of this study as heterogeneous elements among the residues of childhood recollections. As regards the remaining images, we shall probably adopt the simple view that they arise simultaneously with an experience as an immediate consequence of the impression it makes and that thereafter they recur from time to time in accordance with the familiar laws of reproduction. Closer observation, however, reveals certain features which do not tally with this view. Above all, there is the following point. In the majority of significant and in other respects unimpeachable childhood scenes the subject sees himself in the recollection as a child, with the knowledge that this child is himself; he sees this child, however, as an observer from outside the scene would see him. The Henris duly draw attention to the fact that many of those taking part in their investigation expressly emphasized this peculiarity of childhood scenes. Now it is evident that such a picture cannot be an exact repetition of the impression that was originally received. For the subject was then in the middle of the situation and was attending not to himself but to the external world.

Whenever in a memory the subject himself appears in this way as an object among other objects this contrast between the acting and the recollecting ego may be taken as evidence that the original impression has been worked over. It looks as though a memory-trace from childhood had here been translated back into a plastic and visual form at a later date—the date of the memory's arousal. But no reproduction of the original impression has ever entered the subject's consciousness.

There is another fact that affords even more convincing evidence in favour of this second view. Out of a number of childhood memories of significant experiences, all of them of similar distinctness and clarity, there will be some scenes which, when they are tested (for instance by the recollections of adults), turn out to have been falsified. Not that they are complete inventions; they are false in the sense that they have shifted an event to a place where it did not occur—this is the case in one of the instances quoted by the Henris—or that they have merged two people into one or substituted one for the other, or the scenes as a whole give signs of being combinations of two separate experiences. Simple inaccuracy of recollection does not play any considerable part here, in view of the high degree of sensory intensity possessed by the images and the efficiency of the function of memory in the young; close investigation shows rather that these falsifications of memory are tendentious—that is, that they serve the purposes of the repression and replacement of objectionable or disagreeable impressions. It follows, therefore, that these falsified memories too, must have originated at a period of life when it has become possible for conflicts of this kind and impulsions towards repression to have made a place for themselves in mental life—far later, therefore, than the period to which their content belongs. But in these cases too the falsified memory is the first that we become aware of: the raw material of memory-traces out of which it was forged remains unknown to us in its original form.

The recognition of this fact must diminish the distinction we have drawn between screen memories and other memories derived from our childhood. It may indeed be questioned whether we have any memories at all *from* our childhood: memories *relating to* our childhood may be all that we possess. Our childhood memories show us our earliest years not as they were but as they appeared at the later periods when the memories were aroused. In these periods of arousal, the childhood memories did not, as people are accustomed to say, *emerge*; they were *formed* at that time. And a number of motives, with no concern for historical accuracy, had a part in forming them, as well as in the selection of the memories themselves.[1]

---

[1] [The type of screen memory considered here is related to the 'retrospective phantasies' often discussed by Freud later; e.g. in the 'Rat Man' analysis (1909*d*), *Standard Ed.*, **10**, 206–8 *n*., in Sections V and VII of the 'Wolf Man' analysis (1918*b*) and in Lectures XXI and XXIII of the *Introductory Lectures* (1916–17).]

PART II

Discussion of "Screen memories"

1

Screen memories: a reintroduction

Gail S. Reed and Howard B. Levine

Although the clinical interest in screen memories has dropped out of the mainstream of analytic discussion—and with it close study of Freud's original paper—we believe that there is much to be gained from revisiting and re-examining both the phenomenon and the paper within a contemporary context. To this end, we have assembled comments from eight psychoanalysts on the current meaning and value to them of the screen memory concept. These comments come from contemporary psychoanalysts practicing in Italy, Francophone Switzerland, Argentina, Israel, and the US, each of whom has been trained in one or another of a variety of psychoanalytic traditions, among which are ego psychology, a French version of Freud, an American version of Lacan, and at least two variants of Kleinian thought, one British and one Latin American. Their comments range from advocating that screen memories are an important, even central, feature of contemporary analytic work (LaFarge, Cohen), to finding the concept less universally applicable, but nonetheless compelling (Ahumada).

As several of our contributors mention, Freud revealed to us the existence of the screen memory before the turn of the twentieth century and taught us then of its complexity. He demonstrated that the screen memory "owes its value as a memory not to its own content, but to the relation existing between that content and some other, that has been suppressed" (Freud, 1899a, p. 320). Screen memories, Freud explained, were defensively distorted referents of early events, many of them traumatic, in which the principal mechanisms of disguise were condensation and displacement. Their structure required meticulous unravelling because the nature of their defensive disguise led to their appearance frequently being reassuring and their content seemingly benign, even indifferent. While Freud's study of the defensive function of screen memories fit comfortably into his related investigations of neurotic symptoms and latent dream thoughts, it also led him to an extraordinary conjecture that perhaps all memories did not consist of the retrieval of pristinely stored veridical objective, immutable perceptions, and "facts", but were instead assembled and shaped at each moment with a specific set of dynamic needs in mind. Thus, he wondered, in regard to memories in general, whether "we have any memories at all *from* our childhood: memories *relating to* our childhood may be all that we possess" (Freud, 1899a, p. 322; original italics).

Following Freud, analysts saw screen memories as keys that would unlock aspects of the unique, subjective psychic and historical reality in which analytic patients lived. As Thompson reports (this volume, pp. 150–171), Phyllis Greenacre believed that screen memories were organised around core *actual* infantile traumata and so their analysis, including reconstruction of the original, hidden event, was therefore at the very heart of clinical work. Greenacre further believed that screens were distinguished from more ordinary memories by their clear demarcation and intensive luminosity and often contained depictions of the dreamer watching him or herself. Indeed, many of her late writings were devoted to arguing for their clinical importance. She did so because she saw them as essential conduits to the reconstruction of early trauma and recognised that a powerful ego psychological tide was sweeping clinical attention away from them and the infantile trauma they screened to leave in its wake an analysis focused principally on structure and a search for the "correct" interpretation.

Today, many analysts would agree that in many quarters the tide in question has successfully eroded both the importance of screen memories and the reconstruction that Greenacre believed they required. LaFarge (this volume, pp. 36–57) and Ahumada (this volume, pp. 104–117) note that screen memories are rarely today at the centre of analysts' interests. DeMasi (this volume, pp. 58–79) suggests a possible reason for this diminished interest when he argues that screen memories are less likely to be formed by patients who fall outside the neurotic end of the analytic spectrum. His observation makes space for the possibility that the decrease in attention to screen memories occurs because analysts today see fewer neurotic cases.

LaFarge has suggested other cogent reasons for this neglect of screen memories, one of the most compelling of which is that in her experience, as opposed to that of Freud, screen memories, unlike their close analytic siblings, dreams, parapraxes, and symptoms, resist analysis, do not necessarily vanish when they are understood and "require special technical interventions such as the analyst's drawing attention to internal contradictions and discrepancies" (LaFarge, p. 39).

Of course, both the need for specific technical measures and the resisting of analysis may be seen to come from the primarily defensive function of screen memories. Indeed, screen memories may often remain fixed because, by their very purpose and nature, they neither cause discomfort in the patient *nor curiosity in the analyst*. For the patient, their defensive screening may result in a memory that is calming. For the analyst, like a portrait in an historic mansion, the screen memory may hang unnoticed in the shadows of a dimly lit corridor, a kind of formal background "fact" that is accepted and never questioned.

To what extent have analysts ceased to think about screen memories as they work and consequently miss their "unremarkable" appearance on the scene of the session? The following abbreviated account is offered as an example of how a screen memory may develop in the session and may (or may not) be recognised and worked with as it emerges in the flow of analytic material. In the best of circumstances, when recognised and addressed, it might begin to change and offer up material it has heretofore concealed. We believe that is the case in the following example.

Clinical material

Several years ago, one of us treated in a five times per week analysis a young woman who was struggling with conflicts related to becoming independent. These conflicts prevented her from clarifying and working through issues connected to both love and work. She was an only child, small of stature and delicate of build, intelligent and sensitive, psychologically well put together, a professional musician. In the initial consultations three years before the session in question, she had described a happy mid-western family life surrounded by loving parents and relatives. She asserted that there were no upsetting events in her childhood. Her parents had never been sick or forced to be away for a long time. Well, she had been told that her father was in a car accident when she was very small. She had a vague memory of visiting him in the hospital; but there he had looked healthy and happy. There was no further mention of this event.

Three years later, at a time in the analysis when this patient was uneasily discovering positive transference feelings and when she was anticipating a short interruption at the end of the week, she arrived for the second of her five weekly appointments upset and uncharacteristically dishevelled. She had forgotten to attend a theatre benefit to which her former boyfriend had invited her. She was so distressed that she had asked her mother what to say to excuse herself. The act of appealing to her mother made her wonder why she was so worked up.

> *Patient*: Then it hit me. I guess I started feeling like this whole thing with growing up and becoming independent . . . I started getting worked up about that, but I didn't say that to my mother and that bothered me too. .. . . I actually felt sad . . . I have never realised I must have felt sad before . . . It has something to do with my mother telling me why I was stressed and me not being able to tell her the real reasons, why I was distressed.
>
> *Analyst*: Could not or declined to?
>
> *Pt*: [pause] Declined to [silence]
>
> *An*: With separation sadness comes . . .
>
> *Pt*: I felt such a loss yesterday. It was so tied up with . . . all these feelings . . . I don't want to say self hate . . . but I guess part of it was.
>
> *Pt*: [She next thinks of an older friend, one whose husband was away on business, whom she visited the day before.] She

reminded me of my mother, just how she looked . . . like she was burdened by something. I just felt I had to fix it . . . This woman is prone to depressions. Then I felt like an intruder in their family. All this is in my head!

An: You said she reminded you of your mother and that you felt the need to "fix" it.

Pt: I was thinking "he needs to come back! Where is he? She clearly needs him!!" All this thought process is crazy! All going off her not having the biggest smile yesterday and my thinking "she's depressed because her husband is gone for two weeks." The thought I had was: "She needs me here to keep herself together."

An: It sounds as if you were reacting as though she were your mother and you were trying to act a role you couldn't play.

Pt: I thought "was my father ever away?" His job didn't require travelling or anything. On vacations my mother always went with him.

An: Didn't you tell me he was once in the hospital?

Pt: I thought of that just now! That would have been when I was really young. Three maybe. [Silence, a fairly long pause]

An: What is going on?

Pt: You said something about there being a role I couldn't play. I was just wondering if I could probably sense how upset and tense my mother was if my dad wasn't there . . . that I had to fix that—by being him so that she would be ok . . .

An: What do you remember?

Pt: I don't remember being at home without him . . .

An: But you remember going to a hospital to see him?

Pt: Yes. He was sitting on the hospital bed and he looked very healthy, healthier than ever. There was something on his abdomen . . . I don't know what. The memory has been replaced by this image of my father I have from photographs of the time and how young he looked. The image of a handsome young man is clouding my . . . It is as if someone cut out his face and shoulders and glued it on to someone in a hospital bed. I remember not really understanding what was going on. I suppose my mother was there too. I don't see her, but I do see myself looking at him . . . The room was so bright. No hospital is as bright as that. They probably didn't take me to see him until he looked better.

I don't remember much. I keep on thinking of the scar on his chin . . . That's the only scar . . . Maybe they did do skin grafts on the other places . . . My mother had to help him. He did, he had skin grafts. On his abdomen. It was very painful for him . . . I remember as a kid not knowing what the scar on his chin was from . . . wondering . . . Then suddenly I knew what it was. I was much older then. I had been so puzzled. I remember thinking what is that? As if I forgot for a long time . . . .

[She next recounts a series of deaths befalling members of her extended family in the two or three years following her father's accident.] I was just thinking about a book I read where the lead character convinces herself that everything she touches dies.

We begin the session with the patient manifestly upset about forgetting to attend the theatre benefit at the invitation of a former boyfriend, someone with whom her mother wished she would have continued to be involved. It was because of her mother's desires for her that she turned to her mother to provide the excuse for missing the event. By asking her mother, she shows her need for and to her mother, while at the same time the act of forgetting lets her mother know that she resists her mother's ideas about her future. We end the session with the patient close to recognising within herself a painful and guilt-ridden central unconscious fantasy in which she cannot free herself from depending on her parents without killing them. In between, the contradictory (screen) memory of the healthy, smiling father in the hospital emerges, a father whose long absence from the family was possible, but who in the memory is reassuringly well. As the session progresses, however, some of the contents disguised by the screen memory begin to emerge directly—a scar, for instance, which was painful and the memory of which was repressed. Following this opening, other related affects and elements appear in displacement: the woman who may not tolerate absence (of her husband); deaths in the family in the time immediately following the father's hospitalisation; a book in which the heroine fears that everything she touches will die.

The manifest screen memory in which her father, hale and hearty, sits reassuringly on the hospital bed, does not emerge in the session spontaneously by itself. In this case, it is the analyst who reintroduces it and then the joint work of analyst and patient is required for it to be elaborated and the work of dismantling/understanding begun. The patient describes her reaction to her older friend's unsmiling face and connects her friend's upset to the absence of the woman's husband and to her mother's sad face. She is overwhelmed by the need to "fix" her mother in the absence of her father. And overwhelmed, too, by her inability to do it herself. Moreover, as she thinks about wanting to "be" her father to "fix" her mother and the dependency and other problems that issue from these conflict solutions, she takes refuge in the idea that there has been no time when her mother was left alone.

At that point the analyst remembers the remark the patient made during the initial consultations about her father being in a car accident and pursues her memory of her father, hale and hearty, in the hospital. That memory appears to be a screen memory, one which functions to obscure the father's absence from home, his possible injuries, the probable depression of the patient's mother, a depression the little girl could not cure, and the challenge to her little girl's sense of omnipotence. The screen memory is a protection against anxiety, grief, and narcissistic vulnerability and injury; "evidence" that nothing was lost, that there was nothing to fix, no sudden danger or absence. At the same time, it suggests the presence of these very negative features that are being denied: absence, grief, depression, injury, and pain.

In a paper on reconstruction, Reed (1993) pointed out that Greenacre (1975) had argued against treating screen memories as though they were dreams or symptoms and that she had also noted the ineffectiveness of asking for associations to them. Instead, "she advised listening to the associations that occurred around each mention of the screen memory, thinking of those patterns of juxtaposed configurations between sessions if necessary, and using those associations which occur around screen memories to reconstruct appropriately" (Reed, 1993, p. 69).

Although during the session the father's absence from home was never completely acknowledged, the analyst's connection of the father's absence to the patient's description of her current yearning to be the father and fix the mother undoes some of the repression connected to the father's absence. The screen memory of the happy, healthy hospital scene emerges as a second defence, one designed to assert that no one was upset, or in pain, or injured, that nothing upsetting had happened.

There is a specific rationale for not asking directly for associations to screen memories in the way one would do for dreams, parapraxes, or symptoms. As Reed wrote, "The screen memory is the product of a specific defensive operation. That function accounts for the observation that a screen memory will frequently reappear almost stereotypically when the original fantasy or memory threatens to emerge" (Reed, 1993, pp. 69–70; see also Arlow, 1990). Pointing out the associations that occur around the screen memory is theoretically consistent with understanding further the screen memory and proves effective because of the use of isolation and displacement in the defensive process. That is, pointing out the associations that come before and after the appearance of the screen memory breaks down part of the defensive process that characterises it.

Whether one is referring to the concept, the paper by Freud, or the general clinical phenomenon, screen memories are full of rich and complex psychoanalytic ideas. When one begins to contemplate them, they immediately lead to more ideas and richness: the nature of memory, forgetting and remembering, the use of distorted memory to obscure unconscious content, the relation of the structure of the patient's mind to the occurrence of screen memories, and many more.

The papers in this volume delve into many of these questions in a dialogue both with Freud and with modern analysts, even those who tend to dismiss screen memories. LaFarge, for example, notes that because the screen memory itself is the construction of the patient, it is tempting in these two-person days to consign the screen memory to the "classical", or "one person" theory. She points out, however, that the *analysis* of the screen memory requires two people, the patient and the analyst. Indeed, the example offered above shows the screen memory emerging because of the collaboration between patient and analyst. The screen memory may well be the phenomenon of one person; its analysis requires the collaboration of two.

Muller, Eifermann, and Cohen focus on different aspects of Freud's "Screen memories" text. Muller explores the "semiotic features of [Freud's] conceptualisations and clinical interventions" (this volume, p. 135). He argues that "Freud is here suggesting that the mechanism of the unconscious construction of screen memories is a linguistic one, that in some way . . . the unconscious *writes*, it composes a text that tightens and condenses meaning."

Eifermann's primary purpose is to "argue in favour of the Freudian tradition of close listening to the dynamic unconscious, which Freud exemplifies in part in his 'Screen memories' paper, in his attempt to reach the deeper sense of apparently trivial memories" (p. 81). That is, Eifermann reads Freud's unconscious and as a result of realising her first goal, simultaneously accomplishes her second, showing "how certain developments in Freud's generally groundbreaking, creative thought were both hampered and advanced due to early personal experiences—as they were retained, or evolved in memory—and their long-term effect."

Cohen works on Freud's discovery of character and examines mechanisms of both forgetfulness and remembering. Indeed, Freud discovered that "one's memories and the stories they reveal cannot be considered objective historical truths". Cohen imagines him asking, how "are memories selected in the mind of the remembering person?" She concludes that Freud discovered that memories are "complex mental events whose double function is to both reveal and to conceal" (this volume, p. 120). Screen memories, in particular, involve these two layers, the one that eclipses truth, the other where truth is buried.

In two clinical vignettes from the analysis of children, Cohen shows the complex interweaving of the role of interpretation of the past with time and experience. For instance, her comments to readers about an adoptive boy to whom she spoke of "the mother that you had and left you", and the boy acting regressively on the eve of the analyst's vacation, are about the fact that memory does not sort out history from fantasy, what really happens from what is imagined. Rather, memory binds and "grants meaning to the moment in the present" (this volume, p. 127). We hope that for our readers, the encounter with these creative and thought provoking commentaries on Freud's "Screen memories" will similarly grant new meaning to this important clinical phenomenon and stimulate further research and clinical observation into its origins and uses.

2

The screen memory and the act of remembering*

Lucy LaFarge

Screen memories, the durable fragments of childhood memory that accompany us through the life-cycle, were felt to be of great significance by Freud and the early analysts. Pre-formed constructions that patients brought to analysis, screen memories could be seen to blend external reality, fantasy, and defence. They afforded a second set of data which, together with the enacted data of the transference, stimulated the analyst to form his own constructions of the patient's past. With shifts in the orientation of psychoanalysis during the last century, these patients' constructions have receded into the background of psychoanalytic thought, while the enacted data of transference and countertransference, and the constructions made by the analyst, and by analyst and patient together, have taken centre stage. A fresh look at screen memories shows that they can be seen as reflections of a private, one-person mode of thinking: one where the individual remembers and imagines on his own and the *act of remembering* is of equal importance with the *content* of the memory. In the

*Originally published in the *International Journal of Psychoanalysis* (2012) *93*: 1249–1265 and reprinted by permission of the *International Journal of Psychoanalysis*.

analytic process, the content of a screen memory is often played out in transference and countertransference; and the specific screen memory that a patient recalls in a session can be found to reflect current transference developments. At the same time, a patient's recounting a screen memory in analysis also reflects her bringing a private way of thinking into contact with the two-person mode of thinking that she shares with the analyst. It tells us something about the tensions that exist for the patient between these two modes of thought and the patient's fantasies and beliefs concerning each of them; these fantasies may be played out in a second, more subtle current of transference and countertransference.

Freud (1899a) first took note of the group of childhood memories that he would call "screen memories" early in his career, at a time when he was centrally concerned with the processes of remembering and forgetting. Certain memories, he observed, survived relatively unchanged into adulthood. These memories depicted isolated fragments of childhood experience. Although they had a quality of clarity and sharpness, and were held with a sense of conviction, exploration revealed that they were often nonsensical, melding historical elements with imagined elements, and moments from one early era with moments from another. That they were constructed scenes rather than veridical ones was highlighted by the perspective from which they were viewed: often the child whose memory was in question was depicted within the scene as if viewed from outside. Freud saw these memories as a compromise between remembering and forgetting. Traumatic memories, and particularly memories and wishes relating to infantile sexuality, were defensively worked over: they could be remembered only indirectly, in edited and distorted form. It seemed likely that such partial, constructed, or "screen" memories were all that survived infantile amnesia. Conversely, although not all memories retained from childhood had the manifest hallmarks of screen memories—the distinctness and the identifiable evidence of distortion—all childhood memories *were* likely screen memories: "It may indeed be questioned whether we have any memories at all *from* our childhood: memories *relating to* our childhood may be all that we possess" (Freud, 1899a, p. 322, original italics).

Throughout his career, Freud maintained a belief in the importance of screen memories and their value in analytic work. "Not only *some* but *all* of what is essential from childhood has been retained in these memories" (Freud, 1914g, p. 147, original italics). Through the patient's associations and the analysis of resistance, "the memory of [the] significant impressions could be developed out of the indifferent ones" (Freud, 1901b, p. 42). Blending historical memory and fantasy, screen memories promised access to unconscious elements of both. They formed a register of the traumas that an individual had experienced in childhood (Freud, 1939a). Screen memories were implicitly one of the important relics that were available to the analyst–archeologist as he built a picture of the patient's past. Together with the aspects of the patient's past that came alive in the transference, the patient's early memories were both an anchor and a stimulus for the analyst's constructions—constructions which were powerful because, like the patient's own constructions, they contained a piece of historical truth (Blum, 2005; Freud, 1937d; Shapiro, 1993).

Screen memory remained an important topic for early analysts (Fenichel, 1927; Glover, 1929; Kris, 1956; among others). Like Freud, these analysts worked with screen memories by analysing their defensive, screening function, tracing the way they had been constructed and edited in order to reconstruct the "true" memories and fantasies that lay behind them. Greenacre (1949, 1975, 1981), who made the greatest contribution to the study of screen memories after Freud himself, demonstrated the key role that the analysis of screen memories could play in the reconstruction of both external and psychic reality, and explored the way the special qualities of screen memory were linked to aspects of early development. I will return to her contribution later.

During the century after Freud introduced it, the concept of screen memory, used by Freud to denote a group of enduring memories originating in childhood, was broadened to include other kinds of screens such as: "screen defenses" and "screen identity" (Greenson, 1958); the screen memories that arise in response to trauma throughout the life-cycle (Greenacre, 1949); and the screen-like memories that may be newly formed during analysis (Good, 1998).

By contrast, the narrower group of screen memories from childhood described by Freud had by the 1960s gradually ceased to be a significant subject in analytic writing; the term "screen memory" was not included in Moore and Fine's 1968 *Glossary of Psychoanalytic*

Terms and Concepts (Greenacre, 1975). In part, this loss of interest in screen memories may have arisen from the disappointing results of analytic work with them. Contrary to Freud's initial predictions (1899a, 1901b), screen memories do not yield to ordinary analytic work as dreams and symptoms do. Patients do not free associate to them easily; they require special technical interventions such as the analyst's drawing attention to internal contradictions and discrepancies (Greenacre, 1981). Moreover, unlike symptoms or parapraxes, screen memories do not fade once they have been analysed. They participate in the analytic process by serving as templates for transference developments: through analytic work, they can be placed within the broader context of childhood experience, but they are never fully absorbed into it. Screen memories do evolve over the course of development, but they have a quality of "stubborn fixity" (Greenacre, 1975, p. 708), and they retain their quality of specialness.[1]

Greenacre (1980) linked analysts' loss of interest in the screen memory to a loss of interest in the broader area of reconstruction. Both screen memory and reconstruction emphasise the importance of trauma and the link between psychic and external, historical reality. Analysis had moved away from an interest in trauma, she observed, toward an interest in psychic reality, meta-psychology, and the structure rather than the content of the neuroses.

Additional changes in the field since Greenacre's time have led analysts still further away from an interest in the analytic reconstruction of the patient's past, and from the preformed renditions of the past that the patient brings to analysis in the form of screen memories. With the strong shift toward interest in the here and now process that characterises contemporary psychoanalysis, the past that occupies analysts tends to be solely the past that comes alive in transference and countertransference. The parallel current of historical elaboration, which was once thought to anchor identity and transference interpretation, is often neglected (Blum, 1999, 2005; Shapiro, 1993). In this context, screen memories lose their special status and are felt to be important only insofar as they fuel the development of transference.

And from the perspective of two-person psychology that is now dominant in psychoanalysis, it has become increasingly difficult to draw a firm connection between the version of the past played out in transference and countertransference and the patient's historical past, or even the past of the patient's individual psychic reality. With the growing awareness that the analyst is a full participant as well as an observer in the events of the analytic process, it is no longer possible to see the past that is played out in analysis as solely the patient's; to some degree the analyst's past must come alive as well (Racker, 1957).

Changing ideas of the way meaning is constructed in analysis have also acted to move screen memories away from the analyst's attention. Freud (1937d) viewed construction as the task of the analyst. Greenacre saw the work of reconstruction as a collaborative effort, but one in which the patient's subjectivity remained clearly at the centre, and the analyst "held himself in abeyance and . . . [served] as an extra function to his patient" (Greenacre, 1981, p. 37). Current awareness of the analyst's subjectivity (Hoffman, 1998; Renik, 1993) and the interpenetration of the minds of analyst and patient (Schafer, 2000) has led to a heightened awareness of the co-constructed nature of analytic narratives and a further delinking of these constructs from the patient's individual subjectivity and history. Carrying this perspective still further, as some contemporary analysts do, if all we know of the past is a specific instance of its emergence between a unique analyst–patient pair and the story that these two join together to tell about it, it becomes difficult to speak of the patient's past as a fixed, pre-existent entity at all; the past becomes something that is *created* in the session (Stern, 1997).

A second current in contemporary thinking about meaning construction in the analytic situation, the view that the analyst is container and transformer of the patient's inchoate emotional experience as well as interpreter of better elaborated elements of the patient's mental life (Bion, 1957, 1959, 1962a; Botella & Botella, 2005; Brown, 2006; LaFarge, 2000), has not as yet contributed to the understanding of the screen memory, but I believe that it has the potential to do so. From this perspective, the most pathogenic elements of the patient's mental life are not those that are defensively warded off but those that have never been knowable or bearable, that require the analyst's mental apparatus in order to achieve the status of thoughts. Although the analyst's response to the patient's emotional experience evokes pieces of the analyst's own emotional life as well as projected elements of the patient's, the direction of the analytic work in these models clearly points toward the analyst's working through of his countertransference in order to help the patient acquire a more tolerable and knowable version of the patient's own past (rather than an acceptance of the jointly constructed and lived past of some other contemporary models).

Analysts who place containment and the movement toward representability at the centre of their view of the analytic process often think of formulated elements of the patient's experience as less critical than unformulated ones. Hence such crystallised, preformulated elements as screen memories may be neglected in these models, or seen primarily in their function *as* screens, which conceal the unformulated and must be dismantled in order to permit the recognition and historicization of the underlying elements by the analyst or the field (Baranger, Baranger, & Mom, 1988). Their special content and form and their special meaning to the patient have largely receded in importance.

However, models of containment and the movement toward representation, previously used to help us to understand the two-person genesis of the capacity for thinking and the two-person dimension of the analytic process, can also help us to understand the one-person dimension of thinking found in the screen memory. These models bring into focus for us the formal qualities of the screen memory *as a way of thinking and representing* and help us to think about the functions that this mode of thinking might serve.

Screen memories as a mode of representation

Greenacre's careful cataloguing of the special properties of screen memories and her preliminary exploration of the origins of these properties are good starting points for looking at the way these memories may be understood as a way of representing experience. She observed the durability of screen memories: the sense that each memory is a unit in which details are only slowly edited during development; their special intensity and visual quality and their frequent sense of being brightly lit; their sharp boundaries; their onlooker quality, the way the subject often views himself within the remembered scene; and the sense of conviction that accompanies them (Greenacre, 1949, 1975).

Greenacre links a number of these qualities to the way trauma is experienced in childhood: childhood trauma is often visual—the experience of something frightening that is seen—and even non-visual trauma may over-flow into a visual experience, particularly the sense of the memory being brightly lit. The origin of the screen memory in a trauma and the visual also contributes to its having a sharp boundary: unlike the dream screen, which originates in drowsy experience at the breast as Lewin (1946) described, the screen memory arises in a state of hyperarousal, taken in at a distance through the eyes. The hyper-real quality of the screen memory reflects this quality of aroused seeing—the excitement and aggression that are evoked by the trauma—and in addition the inability of the immature ego to distinguish the "real" situation that he has seen from his excited fantasies of it and the defences he erects against it. Like Freud (1937d), Greenacre attributed the sense of conviction with which the screen memory is held to the germ of real trauma that it contains. Screen memories were durable because of their traumatic origins, the instinctual forces that they released, and the stubborn quality of the early defences mobilised to manage both.

Considering the onlooker quality so characteristic of screen memories, Greenacre (1949) attributed it in part to the split in the ego, which other analysts had posited: trauma had evoked panic and depersonalisation, and, in addition the rememberer disidentified from the instinctual wishes evoked by the trauma. And, in a highly original contribution, Greenacre also linked the onlooker quality to a sense of watchfulness associated with superego arousal. A screen memory was not only a memory of a trauma, however disguised, but also a memory of that trauma being *seen* by a part of the self.

Although the analyst's chief concern was with dismantling a screen memory—tracing the forces that led to its formation in order to construct a history of the patient's internal and external experience, Greenacre (1955b) also shows us, through her tracing of the evolution of a screen memory of Lewis Carroll in his literary work, the way a screen memory can serve, especially for the artist, as a valued creation and a frame in which new versions of the self and the imagined world can be developed. This aspect of the screen memory, manifest but not explicit in Greenacre's analysis of Carroll's work, is captured by the title of the chapter of *Alice in Wonderland* in which Greenacre locates a key version of the screen memory: "It's my own invention".

Viewing Greenacre's formulations in the light of the new understanding of trauma and representation that we have acquired since her time, it is possible to see the properties that she described in a different light, one that is complementary to her early formulations. In this new formulation, a screen memory can be seen as a special kind of representation that is formed by an individual under strain and is held because it is felt to organise an experience that might potentially overwhelm the individual capacity to make sense of experience (and along with that his sense of a knowing, organising self). Screen memories memorialise the act of remembering as well as the content of what is remembered. In later life, they are used to evoke a remembered experience and the self who registered that experience, and, in addition, the capacity for invention and construction which that self possessed.

Contemporary psychoanalysis has made us aware of the two-person origin of the capacity to think and represent (Aulagnier, 1975; Bion, 1957, 1959; Fonagy et al, 2002). The child takes in the capacity for thinking through his experience of the mother's management of the child's emotional experience. Thinking, particularly with regard to the sense of self, remains potentially a two-person activity; we go back and forth between our own internalised perspective and the view of our experience that others offer to us (LaFarge, 2008). The two-person quality of thinking is particularly important in traumatic experience: with trauma, we lose the sense of being witnessed and, along with that, the sense that our experience has meaning (Auerhahn & Peskin, 2003; Laub, 1998). From this perspective, the superego to which Greenacre attributed the sense of watchfulness in screen memories could be seen as a very early superego, one whose function is to see and know the child (rather than to judge) and whose presence guarantees the experience of reality and the survival of the experiencing self. Through a split in the self, the child captures a sense of the knowing, witnessing other. The sharp frame, which is often part of the screen memory, further secures a picture of the self as seen and known (LaFarge, 2006; Malcolm, 1970) and serves as an enduring frame in which these images can be re-evoked.

Screen memories are sensuous, pictures rather than words. They evoke whole experiences which can be held to the self. Taking origin in both external reality and fantasy, they preserve the capacity to be in contact with both currents of experience, to recognise both that trauma is real and that the child has the power within himself to transform it. Recalled later on, the screen memory evokes the contents of both currents and with it the memory of the individual's imaginative power; this, for the creative, serves as a frame for further invention.

A literary example of a screen memory

In the early chapters of his childhood memoir, *A Small Boy and Others*, Henry James (1913) describes a number of screen memories. One of these is particularly well elaborated and, because we have a considerable amount of information about it, it is possible to look at it from the complementary perspectives that I have described: Using the biographical information that we have about James, we can deconstruct the memory, as analysts traditionally have done, to understand the way its *content* expresses and screens historical reality and fantasy. Using James's description of the way he remembers and the meaning that remembering has for him, with which he introduces his recollections, as well as glimpses of the memory that we can recognise in his fiction, we can understand something of the way the *form* of the memory, and the *act of remembering*, functioned for James.

James recounts a memory "so infantile . . . that I wonder at its having stuck" (1913, p. 28). He is on "a visit paid with my father—who decidedly must have liked to take me about, I feel so rich in that general reminiscence—to a family . . . in a quite lovely embowered place" (p. 28). There is a sense of luxury and abundance in James's memory of the summer day. The family was numerous and beautiful and they were partaking of a meal out of doors:

> The pre-eminent figure of the group was a very big Newfoundland dog on whose back I was put to ride . . . But the romance of the hour was particularly in what I have called the eccentric note, the fact that the children, my entertainers, riveted my gaze to stockingless and shoeless legs and feet, conveying somehow at the same time that they were not poor and destitute but rich and provided—just as I took their garden-feast for a sign of overflowing food—and that their state of children of nature was a refinement of freedom and grace. (p. 29)

These bare feet, James tells us, remained a fixed feature of the children, as they figured in his later fantasies.

What we know of James's history enables us to place the screen memory in relation to the historical events of his childhood. Although James himself locates the memory only as "connect[ed] somehow with the Pavilion period" (p. 28)—an extended period when the James family used to summer in New Brighton—we know that James's solo visit with his father took place when he was three years old. James's mother was not with them because she was at home in Albany awaiting the birth of her fourth child (Novick, 1996). (James himself was the second child, a year younger than his brother, William.) Thus the happy closeness with the father, and the pleasurable quality of the memory as a whole, wards off the boy's sadness at the loss of the mother. And, one might speculate, James's emphasis on his pleasure at the *numerous* children might likewise be in part a screen for the losses that he felt as his own family increased in number. The facts of James's personal history also help us to understand the image of the bare feet: his father, Henry James Sr., walked with a prosthetic leg, having lost his own leg to amputation as the result of a fire in childhood. Like the other sunny images of the memory, the accentuated bare feet may screen more disturbing sights—here, the memory of seeing the father's stump—a memory which would have become more frightening at an age where castration fears had become dominant.

Using these historical experiences as anchors, it is possible for us to make conjectures concerning the fantasy content of the details of James's memory. His mother pregnant, the three-year-old James was likely concerned with how this had come about. The image of the giant dog with James astride his back could be seen as a representation of the primal scene, with James identified with his father's role. The "riveting" sight of the bare feet might contain an image of his parents' nakedness, and perhaps his father's penis—reassuring in its intactness but also exciting and frightening. The very brightness of the scene in the memory could itself be seen as an aspect of the shock and excitement that James experienced when he viewed the parents in some form of sexual congress (Greenacre, 1947).

The reconstruction that I have just done focuses on the *content* of James's memory; it traces the way discrete elements of the memory reflect historical events in James's early life, the fantasies that these events stimulated, and the defensive operations James used to manage the anxieties that these events and fantasies evoked for him. Approaching the same memory through the *context* in which James presents it enables us to do a second, complementary kind of reconstruction—to trace the meaning and function that constructing, keeping, and re-evoking memories had for James.

James's intention when he began to write *A Small Boy and Others* was to produce a preface to a volume of his brother William's letters, which William's son wished to publish following William's death in 1910 (Novick, 2007). The project soon turned into a memoir about William, one in which Henry James's own act of remembering took centre stage. Gathering his own memories, James is constructing a setting, "the scene of our very first perceptions" (James, 1913, p. 8) in which he can re-experience William's presence. James emphasises that the only way that he can construct a meaningful picture of William is through his (Henry's) own subjectivity. "It was to memory in the first place that my main appeal for particulars had to be made" (p. 1). The memories that James gathers together have the familiar hallmarks of screen memories: the feeling is most often of fragments of memory rather than a continuous narrative; the memories are sensuous, largely visual but incorporating memories of taste as well; they are shrouded in a "golden haze" (p. 3), yet at the same time have a special "distinctness" (p. 3) and "freshness" (p. 4). James describes seeing himself from outside—a literary device, certainly, but one that conveys the dual sense of watching and inhabiting the scenes.

James emphasises again and again the *unitary* quality of his memories. His experience in gathering together "the full treasure of scattered, wasted circumstance" (p. 1) was "to find discrimination among the parts of my subject again and again difficult—so inseparably and beautifully they seemed to hang together and the comprehensive case to decline mutilation" (p. 2).

And a little later: "I struggle under the drawback, innate and inbred, of seeing the whole content of the memory in each enacted and recovered moment, as who should say, in the vivid image and the very scene" (p. 3). The people contained in a memory are also a single unit, connected in an unchangeable way: "We were to my sense, the blest group of us, such a company of characters and such a picture of differences, and withal so fused and interlocked" (p. 2).

For James a memory contains and enshrines the object world, held static in a single moment of feeling; by reconstructing it later on, he can re-evoke both the setting and the objects who have since been lost: "I cherish the moment and evoke the image and repaint the scene," he says, and recalls how "the field was animated and the adventure conditioned for me by my brother's nearness" (p. 3). And at the same time, through the act of remembering, James re-evokes a sense of his own identity, as a presence "interlocked" with the other figures in the scene, and even more as an onlooker—a boy for whom a fundamental part of the self is expressed in the act of looking, taking in the world, and remembering: "For there was the very pattern and measure of all he [James as a small boy] was to demand: just to be somewhere—almost anywhere would do—and somehow receive an impression or an accession, feel a relation or a vibration" (p. 25).

The complementary reconstructions that I have done show us a kind of tension in the way screen memories operate for James and, I believe, for others. Originating in childhood trauma—here, we hypothesise, the mother's pregnancy and absence, the father's amputation, the primal scene—a screen memory tells a visual *story*, constructed by the child to manage the reactions and fantasies the trauma has stimulated; although it can be deconstructed through self-reflection or analytic work, the screen memory is durable because the memories and fantasies that gave rise to it are tenaciously warded off—near to the heart of childhood anxiety and fantasy that can never be fully tolerated. Yet at the same time, the screen memory functions for James as a sensuous story to be held and kept; it is important not as a *specific* story, organised to express and manage *specific* memories and wishes, but as a *piece of the past*—a representation of a whole moment that needs to be durable because it is used to re-evoke both absent objects and moments in self-experience; among the key moments of self-experience that it preserves is the sense of a self as a viewer and rememberer.

Both aspects of screen memory are important for each of us. James emphasises the unitary, evocative dimension of memory in his memoir—and likely this dimension was particularly important to him in a work intended to recall and mourn his brother. However, both currents of the outdoor-meal memory can be traced in his fiction, perhaps most clearly in the opening scene of his great novel,

The Portrait of a Lady, where James (1881) describes first the setting which clearly replicates his childhood memory (Novick, 2007, p. 8)—an outdoor tea on a sunny day, a wealthy family gathered on the grass where carpets have been spread, a feeling of pleasure and discovery—and then brings into it the central figure in the story, a newcomer, Isabel Archer, who like the child Henry James is leaving behind her an unacknowledged loss (LaFarge, 2011).

A clinical example of screen memory

Two sessions from the analysis of a young woman show us something about the way the two currents of screen memory—memory as content and memory as the act of remembering—play out in the analytic situation.[2]

The first session

Toward the end of her first session on the couch, my patient, Miss S, recounted again an important screen memory, which she had brought up in her anamnesis. The session was one where Miss S spoke with some pressure, with a great deal of feeling, and a lot to say. I felt excited with Miss S about beginning the analysis, but I was not fully caught up with her in her feelings. My interventions were brief, largely echoing and restating what she had said to let her know that I was present and listening.

Miss S began the session by speaking of her great anxiety and excitement at starting analysis. The very weekend before we were starting, she had gone out on a date with a new man she had just begun seeing. She had felt immediately drawn to him—pulled to him like a magnet—but she knew somehow that the feeling was really about me, or about me as well as him.

Miss S felt that she was putting herself in a dangerous situation, feeling so excited, she said. It made her want to draw back. She felt that there was so much need pent up, and it might come flooding out. Analysis was something she had wanted for so long! But now that it was actually beginning, she felt like something would be lost or ruined. She felt overwhelmed. It was too good to be true. Everything went so well for her! Things just fell into place! She felt badly remembering that her mother, who had had a serious illness during Miss S's early years, had had a much harder time of things.

Recalling the hard times the family had had when her mother had been hospitalised, Miss S reflected on the way she had managed on her own early on. She had felt some insecurity her whole life that the decisions she made all on her own were not the best ones. Still it was good to be so independent. She now recalled the screen memory she had told me once before:

The memory was of learning to read: all of a sudden, she recognised that the letters on the mailbox spelled out her family name. She could see the red letters on the mailbox clearly in the memory, and herself as a child. She must have been about three years old. She remembered the thought: "I can do it all by myself!"

Recalling the memory now, she said: "I remember the space of time when I had that feeling. I feel that I am in the same space now, feeling the same way—but I don't trust it."

"Why don't I?" Miss S asked herself. Turning back to the feeling of pride and accomplishment in the memory, she listed to herself some of the many successes she had achieved since. "I have done a lot", she asserted. "Over and over wonderful things happen to me. I can accomplish more."

Addressing herself to me again, Miss S said: "For a second I felt not so alone, and I feel that way about the analysis. I can hear the tone of your voice, and it all feels not so scary. I know the analysis will be wonderful. It will be different from the way it was with my parents, with my mother gone so much in the hospital and everything so chaotic. Here is the opportunity again to have what I want, and I want to want it with the same yearning I did then, so I could receive it. But I can't find it again, that yearning. It is muffled."

In Miss S's session, we can see something of the way the two dimensions of screen memory that I have described—memory as a construct in which trauma and fantasy are defensively screened, and memory as a unitary affective experience, summoned up by the act of remembering—emerge and are intertwined with each other in the clinical situation.

The transference situation, Miss S's associations before and after she recounts the memory, and what we know of her history permit us to make a preliminary construction of the content of the screen memory and some of the material that it screens.[3] Although Miss S does not make this connection explicitly, the timing of the memory, when she was three years old, corresponds to the time when her mother was away for prolonged periods at a hospital in a distant city. The feeling that "I can do it by myself" wards off the flood of neediness that Miss S is feeling now and must have felt then. Likely the mailbox also reflects an aspect of the mother's absence—her sending letters home to the family. And we can see in the memory an edge of the excitement that Miss S is feeling in the session and with her new boyfriend. It is a memory not simply of accomplishment but of a magical moment of understanding, and one wonders what Miss S has learned—whether, for instance, with the family name on the mailbox, the knowledge has something to do with how the family came to be, with sexual secrets, or with fantasies of what it meant for Miss S for her mother to be gone and herself to be left with her father. We can begin to conjecture that the conflicts that make Miss S unable to revive her old yearning so that it could at last be satisfied, have to do with neediness, loss, guilt, and sexuality. Even in this first session, we can see the beginning of my being cast in the transference in the roles of the characters who stand just on the periphery of the "by myself" memory—the mother who is longed for, and, a little further away, displaced onto the figure of the boyfriend, the exciting father.

At the same time, in this first session, I think Miss S is also showing and telling us about the memory as something more unitary and concrete—a space, or a feeling to be summoned up and held on to at a frightening time, which serves to evoke a particular sense of self and objects. From this perspective, the unfolding of the session involves Miss S's creating a state of mind where she can feel like herself and feel heard and begin to connect this place with a feeling of my presence—a background, or starting place where she can begin to do the work of analysis. When we look at it this way, we see Miss S launching herself forward full speed into the analysis, telling me about her pressured feelings of need, excitement, and anxiety until these become overwhelming. The memory is a pause in this movement, an evoked picture, and with it a particular feeling state of entering the memory, as "a space of time when you have that feeling", where she is now. The first time she tries to establish this state, it breaks down—"I cannot trust it". In order to shore it up, she turns inward to herself; only then does she feel settled enough to put me in the picture, to feel that I am the one who is hearing and seeing the memory. She turns back toward me, feels less alone and is soothed by the sound of my voice. From this perspective the development of transference in the session is less busy, less inhabited by the figures of parents and self, playing out a story, and has more to do with the quieter figure of a listener who makes the story real and known, a role that Miss S first takes into herself by recalling a childhood memory and ultimately is able to delegate to me.

The second session

A session one year later, where Miss S brought up a related screen memory, shows us the way the content of the memory and the act of remembering and telling it continue to unfold and play out in relation to each other. The session I report followed a very lively session where Miss S had spoken for the first time about her fantasies about my life outside the consulting room.

Miss S began the session by reporting a dream: *she had come to my office for her session. My office was different—grand and palatial—and I was unexpectedly absent. A man was filling in for me. She began the session with him but felt disappointed that I was not there.*

Associating to the dream, she said that the man was an older man she knew who was very kind and sympathetic. She wondered why the office was so fancy. Yesterday she had been imagining my apartment; it had not been so grand in her fantasy.

I said that perhaps the dream continued that session and her fantasies about me.

Miss S did not respond directly but continued on the theme of the grand office. A friend of hers went to see a woman analyst who was reputed to have a grand office. That friend's appearance had changed entirely: she had become glamorous and expensively dressed!

I said that she might wish that I was more glamorous and had a fancier office so that she could model herself on me and become more glamorous as well.

Miss S demurred; she had talked about this with another friend and decided that it was better not to see someone so imposing. My house as she imagined it was cosier and very nice ... Yesterday's session had been exciting, she said, but it had left her feeling angry. This was the best session she had had in analysis; she felt that she was doing it just right and everything was opening up! Why hadn't *I* shown her how to do it so well earlier?

Throughout this part of the session, I felt that I was watching an oedipal drama in which I was cast as the mother; I felt a lively connection with Miss S, and interested in the drama, but not strongly pulled to take part in it.

Returning to imagining my apartment as she had yesterday, Miss S now found herself seeing an image from an early memory: Miss S was three years old. She was reading a story from a picture book to her mother, and she made up a story to tell her mother about the picture in the book, a picture of a little girl in a pretty dress.

With Miss S's recounting of the memory, I felt a shift in the tone of the session, as if she had joined me outside the drama, and we were looking at it together. Then, as she associated to the memory, she seemed to move back and forth from playing out the memory (and the same oedipal drama, reconfigured within the memory) to looking at it with me.

"I have a thought like, 'See! *I* can do it," Miss S said. "It's something I always knew how to do but was just beginning to do here—to tell you the kind of stories I was telling yesterday."

In the memory, the picture in the book was very vividly coloured, Miss S said—yellow and white and red. And as she looked at the background now she could see that the setting of the memory was the home of another little girl, an elementary school classmate who had a very doting mother. That mother would dress her daughter beautifully every day for school! Everything matched and was frilly. Miss S remembered how she had wished that she were that little girl, with that mother.

She turned again to the dream, and the man analyst. "I heard recently that you are married to another analyst. I don't know anything about the rest of your family. But I wish I didn't know about your husband. I can make up stories about you, your children, even your grandchildren. But even when I do, I still wonder where you really live, who your family is—I still want to know all about you. I miss the time when the stories I formed were enough."

I now felt drawn much closer to Miss S, aware of how strongly she wanted to connect with me, how she struggled against that wish and wished that she could stay with her fantasies instead. I said that her wanting to know about me disrupted her imagining me.

"Yes," Miss S said. "Wanting to know makes me anxious. I used to just want the stories."

She thought again about the memory of the picture book and her telling a story. "I have many feelings as I see that picture. It is comforting, familiar, enchanting. It reminds me of happy moments with my mother—how she loved me to read to her and tell her stories—how enchanted she was by my stories! But as I look at the picture now, I feel angry that *you* weren't asking me to tell you—*you* weren't trying hard enough to know! And that makes me feel like not telling you stories at all. It makes me want to keep my stories private.

"I am three years old in the memory. My mother was gone most of the time for a year. I think this might be a memory of when I got her back and we were close again. And it is coming up with you now, just a year after we have begun together. Now I can begin, suddenly, to tell my stories to you."

In this session, I think we can see the way the transference themes that were glimpsed in the first session have begun to be drawn into a single, powerful maternal transference; and the more elaborated screen memory recalled in this session gives us a more complex view of the same themes. At the same time, the act of remembering and the telling of the memory continue to serve another important set of functions for Miss S.

Once again, drawing upon the transference situation, Miss S's associations, and the history that we have learned, we can build a complex reconstruction of the content of the memory—a construction in which some of our hypotheses from the beginning of the analysis are borne out. This time we can clearly connect the "reading" memory to oedipal material. Miss S recalls the memory in a session where I am cast as the oedipal mother; curious about my private life, she dreams of replacing me with a fatherly man. (It seems likely that this reflects not only a wish but an actuality for Miss S, who was left with her father when her mother went to the hospital.) She denigrates my femininity and berates me for not telling her important secrets. In this context, the screen memory that she recounts can be seen to represent a disguised solution to these oedipal conflicts. Miss S is close to me but superior—reading to *me* and telling *me* a story rather than the other way round—and I am happily accepting this situation. There is a snug regressive tone to the memory, and sexuality and feminine aspiration have been placed, as in a dream within a dream, within a second, interior frame—in a picture, inside a book, of a beautifully dressed little girl.[4]

The figure of the listening mother, who seemed to hover on the periphery of the earlier screen memory, is incorporated in this second memory, where Miss S's mother is shown listening to her story; and we can begin to understand it better in the transference as well. The memory represents the reunion of Miss S and her mother after the mother's long absence; the happiness in the memory screens the loss; and the "anniversary" session where the memory is recounted reflects both Miss S's wish to place me in that early, listening role (and likely her awareness that as I have listened to her in our sessions she has begun to do so); and the way her anger and disappointment at my earlier failures intrude on that wish. In the interconnection between oedipal and pre-oedipal, "listening" images of the mother, we can also begin to see the way these two maternal themes may be related—that, for Miss S, the mother's absence, which left Miss S in possession of the father, was likely felt as both an oedipal triumph and a punishment for oedipal wishes, framed as an abandonment by an earlier, "listening" mother (Kulish & Holtzman, 2008).

At the same time, we can trace in this session a second line of meaning—one that has to do with the acts of recalling memories and telling them to others. In telling the memory, Miss S moves from a situation where conflict and anger at me are mounting to a situation where we are looking at something together; Miss S can only intermittently permit me to look at it with her. To share it with me means to give up her anger at me—to forgive me—while keeping it to herself is a kind of revenge. However, for Miss S the greatest danger to the screen memory lies not in its being shared, but in its losing the power it possesses as a world of fantasy. The screen memory, like Miss S's stories, represents a private world in which Miss S is in omnipotent control, a place she has invented, which stands as an alternate reality to the one she encounters in the external world; pulls to have real satisfactions in the external world disrupt it. Becoming closer to me means not only forgiving me and allowing me to share the screen memory but re-entering the world that prompted the construction of such memories—a hazardous, traumatic world where fantasy does not reign. It is no wonder that Miss S wishes that her stories were still enough!

Discussion

Contemplating the difference between screen memories and other psychic formations such as parapraxes, Freud observed the permanence and constancy of screen memories, "which seem to have the power of staying with us through a large part of our life" (Freud, 1901b, p. 44). I have tried to show that the special power and durability of the screen memory have to do with its dual function, as an organisation in which the demands of external reality, fantasy, and defence are reconciled, and as a memorial to a particular act and kind of remembering.

The first dimension of screen memory—screen memory as content—is more familiar to us. Although each screen memory has the form of an isolated moment in a child's experience, its content is highly condensed, containing in disguised form central themes and traumas of an entire childhood: parental privation and loss, the primal scene, oedipal rivalries, and solutions. As I have shown with the screen memories of Henry James and Miss S, the deconstruction of a screen memory can give us a window into the mind of the child who drew together its disparate elements into a unique organisation, and enable us to understand the way that child's development took place within a unique historical context of people and events.

The organised content of the screen memory acts as a template for object relations throughout life (Reichbart, 2008). In analysis, the object relationships mapped out in the screen memory emerge in transference and counter transference and can be interpreted.

Advances in psychoanalytic understanding of the processes and fantasies associated with thinking and the development of the capacity for thought permit the contemporary psychoanalyst to recognise a second dimension of the screen memory—a dimension that has to do with the screen memory as a *particular kind of representation* and the recollecting of a screen memory as a *particular kind of thinking*. This dimension of the screen memory, which we can trace in Henry James's writings about memory, and in Miss S's fantasies about remembering as they emerged in the analytic situation, gives us another window into the mind of the child—in this case, a view of the child in his role as constructor and rememberer of his own experience. From this perspective, the special properties of the screen memory—its brightness and sharp frame, its stubborn, unitary quality, the sense of watchfulness that may be embedded in it—can be seen as aspects of a representation created by a child whose capacity for constructing a coherent picture of himself and his experiences is under strain. In this situation, the child manages the *content* of trauma and wish by creating a *specific organisation*; but it is also of paramount importance for him to create a *feeling of organszation*, a sense that his experience is real and knowable—concretely, that it is happening and that it is being seen and known. The screen memory marks the child's establishment of this feeling and commemorates it.

The screen memory is a solo construction, one in which the child does not rely on the object's mental functioning to manage his emotional life, but rather seizes as much of that functioning as he has taken in, and reinforces it. The sense of individual identity associated with each person's store of screen memories (Reichbart, 2008) has to do, I think, not only with their durability and their capacity to represent in condensed form so many of the essential themes of childhood, but also to the act which they embody, of bringing together the two essential currents of identity (Greenacre, 1958)—the experiencing self and, in imagined form, the self as known to others.

The recollection of a screen memory in later life evokes both the memory itself, as a concrete unit in which a sense of self and others can be placed, and the individual's capacity to construct and evoke a world of his own. In the analytic process the act of remembering a screen memory brings up fantasies concerning the meaning of this private world, and the meaning of sharing it. Like the fantasies about the content of each screen memory, fantasies about the act of remembering and the private world of memory play out in transference and countertransference and can be interpreted. Like the content of screen memories, however, these fantasies and the private world connected with them never entirely lose their special quality; they remain markers of the individual's capacity to establish and maintain alone a steady view of his own emotional experience.

Notes

1. Mahon and Battin-Mahon (1981, 1983) express a rare dissenting view on this point, arguing that screen memories lose their psychological significance and salience in a successful analysis and that this decathexis can be used as an indicator of readiness for termination.

2. Miss S was treated in analysis four times a week on the couch.

3. I am in agreement with Greenacre (1981) that such preliminary constructions by the analyst should not be communicated to the patient; rather they should serve as hypotheses which organise the material and may be tested later on.

4. The setting of the age three memory, in the home of an elementary school classmate seems to indicate the kind of "portal aspect" described by Spero (1990), where later elements introduced into an earlier screen memory represent moments when the original conflict that gave rise to the screen memory threatens to re-erupt.

3

Screen memories: the faculty of memory and the importance of the patient's history

Franco De Masi

Freud's essay on screen memories (1899a) is a milestone in the development of psychoanalytic thought and contains the seeds of a number of concepts that lie at the root of analytic theory. A huge volume of literature has been inspired by this paper.

In my contribution I shall attempt to connect Freud's intuitions on screen memories with some of the approaches to clinical analysis that have evolved in recent decades and can, in my view, be applied in the therapy of patients with severe pathology. The new insights do not conflict with Freud's discoveries, but complement them. From this point of view Freud can aptly be compared to Columbus: the Genoese navigator also discovered a new world, but was able to explore only a part of it.

In the contemporary literature certain schools that take up a position beyond the dynamic unconscious and attach relatively little importance to repression are contrasted, sometimes artificially, with classical conceptions. It seems to me that the various approaches should not be seen as antithetical because each may prove legitimate when applied in a particular clinical field. Specifically, I believe that theories that disregard the dynamic unconscious are applicable principally in severe (i.e., borderline or psychotic) pathologies, in which the relationship between conscious and unconscious is gravely compromised. In this paper I shall also reflect on memory of the past and on the therapeutic importance of reconstructing the patient's personal history.

Screen memories

Phyllis Greenacre (1949) sees Freud's essay on screen memories (1899a) as a crucial turning point because for the first time it recovers the lost continent of infantile experience. After all, even if Freud's investigation is seemingly confined to the problem of the hidden meaning of memories, far-reaching perspectives are thereby opened up for the reader.

Freud begins by noting that in most cases infantile memories do not appear to be particularly significant. Those which later prove to be important and imbued with powerful emotions are, as a rule, not consciously remembered. The surviving conscious memories are in fact modified by displacement and repression. Psychoanalytic investigation reveals them to be unconsciously linked to significant and sometimes traumatic events. Freud holds that repression is not merely specific to the memory of a given event, but extends to the whole of infantile emotional life.

Personal memories are deceptive because memory is not a faithful transcription of what happened, but is subject to continuous revision.[1] Moreover, it is in this phase of reconstruction that memory undergoes transformations consistent with the subject's wishes or defences.

In his later writings Freud recognises that screen memories have a similar dynamic to parapraxes and must also be regarded as analogous to dreams, which are the product of repression, displacement, condensation, and symbolisation. For this reason too, the dynamic of screen memories is found to parallel the formation of neurotic symptoms. Freud was never to underestimate the value of his discoveries concerning screen memories, to which he still alluded indirectly in "Constructions in analysis" (1937d).

The 1899 essay addresses two factors that were to assume fundamental importance in psychoanalytic thought—namely, memory and infancy. Freud later had the following to say about the importance of infantile life and memories:

> This is often the way in which childhood memories originate. Quite unlike conscious memories from the time of maturity, they are not fixed at the moment of being experienced and afterwards repeated, but are only elicited at a later age when childhood is already past; in the process they are altered and falsified, and are put into the service of later trends, so that generally speaking they cannot be sharply distinguished from phantasies. (Freud, 1910c, p. 83)

> What someone thinks he remembers from his childhood is not a matter of indifference; as a rule the residual memories—which he himself does not understand—cloak priceless pieces of evidence about the most important features in his mental development (p. 84).

Again:

> ... analytic work deserves to be recognized as genuine psychoanalysis only when it has succeeded in removing the amnesia which conceals from the adult his knowledge of his childhood from its beginning (that is, from about the second to the fifth year). This cannot be said among analysts too emphatically or repeated too often. The motives for disregarding this reminder are, indeed, intelligible. It would be desirable to obtain practical results in a shorter period and with less trouble. But at the present time theoretical knowledge is still far more important to all of us than therapeutic success, and anyone who neglects childhood analysis is bound to fall into the most disastrous errors. The emphasis which is laid here upon the importance of the earliest experiences does not imply any underestimation of the influence of later ones (Freud, 1919e, p. 183).

Freud's consideration of memory dates from very early in his career. In a letter to Fliess written in 1896, he had written:

> As you know, I am working on the assumption that our psychical mechanism has come into being by a process of stratification: the material present in the form of memory-traces being subjected from time to time to a *re-arrangement* in accordance with fresh circumstances—to a *re-transcription*. ... memory is present not once but several times over, [and] is laid down in various species of indications .... (Freud, 1896b, p. 233)

> I should like to emphasize the fact that the successive registrations represent the psychical achievement of successive epochs of life. At the frontier between two such epochs a transition of the psychical material must take place. (p. 235)

Furthermore, he had anticipated the stabilising function of memory (Freud, 1901b). Mnemic impressions are preserved both in their original form and in the successive formulations assumed in the course of later development. These subsequent impressions arise from the interweaving of acts of fantasy with real facts, while the individual intersections impress their stamp on memory (1908e). By virtue of this particular quality, memory is timeless.

Given this mixture of fantasies, screen memories, and real events, the analyst has wide-ranging scope to distinguish the various elements involved.

The idea of a hierarchical structure is admittedly a central aspect of Freud's conceptualisation of screen memories (1899a, 1901b, 1917b), which, however, came to be seen as even more significant in his later writings. Screen memories may on occasion conceal disturbing images attributable purely to fantasy (in this case Freud (1908b) uses the term "screen-phantasy"). Alternatively, they may be clearly perceived psychical creations (1914g) that serve to conceal the traumatic significance of sexual or other kinds of events (1917b, 1918b). Freud is evidently postulating that the distortions accompanying the transformation of a memory may extend even to alteration of the perception of reality.

At any rate, fantasy as conceived by the Kleinians (Isaacs, 1948) must be distinguished from screen memories in that the latter still contain a fragment of objective perceptual material, whereas fantasy is a purely endopsychic creation originating in the drives.

Considered in these terms, a screen memory not only has the significance of a defence against a historical fact, but also represents a qualitative alteration of the reality sense affecting memory itself, its objects, and the experience of self (Spero, 1990).

Memory as seen by the neurosciences[2]

The neuroscientific view of the unconscious differs from the psychoanalytic conception of a dynamic unconscious governed by repression. The neurosciences are instead concerned with mental phenomena of which the experiencing subject is unaware and which are by their nature unknowable to him.[3]

In the neuroscientific approach, working memory is distinguished from long-term memory. The former, which depends on the prefrontal cortex, persists for a few minutes and furnishes information on what we perceive. An example is the ability to repeat a list of names or telephone numbers. The information contained in working memory disappears after a short time, but may also be recorded in long-term memory, which provides for permanent storage. Working memory allows us to search for and retrieve memories from the past. Many cognitive skills, such as the selection of memories, simultaneous comparison of different memories, and the capacity for reasoning and planning, depend on working memory.

As to the process whereby memories are recorded, according to the neuroscientists human beings possess two different types of memory that operate in parallel—namely, explicit or declarative memory and implicit or procedural memory.

An example of declarative memory is remembering the place where one married. Procedural memory, on the other hand, concerns an acquired skill such as riding a bicycle or a characteristic individual behaviour, the reasons for which, however, remain unknown because they depend on experiences dating from before the operation of declarative memory and the capacity for representation. Declarative memory refers to something that has been learnt and of which it is possible to become aware; it is permeable and enables an event to be recalled at will, whereas procedural memory is incapable of being remembered.

In evolutionary terms, the brain system governing procedural memory, which resides in the basal ganglia, is also present in lower animals (e.g., reptiles), whereas declarative memory, whose principal organ is the subcortical structure of the hippocampus, is unique to mammals. Some authors (e.g., Grigsby & Hartlaub, 1994) believe that character—that is, a person's routine behaviour—may be supported by procedural memory, even if it also involves attention and declarative memory.

As stated above, the two types of memory reflect distinct brain systems, which differ in terms of both development and anatomy. Declarative memory depends on the functioning of the hippocampus, the bilateral destruction of which entails loss of the capacity to memorise an event. The emotional component that accompanies a memory—in particular, fear and anxiety—is recorded in the amygdala, a small organ at the base of the brain.

Visual, auditory, and other memories are stored in the same areas of the cortex as the original perceptions. For example, visual memory is stored in the occipital areas that process incoming visual stimuli, whereas auditory memory is located in the temporal areas responsible for the reception of auditory stimuli. The hippocampus activates and connects the various areas of the brain that have recorded memories. An important part is also played by the frontal lobes, which are involved in the selection and organisation of memories.

The function of the hippocampus and the frontal lobes is to select and activate the selective "points" of memories (sounds, sights, or images) recorded in the various areas of the brain so as to create the experience of remembering (Nadel & Moskowitz, 1997). The fronto-hippocampal complex assembles the sensory experiences recorded in the various areas of the cortex and links them to the time and space when and where they were recorded. *What is remembered is therefore a reconstruction and not an exact replica of what happened in the past.*

It is important to note that in the first years of life declarative memory is not present owing to the delayed maturation of the hippocampus, whereas procedural memory is active because the basal ganglia are already operational (Joseph, 1996). This is a possible explanation for infantile amnesia. However, neurophysiological factors alone cannot fully account for the lack of memories of early infancy, since mother–child affective and communicative relations in the first years of life have been shown to reinforce declarative memory (Siegel, 1996). Those who have difficulty in recalling the early years of their infancy may have had insufficient communicative experiences of this kind.

Declarative memory also includes autobiographical memory, which concerns memories of the subject's personal life. In his investigation of screen memories, Freud was mainly concerned to discover the corresponding real event or infantile fantasy concealed behind the false memory. For this reason the focus of his interest was on autobiographical memory—that is, the part of memory retrievable by conscious effort. This approach was consistent with his hypothesis on the nature of neurosis (screen memories having the same dynamic as symptoms), but also had important therapeutic implications. Freud considered that emotional facts that lacked access to consciousness and had been repressed lay at the root of neurosis.

His therapeutic technique was therefore directed towards facilitating the emergence of the repressed wishes and thoughts, and for this purpose it was extremely important to decipher and render conscious the conflicts hidden behind screen memories.

In other words, Freud believed it essential to overcome the repression and make the patient aware of the unconscious thoughts concerning not only the present, but also the past. Recovery of the past was fundamental to integration of the individual and to restoration of mental health. Freud's aim was rediscovery of the historical truth freed from the distortions wrought by the patient's defences. Dismantling the false memory meant bringing the patient closer to the truth and releasing him from the power of illusion and unconscious manipulation. The hitherto concealed facts had to be consistently and progressively accommodated within autobiographical memory. That is why Freud likened the analyst's work to that of an archaeologist excavating the remains of an ancient city for the purposes of reconstruction.

Some neuroscientists have even postulated a possible neuronal route for conflict and repression within the brain: if information bound up with painful memories is stored in certain areas of the brain, a mechanism that inhibits declarative memory might be activated (Schacter, 1996). In this case, the right prefrontal lobe sends inhibitory stimuli to the left hemisphere and the temporal lobe, thus preventing translation of the relevant memory into words (Joseph, 1996).

Another important aspect is the action of trauma on memory. Trauma may give rise to hippocampal dysfunctions, sometimes resulting in permanent damage. It also causes altered states of consciousness that inhibit attention by means of dissociative mechanisms. The outcome of these various mechanisms is that declarative memory is inhibited or excluded from the recording process, while procedural memory retains the connection with the traumatic memory and may therefore generate disturbances associated with the trauma (emotional states or psychosomatic symptoms) even though no memory of the traumatic event emerges into consciousness.

Memory of abuse: true or false?

As we know, however, the problem of the veracity of the history as remembered is never so simple. Sometimes not screen memories but actual falsifications of reality are involved.

After the passage of many years the issues raised by Freud's 1899 essay have given rise to a vigorous debate, which has not lacked a dramatic aspect owing to the legal and social consequences of false memories. When instances of sexual abuse in infancy are recalled, did these happen in reality or are they constructions—false memories—on the part of the patient?

Notwithstanding the enormous volume of literature on the subject (Brenneis, 2000; Brown, 1999; Good, 1999; Good, Day, & Rowell, 2005; Greenacre, 1949; Harris, 1996; Kris, 1956; Sandler & Fonagy, 1997; Spero, 1990; Target, 1998; Yovell, 2000), the matter has not been settled once and for all. The problem, it seems, can be solved only after the event and must be addressed by in-depth exploration of the specific dynamics of each individual case. There are no hard and fast rules for establishing whether the history as presented is true or false.

At any rate, one should be suspicious of over-explicit accounts by certain patients, especially if forthcoming early in the therapy, because real memories of abuse are very often dissociated, emerging only late on and frequently mingled with a sense of guilt.

> For instance, towards the third year of her analysis, a forty-year-old patient of mine suddenly recalled an incestuous relationship with her father at a time when she had grown into a beautiful young girl. She remembered that her father had kissed and caressed her in her bed for a long time on many occasions. The patient was certain of the accuracy of this memory, but felt very guilty because she was convinced that it had been her fault. She was obviously unable to admit that her father was also to blame because she respected and idealised him—unlike her mother, whom she despised. When her younger sister told her that she too had been the object of his erotic attentions, the patient realised that it had not been her fault alone and that her father had perhaps not been so ideal after all.

An important criterion, in my view, for distinguishing true from false memories is the analyst's acquaintance with the patient's conscious and unconscious dynamics, as well as appraisal of the patient's family background. All such evaluations can, of course, only be hypothetical and the analyst must remain in doubt for a long time. These patients have frequently undergone emotional traumas within their families and developed intense reactive aggression and vengeful wishes towards their parents, who may be accused of committing acts that never happened.

> A paedophile sadomasochistic patient of mine (see De Masi, 2007) believed that his mother had masturbated him on many occasions. He said that this happened when she decided to sleep in his room to calm him down, because he often suffered from insomnia. There may have been some substance to this memory because the mother, a hysterical character, eventually fell in love with some of her son's friends. Although I did my best to keep the patient's memory in mind, it failed to convince me because the mother did not seem to me to be so ill as to engage in incest. The memory in fact later proved to be false, having been generated by the patient's characteristic processes of mental sexualisation which had altered the memory of the past, as well as being an attempt to project the guilt of his paedophilia on to his mother.

This example may facilitate understanding of the retroactive power of certain mental states over past events.

Meltzer (1973) describes the process of mental sexualisation observed in some psychotic states, perversions, and cases of drug addiction. Such patients succeed in creating an aroused masturbatory state that distances them from reality: the transformation is so pleasurable that they cease to be aware of the dangers of the process that alters their perception of reality.

Sexualisation corresponds to a withdrawal of the mind into the aroused body and is characteristic of the perverse mental state. My patient's state of mental sexualisation caused him to experience as sexual even things that had nothing to do with sex: for instance, it seemed to him that all little boys wanted sex and were constantly masturbating each other. The adolescent experience with his mother, too, had undergone subsequent sexualisation. This case is another demonstration of the importance of Freud's discovery that memory is a reconstructive phenomenon subject to possible distortion.

Actual sexual abuse usually results in such powerful dissociation that the subject is no longer aware of it. It may sometimes be revealed in dreams, which are so inexplicit and camouflaged that they appear to be actual screen memories, as in the case presented below. Yovell (2000) here describes the emergence of the emotional memory of a trauma in the therapy of a female patient who had been repeatedly abused by a young friend of the family at about the age of four.

> In addition to eating disorders and a constantly depressed mood, the young patient, Tara, had developed an emotional inhibition that had prevented her from engaging in a meaningful relationship with a man. During the course of her therapy she had become more open to the possibility of a relationship and had met a partner whom she liked.
>
> Following an intimate evening with him at her home, Tara had come to her session the next day in a very depressed and anxious state, saying that, immediately after parting from him, she had felt impelled to rush to the bathroom to wash and then to stuff herself with food—something that had not happened to her for months. She had also had an anxiety-filled dream that had woken her up and prevented her from falling asleep again. In the dream she saw herself as a little girl playing in the garden with her friends. Eventually a great big snake appeared in the grass; at first it seemed quite nice, brightly coloured, moving about happily and even crawling between the girls' legs. It then crawled towards Tara, coming so close that it threatened to suffocate her. Looking round in terror, Tara saw that all her friends were dead.
>
> In the second part of the dream, Tara turned back to the house and went into the kitchen, where she saw her mother from the side desperately trying to slice the snake up and kill it. On noticing that she was there, her mother looked at her with hate in her eyes as if she had discovered a secret.
>
> Hearing the account of the dream, Yovell began to suspect that the intimate contact with Tara's boyfriend (they had kissed passionately the night before) had aroused the dissociated memory of an abuse. That is why she had felt terribly anxious and guilty on his departure.

On subsequently questioning her brother, Tara learnt that, as a little girl, she had indeed been abused by a neighbour who played with them, but that all members of the family had been forbidden to talk to her about it. The dream had caused Tara to relive the old trauma of having to yield to the penis–snake and be enveloped and penetrated by it. Note, too, that the dream shows that Tara was aware that her mother knew about the abuse but persisted in keeping silent about it.

An elegant neuroscientific experiment (Schacter et al., 1996) demonstrates the fallibility of memory and its alterability by brain structures responsible for mental deception. An interviewer presented a list of names of objects orally to a number of experimental subjects. The same subjects were subsequently shown another list containing some of the names included in the first list (which they had heard), as well as others in which the same objects as those in the first list were given different names, which, however, had the same meaning (e.g., "sweet" instead of "cake"). Finally, the subjects were asked if a particular word was or was not included in the first list. The subjects sometimes mixed up the names in the second list with those in the first, while on other occasions they recalled the names in the first list perfectly. Using neuroimaging techniques, the researchers observed that the hippocampus was activated both when the subjects' memory was correct and when it was wrong.

The difference was that in the case of accurate recall the auditory cortex (the seat of auditory memorisation) was also activated, whereas when the subject remembered wrongly even when convinced that this was not the case, the hippocampus was activated but not the auditory cortex. The authors concluded that the hippocampus furnished the conviction that a memory was real whether or not this was actually the case.

Hence a person may be convinced of the reality of a false memory of abuse even if the abuse never occurred (Pally, 1997b).

Precursors of thought and emotion

As stated earlier, in his examination of screen memories Freud necessarily concentrated on autobiographical memory, which forms part of declarative memory. It is in this sphere that repression operates.

The (repressed) dynamic unconscious described by Freud can operate by repression because a form of recording of events that belongs to declarative memory has developed: before being repressed, an emotion must be accepted and recorded by a psychic receptor. In other words, the dynamic unconscious can repress the incompatible affect only if that affect has been received by the emotional receptors. The subject first records the emotions without being aware of so doing and then renders them unconscious if they are felt to be incompatible.

The discovery of procedural memory in particular permits an alternative conception of the way in which the non-conscious influx of past experiences informs certain aspects of the personality (Schacter & Scarry, 2000).

On the basis of the existence of non-declarative processes, it has been postulated that the precursors of thought and affectivity are formed by way of non-conscious processes that are recorded in procedural memory and do not have access to consciousness. These precursors structure a child's personality and may be compromised in the event of deficient care.

Of the many recent contributions on non-declarative processes, I shall mention only that of Beebe, Lachmann, and Jaffe (1997). These authors seek to throw light on the early interactive processes that arise from the forms of mother–child emotional communication in the first year of life prior to language use. The interaction between the two organises experience and creates patterns, which the infant learns to recognise, expect, and remember. These dyadic experiences will later constitute the unconscious organisational structures that underlie personality. The authors invoke a "prereflective" rather than a dynamic unconscious, because in their view a newborn's representations are symbolised mainly in the non-verbal representational system.

A large number of studies have shown that non-verbal emotional communication between mother and child (prosody, gesture, and facial expressions) of the kind that occurs constantly in the first few months of care constitute the foundations of the developing personality.

Such insights (stemming also from infant research and attachment theory) totally bear out Bion's container–contained model. In order to live, the human mind needs a place in which to deposit wishes and anxieties. An infant does this constantly by projecting into the mind of the mother, who accepts his projections and returns the meaning of his non-verbal communication to him. It is the quality of the mother's response that will be introjected by the child and provide him with the means to understand and strike a balance between his sensory or emotional experiences.

Early emotional trauma

It may be postulated that the unconscious does not exist from the beginning, but is a system that develops progressively provided that the necessary emotional conditions are satisfied; this process is not always guaranteed and if it is deficient serious consequences may ensue for the individual's mental health. As stated earlier, this basic emotional network is structured long before verbal language. Failing the necessary emotional experiences, an unconscious that uses symbolic language and can forge emotional links cannot develop.

On the basis of such considerations, Fonagy (1999) takes the view that borderline states stem from early traumas incorporated at a time when they are not representable. Borderline and psychotic patients are therefore unable to mentalize—that is, to represent—emotions, psychic events, and mental states, since they are ignorant of their meaning.

An extreme example of a screen memory in a patient with severe pathology was presented by a patient of mine who exhibited a psychotic transference (De Masi, 2006).

> When I asked the patient for information about his parents at his initial interview, he told me that his memories of infancy with his mother were wonderful, whereas those involving his father were very negative and traumatic. During the course of the analysis the traumatic relationship with the father was confirmed by the development of a violent and persecutory transference, but the enactment of his relationship with his mother was even more dramatic: having been admitted to hospital several times for psychotic episodes, when she was at home she would waylay her son and confide her anxieties and delusions to him. One of these was that she was dead and that the patient had been entrusted to a stepmother; in desperation, he had then gone to her grave to

bring her back to life. In reality, the mother eventually committed suicide even though the patient was told that she had had a heart attack.

I believe that the more complex psychopathologies are underlain by damage to the unconscious functions—in particular, those of emotional awareness.

Whereas neurosis is the outcome of a lack of harmony in the operation of the dynamic unconscious, borderline or psychotic structures are fuelled by an alteration of the emotional and receptive unconscious—that is, of the mental apparatus capable of symbolising affects and of using the emotional function of intrapsychic and relational communication.

In other words, screen memories are more common in patients who have developed a dynamic unconscious and make use of defences such as displacement and repression. The patient with wonderful memories of his psychotic mother was on no account resorting to repression, but instead to para-delusional transformations in which the mechanism of projection rendered the original figure unrecognisable.

Screen memories involve a transformation of the infantile experience of the past, which, however, retains a correspondence with the figures of reality. In the psychotic state, on the other hand, there is a radical, para-delusional transformation of memory in which any relation to the original object is lost.

Value of the history

Another issue arising out of Freud's work on screen memories concerns the reconstruction of the patient's personal history and its therapeutic value. Reconstruction of the past was of central importance to Freud (1937d), and although his ideas on the matter were by no means clearly defined, he was convinced that the truth of the patient's infantile vicissitudes could be established.

Following in his footsteps, most analysts have taken the view that precisely the transference, given that it is a repetition of the past, guarantees the veracity of these infantile vicissitudes.

The validity of historical reconstruction has, of course, been called into question by some analysts, who have introduced the concept of narrative truth in preference to historical truth (Schafer, 1983; Spence, 1982).

However, denial of the importance and reality of historical truth carries the risk of underestimating the significance of the child's mental and emotional environment and its contribution to his development. A hypothesis specific to psychoanalysis is that our relations with the care-giving objects of our infancy are fundamental to our development and future life. As stated above, the quality of the responses received at the beginning of our lives dictates our subsequent emotional disposition. The concept of emotional history has expanded substantially and now extends to the level of procedural processes and the role of the care-giving figures.

Not all analysts accept the therapeutic value of reconstruction of the past. Fonagy (1999), for example, considers that there is no evidence of a direct correlation between improvements and reconstruction of the past. In his view, reconstruction is necessary for the therapeutic process because it supplies the instruments to put the patient's mind in touch with what was previously intolerable and because it generates a narration of self consistent with a historical continuity.

Blum (2003), on the other hand, emphasises the importance of infancy and its psychoanalytic reconstruction, holding that it is interpretation of significant facts from the past that gives rise to transformation in the course of therapy. Memories, including screen memories and distorted memories, as well as lapses of memory, fragments, and forgetting, become grist to the mill of the psychoanalytic process. The transference too is a return to the past, with repressed memories deeply embedded in a fundamental constellation of unconscious fantasies, and constitutes the main, if not the only, path towards understanding and analysis of the patient. This author does not believe that the psychodynamic unconscious can be set aside in favour of procedural memory.

Eric Brenman is one of the analysts who set store by the reconstruction of the past for therapeutic purposes. He writes:

> It is inherent in man to seek knowledge, to enquire and discover. It seems important for him to pursue enquiry about his origins, to find his roots; he needs roots and objects, he cannot function alone. To my mind, knowing his background provides him with a sense of continuity and meaning. Only if he feels he belongs can

he achieve his own identity. Reconstruction is of value as a means of rediscovering roots, past objects and lost parts of the self (Brenman, 2006, p. 11).

Brenman also notes that the reconstruction of the past may differ according to one's individual approach. For instance, reconstruction of the Oedipus myth may take either a drive-based or a traumatic form. In the former case Oedipus kills his father because he wants to take possession of his mother, whereas in the latter the parricide is due to the parents' prior abandonment of their son. It has been pointed out that it is hard to imagine an Oedipus in possession of good enough objects to confront his Oedipus complex.

Emotional history

In order to understand the complexity inherent in a patient, it is essential to reconstruct his emotional history. By "emotional history" I do not mean reconstruction of events of the past with the aim of achieving a definite, shared objectivity. I have already stated that memories may be distorted by present conflicts and emotions. I am referring instead to the possibility of formulating meaningful hypotheses, which, by reconstruction of the relationship with the primal objects, can facilitate understanding of the precarious equilibrium of the present situation. By means of his intuitive work, conducted silently and apart from the analysand, the analyst can develop hypotheses to explain the possible distortion of emotional development and the traumatic character of early infantile experiences.

The other aspect must of course also be explored. Disturbances of development are attributable not only to deficiencies or distortion of the primary objects' responses, but also to the child's subjective disposition to create defences or psychopathological structures that eventually become very significant. For instance, a child faced with an unreceptive mother may be compelled to withdraw into bodily fantasies that can give rise to a state of mental arousal and take the place of dependence on a human object conducive to development.

Some of our patients have sustained various forms of emotional trauma in infancy and are usually unaware of them. These traumas may have the consequence of emotional inhibitions of one kind or another, whose outcome may be a lack of vitality and in some cases even a "psychic retreat" (Steiner, 1993). This is a psychopathological construction characterised by a pleasurable (omnipotent, perverse, or sexualised) psychic reality that sometimes exists in parallel with a seemingly normal social life.

It is my conviction that hypotheses about the past must be formulated on one's first meeting with a patient—that is, well before any relevant transference manifestations. Right from the initial interviews it is my practise to listen to the patient's account of his history and problems while at the same time using my analytic receptivity to gain an impression of his primary objects or his parents' manner of facilitating or, conversely, inhibiting the development of his personality. In other words, I frame to myself the questions that enable me to postulate the nature of the external and internal factors that have potentially blocked or distorted the patient's emotional development. In particular, I reflect on the parents' capacity to help the patient to confront life and to develop a genuine identity. I use intuition to attempt a reconstruction of the patient's emotional trajectory, by comparing his conscious memory with his present state of difficulty. The discrepancy between his conscious account and his actual awareness enables me to hypothesise about the extent of the patient's ignorance of the past, the character of his primary objects, and even his mental functioning.

The formulation of reconstructive hypotheses about the past is useful in order to facilitate insight into some of the possible transference dynamics, the anxieties that may emerge in the relationship and the emotional distance to be covered by the patient in the course of analytic treatment. Caution must, of course, be exercised with the reference to the past, which must not be used as a defence against conflicts or turbulence in the analytic relationship.

Once formulated, these hypotheses may be modified or integrated with other material that emerges during the course of the analytic process. In all cases the forms assumed by the analysand's progression will be entirely novel and likely to surprise the analyst, who must be prepared to forget his hypotheses and to open his mind at all times to the new and the unknown.

If the analyst has been able to apprehend and internally evaluate the history of the patient's emotional development, then the pathogenic relationship with the primary object that is immediately manifested in the analysis will elicit an appropriate response from him. This position, which helps the patient to tell the analyst as an object from the past apart from the analyst who facilitates understanding of the past, is part of the technique that I apply as early as possible. Transference interpretation is useful in this case in attempting to disentangle the figure of the analyst as a potential new object from the patient's experience with the internalised objects of the past. It is, after all, the analyst's task to transform the role in which he is cast by the patient into that of a potential new object.

As stated earlier, in patients who have attained a more advanced level of development (neurotic patients) or who become capable of representation, traumas in the primary relationship may also find expression in dreams (as in the case of Yovell's patient).

It will be seen that my approach differs from that of many other analysts (e.g., Joseph, 1985), who consider that reconstruction of the infantile history becomes useful only at an advanced stage of an analysis and may indeed be used as a defence against analysis of the transference. The analyst must obviously be aware of the defences deployed both by the patient and by himself. He must always communicate his hypotheses only when the patient is capable of understanding them; that is to say, he must choose the optimum time having regard to the patient's personality and capacity for understanding, the latter often bearing no relation to the length of the analysis.

A relationship conducive to development

According to the traditional view, the cornerstone of analytic work consists in transference interpretation and reconstruction of the past. My own opinion is that interpretation of the transference and reconstruction of the past are a necessary but not a sufficient step. To develop a bond of dependence directed towards mental growth, trust in the analytic relationship is required. After all, the therapeutic process depends largely on the ability of the two protagonists—analyst and analysand—to forge a relationship conducive to psychic development.

For this reason I distinguish the transference and countertransference from the analytic relationship. Put simply, whereas in my view the transference is attributable to the patient's projections, split-off aspects, and infantile past, the analytic relationship is the result of the meeting of the receptive parts of the analysand and the analyst and develops with the contributions of both. In particular, while the analytic relationship is based on the natural need to depend on an object for mental growth, the character of that relationship depends on the analyst's interpretative capacity—that is, on his receptivity and the appropriateness of his response to the patient's communications. (In this connection, Freud's notion of the unobjectionable transference was the first attempt to theorise the area of the analytic relationship and mental growth.)

Insight and emotional understanding of the past, which eventually become possible in an analysis, bear witness to the fact that the analysand's system of empathic receptivity has expanded. The valuable new acquisitions throw light on the past. What we recover is not the memory, but the capacity to remember and to integrate. In other words, analysis helps the analysand to develop his formerly inhibited capacity for intuition, thus enabling him to understand not only the present, but also the past after the event. Discovery of a truth about the patient's personal past in my opinion permits the restoration of what was rendered unconscious by means of defences, idealisation of the self, or the projection of responsibility on to the primal objects; reconstruction of the past thus helps to structure the patient's identity.

However, can the past really be recovered in all instances? In the treatment of neurotic patients, the experience of the past is present in unconscious awareness and is therefore destined to emerge in the course of analytic work. In more serious cases (e.g., borderline or psychotic patients), the difficult experiences of infancy compromise personality structure and encourage the formation of pathological structures that obliterate the memory of the infantile experience. In such instances a more complex road must be travelled, as the link between psychopathology and trauma is more deeply buried and more indirect.

Reconstruction of the past is conditional on the patient's possession of an unconscious capable of metaphorical thought and of associative memory—that is, of an emotional and receptive unconscious. While this function is substantially operational in neurotic analysands, it proves to be badly damaged or even completely absent in borderline or psychotic patients. This finding is at variance with certain statements by Freud (1937d), who could not readily credit that a psychic structure could be totally destroyed and implicitly believed that reconstruction was always possible.

In the course of the pathological processes and repeated traumas from which borderline or psychotic states seemingly arise, the unconscious pre-representational functions undergo various transformations that completely destroy their role of intrapsychic and relational communication.

If the emotional and receptive unconscious is likened to a language, it follows that in neurosis the language that enables us to read its contents is preserved. In this case reading within the hidden content of screen memories is possible. The need is to identify the defensive purpose of these memories and to assemble them in a better way so that they can be understood.

A borderline patient is like a civilization which has not been able to evolve language—that is, the ability to structure and understand its own history. Psychic reality is so drastically distorted that no relationship with historical truth can be established. We then lack a language that we can understand, because the capacity for narration and communication is absent. A distortion of this kind is also observed in psychosis, in which violence is constantly inflicted on a communicative structure such as the unconscious by the construction of a solipsistic and grandiose world in which the receptive and communicative channels of psychic reality have been destroyed.

In such patients, enormous problems lie in the way not only of therapy, but also of shared reconstruction of the past, which can be achieved only by means of hypotheses.

Conclusions

In this contribution I have sought to show that Freud's essay on screen memories paved the way for wide-ranging fields of psychoanalytic inquiry that are still relevant today. It may justifiably be claimed that no theory of the mental apparatus could have been forthcoming without the observations which that paper contains.

In it Freud gives an outline of the fundamental aspects of mental functioning, and of the anterograde and retrograde particularities of memory (the selection and construction of memories, and the recalling and later—*nachträglich*—transformation of mnemic data, respectively). Already in 1893, Breuer and Freud had noted that the components needed for the construction of a theory of mental disorders and their treatment could be found in the functioning of memory. The famous adage "Hysterics suffer mainly from reminiscences" (Breuer & Freud, 1895d, p. 7) is among their descriptions of the non-linear nature of the relationship between the external reality of the trauma and the internal reality of the process of construction of symptoms and of psychic reality.

Precisely by taking memories as our starting point, we have succeeded in gaining an impression of the extent to which the human mind is capable of falsifying reality. If memory is seen as subject to continuous reformulation, it is clear that in the process of reconstruction internal reality may be altered even to the point of falsifying the entire personality. It is thus no longer a matter of screen memories but instead of the falsification of memory in which the connection between what is remembered and what actually happened is completely broken. As already stated, false memories of abuse present highly complex problems that cannot easily be solved in the clinical situation.

Brenman writes that a patient's history may be falsified for an infinite number of reasons and that the patient will never arrive at the truth without a supporting object to help him confront the intolerable: "Analysis does not answer historical questions but provides the security to explore them" (2006, p. 12). Once we become able to tolerate reality, the reconstruction of memory may also facilitate the attainment of a deeper level of personal experience, thus rendering us better able to confer meaning on our past life.

I have concentrated in the final part of this contribution on the importance of reconstructing the past for therapeutic purposes. I have endeavoured to show that certain patients who have sustained very early emotional traumas fail to develop a system of emotional competence—a receptive and emotional unconscious—that enables them to comprehend mental life. These patients lack the foundations needed for the possibility of reconstructing the past.

As stated earlier, understanding of the past is a process that develops during the course of life in parallel with the capacity to broaden our understanding of our mental processes themselves. Discovery of the truth is an ongoing process, whereby we come into contact with the emotional truth that exists inside us and survives in our unconscious. This experience is particularly necessary as we approach the end of our lives; when our future is seen to be limited, reflecting on the past is a useful tool for conferring meaning on the previous course of our existence. The ability to rethink the past in the light of experience is a part of the work of construction that can make for a creative old age.

Memory then becomes the epitome of a reparative experience.

Notes

1. Significantly, Freud's insight that memory undergoes constant revision has been confirmed by the neurosciences.
2. This account is based on Regina Pally's paper on the subject (1997b).
3. For convenience, the masculine form is used here for both sexes.

4

The screen and behind it: manifest and latent themes in Freud's *Über Deckerinnerungen*[1]

Rivka R. Eifermann

It has become common knowledge (Bernfeld, 1946), that Freud is himself the anonymous patient in his 1898 article "Screen memories" (*Über Deckerinnerungen*) (Freud, 1899a). This discovery has allowed me to re-read the paper paying close attention to the verbal associations and symbolic connections suggested by this additional context. The presence in the screen memories paper of Freud, the patient, allowed my associations to extend beyond the 1898 article to events and personae from Freud's early life as he reports them in his letters to Fliess, in *The Interpretation of Dreams* (Freud, 1900a), and in his 1901 paper, "Childhood memories and screen memories" (1901b).

The relevance of these extended associations to his "Screen memories" paper became ever more important to me as I realised that the memories as described in these sources were alive in Freud's mind while he was writing his paper. Indeed, just before reporting and analysing his "meadow memory", Freud briefly refers to every one of the personae and events in the adjacent texts I have mentioned that I consider highly relevant (Freud, 1899a, p. 310).

These associations, insights, and discoveries came to me unpredictably, in no discernibly systematic way (Eifermann, 1997). They gradually built up into a recognisable network which expanded in complexity and depth as my work on Freud's article progressed. In the interest of clarity, I shall present the network in linear fashion under five main headings following more or less the structural sequence of Freud's article. The headings are:

1. the two illustrations which Freud presents from the Henris' research
2. Freud's recollection of his calf love
3. the part of Freud's meadow memory describing events which occurred on the meadow
4. the two women present in the meadow memory
5. Freud's father's underlying presence in his article.

As my discussion within each section evolves its connection to the larger network of themes unfolds. The network thus becomes more and more apparent as the paper expands. The final section ends with a discussion of the theme of loss, or transience, which emerges as the motif underlying the article as a whole.

My main purpose in this exposition is to argue in favour of the Freudian tradition of close listening to the dynamic unconscious, which Freud exemplifies in part in his "Screen memories" paper, in his attempt to reach the deeper sense of apparently trivial memories. Such close listening has, in my view, often been neglected in clinical as well as theoretical psychoanalytic work over the last few decades (Eifermann, 2007). The corresponding process illustrated in this paper, of listening to Freud's paper is, of course, a product of subjective interaction between reader and text (Eifermann, 1989). It inevitably involves my selective attention and blind spots. Nonetheless, and notwithstanding the more or less tentative, even speculative, nature of some of the connections that I reach, I believe that the cumulative weight of the evidence I put forward suffices to illustrate how certain developments in Freud's generally groundbreaking, creative thought were both hampered and advanced due to early personal experiences—as these were retained, or evolved in memory[2]—and their long-term effect. This, then, is my secondary aim.

Two illustrations from the Henris' research

The first illustration

Although Freud's nurse is only once explicitly mentioned in the article (1899a, p. 310), and his mother not at all, I propose that his nurse, and mother, nonetheless play a major role in Freud's latent thoughts in the paper. It is worth pointing out that these two figures, Freud's nurse and mother, emerge explicitly in his 1901 article "Childhood memories and screen memories". In the latter, the Henris' examples are dropped, while Freud presents, in a section added in 1907, an extensive, "single example" (Freud, 1901b, p. 49) from his own early life "of the way in which a childhood memory, which previously appeared to have no meaning, can acquire one by being worked over in analysis" (p. 49). There, his nurse plays the central role, his mother being the reporter and commentator on the nurse and on the background to the event that Freud relates and discusses.

Freud presents the first of the two cases taken from the Henris' as follows:

> [a] professor of philology whose earliest memory, dating back to between the ages of three and four, showed him *a table laid for a meal and on it a basin of ice*. At the same period there occurred the death of his *grandmother* which, according to his parents, was a severe blow to the child. But the professor of philology, as he now is, has no recollection of this bereavement; *all that he remembers of those days is the basin of ice*. (Freud, 1899a, p. 306, my italics)

I propose that this memory, rather than being inconsequential and inexplicable, as Freud suggests (p. 305–306), could represent for the child-now-professor a familiar, repeatedly observed disappearance: that of ice cubes, which vanish once dissolved. This phenomenon could have symbolised, and replaced his grandmother's painful disappearance in the professor's memory. While in his paper Freud comments regarding this memory that he "can make nothing" (p. 319) of it, he does interpret it, in symbolic terms, in a footnote, in his 1901 paper. He writes, "[O]ne of the Henris'informants instanced a piece of ice as a screen memory for his grandmother's death", that is, turning cold and hard following death (1901b, p. 51, n. 2).[3]

It seems that Freud's choice of this particular example, even prior to its explicit association with a dead person, was (unconsciously) associated in his mind with his own early experience with his nurse: she also disappeared from his life suddenly, an event which greatly upset him.

Freud's nurse is described in one of his letters to Fliess as "an ugly, *elderly*, but clever woman" (Masson, 1985, p. 268, my italics) and is further referred to as "the *old* woman" (p. 269, my italics), one could say, like a grandmother.[4] Just as the professor did not retain the memory of his grandmother's disappearance even though it "was a severe blow" (1899a, p. 306) to him as a child (or, perhaps *because* it was such a blow), so too, Freud failed to remember the disappearance of his nurse, or its painful, anxiety-provoking effect on him. But he did recall a subsequent scene, of great distress, involving his mother. Freud describes it in a letter to Fliess written on 15 October, 1897, that is, less than a year prior to the publication of his "Screen memories" article, and again in his 1901 article, "Childhood memories and screen memories". In his letter he describes how, in the course of his self-analysis he wondered about the impression the sudden disappearance of his nurse made on him. Whereupon a scene occurred to him that emerged in his mind without understanding it:

> My mother was nowhere to be found; I was crying in despair. My brother Philipp (twenty years older than I) unlocked a wardrobe [*Kasten*] for me, and when I did not find my mother inside it either, I cried even more until, slender and beautiful, she came in through the door. What can this mean? Why did my brother unlock the wardrobe for me, knowing that my mother was not in it and that thereby he could not calm me down? Now I suddenly understand it. I had asked him to do it. When I missed my mother, I was afraid she had vanished from me, just as the old woman had a short time before. (Freud in Masson, 1985, p. 271)

He goes on to describe the meaning of the memory, which then suddenly came to him. He had asked his brother to unlock the wardrobe for him since, when he missed his mother, he was afraid she had vanished just as his nurse had a short while before. (She was imprisoned for stealing coins from him, as well as objects from the household, his brother Philip having reported her to the police.) "So

I must have heard that the old woman had been locked up and therefore must have believed that my mother had been locked up too—or rather, had been 'boxed up' *[eingekastelt]*" (Freud in Masson, 1985, p. 272).

The basin of ice as a representation of the transience of life reappears in these memories once again, in a more direct representation of death itself. In Austrian–German, *Kasten* (box) is a term used for *coffin*, and *eingekastelt* to being "boxed up" in a coffin. It is possible that even as a small child Freud had heard about coffin and death being connected, with only a vague grasp of what that meant. This possibility together with Freud's vague understanding and fear regarding his nurse and mother who had disappeared (even if only *nachträglich* [as "deferred action"]), suggests a further mental link between the professor's case and Freud's self-analytic recollection and understanding of his childhood experience, as well as his choice of this particular illustration from the Henris': his nurse, like the professor's grandmother, was (declared) dead. This triggered the anxiety regarding the disappearance of his mother.[5]

Perhaps Freud's latent preoccupation—even as a small child—with a fear of his mother's death is linked not only to the early and sudden disappearance of his nurse, but also to the fact that the mother of his far older half-brothers had "disappeared" (i.e., died). While the mixture of generations in his family has often been pointed to as a confusing experience for the child Freud, I am proposing that the shadow of the death of mother must also have been present in his life from the start as a by-product of this confusion. It may well have led Freud to fantasise the dead mother of his half-brothers as having been his *grandmother*.

The second illustration

In Freud's second illustration from the Henris', we find further latent recollections of his nurse embedded. The case is of

> [a] man reports that his earliest memory is an episode upon a walk in which he broke off a branch from a tree. He thinks he can still identify the spot where this happened. There were several other people present, and one of them helped him. (1899a, p. 306)

The Henris' second report, written in French, evoked a far from trivial, colloquial sexual meaning in Freud's mind. He connects breaking off a branch from a tree, to the phrase "to pull one out" ("*sich einen ausreißen*", 1899/1952, p. 550] which, in the Austrian–German of his day was "a very common vulgar term for masturbation" (1899a, p. 319). This verbal bridge rescues the memory from its apparent triviality, thus making sense of its retention.

Once again, as with regard to the first illustration, Freud's nurse, as she emerges from his letters to Fliess, comes to mind. Thus in a letter of 4 October, 1897 he gathers, based on a dream he has had on that day, that "she was my teacher in sexual matters and complained because I was clumsy and unable to do anything", and that, "she washed me in reddish water in which she had previously washed herself" (Masson, 1985, p. 269). Specifically with regard to *seduction*, Freud reflects in a letter to Fliess written on the previous day (3 October, 1897) that, in my case "the '*prime* originator' " (my italics) was his nurse.

Moreover, Freud unreservedly interprets the memory taken from the Henris' case, "There were several other people present, and one of them helped him" to mean "Nothing more nor less than *secrecy*" (1899a, pp. 306, 319–320, my italics). My understanding of the associative flow in Freud's writing gains support when looking more closely at the thoughts Freud attributes to the "patient" in this part of their imaginary dialogue, as against thoughts he attributes to himself; it is the "patient" who links the breaking of a branch to a crude sexual verbal expression for masturbation, while his analyst, Freud, explains that the fact of having masturbated had to be kept secret since it was too embarrassing to expose.

Freud expands further that hence, "his seduction to masturbate must have occurred in *solitude and secrecy*" (p. 319, my italics) later in the man's life, and been displaced onto an innocent childhood event: "it [the distorted memory] serves once again to make the scene innocent" (p. 319). This statement is puzzling not only because Freud again speaks of seduction, but because "seduction" and "solitude" do not go together; unless one *fantasises*—in solitude—that such seduction is taking place. This possibility may be regarded as supported by the fact that whereas when writing of the "seduction to masturbate" Freud uses the German word *Verführung*, he uses the less forceful word, *Verleitung*, when he refers to a fantasised event, in solitude and in isolation which, as I am about to show, connects to himself.

Calf love

To my mind the puzzle of Freud's use of the term seduction is resolved, if Freud's early memories of his nurse as his seducer are connected with his description of the unconscious fantasies which accompany his calf love. I propose that, presumably unaware, Freud adopted the Henris' example as his own. It served him as a kind of screen memory—one that covered up for his own less "innocent" early childhood memories involving his nurse—and mother, as I shall later expand—as his seducers. *Freud's paper thus contains a personal illustration which is a variant of the kind of screen memory he aims to conceptualise in it.*

For strikingly, it seems to me, *secrecy* and *solitude* characterised his own experience of this first calf love: Freud's first association to his memory of his childhood meadow scene was of his experience of that unrequited love. He describes (p. 313) how, upon his first visit back to his birthplace, when aged seventeen (he was in fact sixteen), he was "powerfully" excited, and felt "passionately" in love with the fifteen-year-old daughter of the house. He "kept it completely *secret*". Following her departure he went on "*solitary* walks through the *lovely woods*" spending his time "*building* [*erecting*] *castles in the air*" (p. 313, all italics mine). His description speaks of lonesome masturbatory day dreaming, in secrecy and isolation, involving sexual fantasies of intercourse: normal adolescent contents when masturbating (or desperately trying to avoid the act), the more so when passionately in love.[6]

It should be noted that Freud never saw the girl following his leaving Freiberg when he was about three, until they re-met when he was sixteen. This separation was for him "[a] catastrophe [that] had involved my whole existence" (p. 314). Except for his parents and baby-sister, he lost at that time all that was familiar and close to him: home and countryside, extended family as well as playmates. When he finally returned, he lost a one-time playmate again, who left for her school. He writes, "it was this separation after such a short acquaintance that brought my longings to a really high pitch" (p. 313). Awakening, I daresay, a far more extended feeling of loss.

Masturbation screened

My understanding of the latent meaning contained in Freud's report of his unrequited love is partly confirmed by Freud in his text. He assumes, though, that the fantasised content of his day dreams remained unconscious and furthermore, does not refer to any accompanying masturbatory activity. Freud writes that, due to a collapse of the branch of industry with which his father was concerned, his family had left the area to which he returned on a visit for the first time since he was three. Having fallen in love with the fifteen-year-old daughter of the family who were hosting him, he ruminated how, if his father's economic collapse and consequences mentioned before had not occurred, he would have grown up close to the girl and married her. "The most seductive [*verlockendste*, viz. tempting, enticing] part of the whole subject for a young scapegrace is the picture of the marriage night. (What does he care about what comes afterwards?)" (p. 316). Freud adds, that this fantasy remains unconscious because of its disrespectful, "coarsely sensual element" (p. 317).

Even though Freud the analyst thus uncovers meanings that lie beyond the young scapegrace's "pure", romantic fantasies, memories of any pleasure or struggle around masturbation remain unrevealed in his self-analysis or perhaps, undisclosed to the reader. Except for the various verbal links that strongly suggest the connection, it remains as though the issue of masturbation concerns the Henri's hypothetical case alone.

Freud exposed himself a great deal in *The Interpretation of Dreams* (Freud, 1900a), frankly physically as well mentally (e.g., in the dream of his peeing, the dream regarding a huge boil at the base of his scrotum, the dream of dissecting his own pelvis). Yet masturbation seems to have been beyond the limits of his direct self-exposure, apparently terribly embarrassing, as "*we* feel" in dreams of nakedness in which "a lot of strangers" (his readers?) (1899a, p. 319, my italics) are present. This fact may well connect to his early experiences, as remembered by him, with his nurse and mother, on which I shall expand further below. In spite of questioning his so-called "seduction theory" in a letter to Fliess written already in 1897, to the point of entirely rejecting the validity of such memories altogether, they continued, as I shall show further in the chapter, to affect his thought and theorising, whether as realities or as fantasy-creations (Schimek, 1987).

Freud does describe a childhood memory of an occurrence involving symbolic masturbation, concerning himself and his sister, though again without interpreting its symbolism. It does not appear on his "list" which contains only memories from his early years, in Freiberg. No memories of events recalled from later in childhood are on the "list".[7] Yet the particular event to which I refer connects to the "Screen memories" paper, since Freud himself refers his readers back to it in a footnote. Moreover, he writes of the event that it is "almost the only plastic memory that I retained from that period of my life" (1900a, p. 172); he was eight at the time. Here is the description, in *The Interpretation of Dreams*, in the context of his analysis of his "Dream of the botanical monograph" (1900a, p.169 *ff*):

> a recollection from very early youth. It had once amused my father to hand over a book with *coloured plates* (an account of a journey through Persia) for me [aged eight] and my eldest sister [two years younger] to destroy. Not easy to justify from the educational point of view! . . . the picture of the two of us blissfully pulling the book to pieces (leaf by leaf, like an artichoke, I found myself saying). (p. 172)

"Pulling the book to pieces . . . leaf by leaf" is a direct reminder of "to *pull* one out". The German expression Freud uses is *zerpflücken*; literally, to *pick* (pluck) to pieces, to me sounding more expressive of the extremity of aggression also contained in "to pull one out". Self-castration is implied: as though condensed in the expressions is also punishment for the act. I shall later discuss other aspects of this expression in connection with Freud's childhood memory of events on the meadow.

Perhaps in using the verbal expression *zerpflücken*, meaning to tear to pieces, but also carrying the meaning "to criticize severely" (as "tear to pieces" does in English), Freud conveys, unawares, his severely critical stance towards masturbation due to its damaging effects—a view he held strongly and expressed over years. The word he used may also reflect a critical stance toward his father's tolerant, even inviting, attitude to his children's playful, latent sexuality, and no less to the manifest tearing of a book to pieces. Freud's later turning into a "book worm" may have involved more than a tinge of protest against his father's tolerance. Indeed, when Freud years later, as a university student, acquired "a passion for collecting and owning books" (1900a, p. 172) his father did not support this passionate hobby, having to meet the largish account at the bookseller for his son. Reporting on it, Freud comments, "my father had scarcely taken it as an excuse that my inclinations might have chosen a worse outlet" (p. 173).

As Freud relates in his "Screen memories" paper, upon his visit to his "uncle" (half-brother) three years following his return to Freiberg, he "had nothing left over" (Freud, 1899a, p. 314) for his niece (the once little girl we shall meet forthwith in the "meadow memory"), having become "slave" (p. 314) to his books. Freud there comments on his father's disapproval of the debt he accumulated at the bookseller's, "I had early discovered, of course, that passions often lead to sorrow" (1900a, p. 173). The agonised longing that the separation from his secret love during his visit to Freiberg evoked in him had, presumably, a great deal to do with the subsequent displacement of his passion on to books.

Notwithstanding his extensive discussion on masturbation in his 1905 groundbreaking *Three Essays*, Freud refers to genital masturbation even there as an act "which scarcely a single individual *escapes*" (Freud, 1905d, p. 188, my italics). In a paper published in 1908 Freud writes that originally masturbation was purely autoerotic, then later merges with object-love but, "[W]hen, subsequently, the subject renounces this type of satisfaction, composed of masturbation and phantasy, the action is given up, while the phantasy, from being conscious, becomes unconscious" (1908a, p. 161). Freud maintains that unless abstinence supervenes and the subject succeeds in sublimating his libido, pathological symptoms take over.

Freud briefly described, already in 1905, an "instinct for knowledge or research" which, he says, cannot be classed exclusively as belonging to sexuality, though its relation to sexuality is particularly important: a sublimated manner of obtaining mastery, at the same time making use "of the energy of scopophilia" (1905d, p. 194). It is to this early, at times aggressive, sexual curiosity in children and its aftermath, as it emerges from the events on the meadow remembered by Freud from his early childhood, that I now turn.

Events on the meadow

Freud recalls:

> Three children are playing in the grass. One of them is myself (between the age of two and three); the two others are my boy

cousin [in fact his nephew], who is a year older than me, and his sister, who is almost exactly the same age as I am. We are picking the yellow flowers [of which there are a great many] and each of us is holding a bunch of flowers we have already picked. The little girl has the best bunch; and, as though by mutual agreement, we—the two boys—fall on her and snatch away her flowers. She runs up the meadow in tears and as a consolation the peasant-woman gives her a big piece of black bread. Hardly have we [little Sigismund and his nephew] seen this than we throw the flowers away, hurry to the cottage and ask to be given some bread too. And we are in fact given some; the peasant-woman cuts the loaf with a long knife. In my memory the bread tastes quite delicious—and at that point the scene breaks off. (1899a, p. 311)

Freud comments in a letter to Fliess dated 3 January, 1899, in which he refers to the fact that he was working on the paper under discussion that, "[T]o the question 'What happened in earliest childhood?', the answer is, 'Nothing, *but the germ of sexual impulse existed*' " (Masson, 1985, p. 338, my italics). Indeed, it appears that such budding sexuality finds expression in the scene played out on the meadow, even if not in full awareness of the participants. "We are picking the yellow flowers" associatively connects to "picking" the artichoke (a flower too!), and suggests, in conjunction with the act of the boys that followed, an evocation of the germ of sexual impulse and curiosity. As suggested by Anzieu (1986, p. 410) most likely curiosity regarding the differences between the sexes was not far from little Sigismund's mind, and particularly evoked at that time, when his sister had just been born. It may further be noticed that Freud specifies that the two boys snatch the little girl's bunch from her upon observing that hers is the best bunch. Taking into consideration that the flowers also had stems, the possibility that envy for the girl who seemed to have the best of all—stem and flower—has also motivated their attack (see Freud on children's denial of what they see in "On the sexual theories of children", 1908c).

The snatched-away flowers were soon dropped in favour of the country bread, which his crying niece received as consolation. Remarkably, Freud remembers and specifies that she was given "a big piece"; the boys—upon request—received (only) "some". Freud furthermore recalls how the bread tasted—that it was particularly delicious.[8] Freud remembers, and further recalls the detail that, "the peasant-woman cuts the loaf with a long knife" (1899a, p. 311). Thus the delicious taste of the bread may well have been enhanced for the child, unconsciously, by the fact that the long knife was used for cutting the bread only. The very fact that the adult Freud remembers and includes the act in his description, suggests as much. Its later, fully formulated conception would run: *deflowering (robbing) the girl might have ended in castration* (viz. *in robbing him of his penis*). The threat contained in pursuing pleasures beyond one's reach finds further, succinct expression in Freud's paper. The last in the list of childhood events he mentions (on p. 310, already referred to herein), is the exception in the "list", in that it is the only one described in detail. He writes of "an injury to my face which caused a considerable loss of blood and for which I had to have some stitches put in by a surgeon. I can still feel the scar resulting from this accident" (1899a, p. 310). Allusions to this event in a number of his publications indicate its special significance for Freud. It occurred, as Freud describes in his *The Interpretation of Dreams* (1900a),

> when I was more than two and not yet three years old. I had climbed up on to a stool in the store-closet to get something nice that was lying on a cupboard or table. The stool had tipped over and its corner had struck me behind my lower jaw; *I might easily, I reflected, have knocked out all my teeth.* (1900a, p. 560, my italics)

The memory speaks of desire unfulfilled, and of the heavy cost that desiring beyond one's reach may lead to, ultimately castration. "The recollection", Freud adds, "was accompanied by an admonitory thought: 'that serves you right' " (p. 560).[9] While the retrieval of this experience, not consciously recalled, evoked the thought of deserved punishment in Freud, the early recalled experiences on the meadow contain, it seems to me, the kernel of such feelings already alive at the time. While castration anxiety was only gradually identified by Freud, he makes the following relevant comments already in the first (1900a) edition of his *The Interpretation of Dreams*, partly repeating those on masturbation appearing in the "Screen memory" paper: "[I]n our part of the world the act of masturbation is vulgarly described as '*sich einen ausreissen*' or '*sich einen herunterreissen*' [literally, "pulling one out" or "pulling one down"]" (1900a, p. 388). Freud adds, "I know nothing of the source of this terminology or of the image on which it is based; but 'a *tooth*' would fit very well" (p. 388, my italics). He thus condenses, by means of common linguistic usage, masturbation and punishment by castration, as well as regarding the tooth as a symbol, already at a time when sexual symbolism was as yet not systematised in his work (see the editors' comments to Section E of Chapter Six of *The Interpretation of Dreams* in this connection).

Two women

The "group" of children's nurse and peasant-woman

Surprisingly enough—both the nurse, as well as the peasant-woman, escape any mention in Freud's analysis of his childhood memory, in which they appear. Freud is, of course, aware of this gap, and indeed, asks his "patient", "[C]an you make any sense of . . . [the group] of the peasant-woman and the nurse in front of the cottage?" (1899a, pp. 318–319; the words "the group" are dropped in Strachey's translation). Surprisingly again, *nothing* occurs to his "patient" regarding either of the two women. Freud the analyst ignores this—to my mind a telling "mental block"—arguing that the (unacceptable unconscious) fantasy that lies behind the (innocent) screen memory does not coincide completely with the memory as a whole, "It is only based on it at certain points" (p. 319). The fact that some points in the memory evoke no associations in the "patient" simply means that they are irrelevant to the memory's function as a screen. To this circular argument Freud adds that the incomplete fit "argues in favour of the childhood memory being genuine" (p. 319), since it is shown to be preserved as a whole. This argument also begs the question. For why, one may ask, is the memory fully rather than selectively preserved, with its irrelevant parts forgotten, so it can serve as a pure screen for the later repressed memory?

As a matter of fact, the memory seems to change as it is re-told even within the confines of the paper, and just at the point where its genuineness is argued for. Above I focused on Freud's question regarding the two women. The question begins with reference to another issue, namely, "For instance, your boy cousin *helping you* to *rob* the little girl of her flowers—can you make any sense of the idea of *being helped* in deflowering someone?" (pp. 318–319, my italics). The original description of the scene says, however, "*as though by mutual agreement we—the two boys—fall on her and snatch away her flowers*" (p. 311, my italics).

In my understanding there is a general case for assuming that the two women, as a "group" and as separate individuals, are strongly and variously linked in Freud's mind to his mother and nurse, two "mother figures" (Anzieu, 1986, p. 371). Any attempt to point to one as representing his mother, the other, his nurse, would however, be grossly over-simplistic. I view them rather as forming a reflection of a variety of experiences of motherhood and womanhood that belong to Freud's early childhood, that subsequently influenced his psychoanalytic investigations.

In the earlier sections of my chapter I claim, and aimed to demonstrate in some detail, that Freud's nurse is embedded in his selected illustrations from the Henris'; I also regard her as being latently present in Freud's associations concerning his calf love. We have also already met his mother and nurse as interconnected in Freud's mind around the theme of their alarming disappearance, which he relates in a sequence.

My conviction, that the two women are strongly linked to Freud's nurse and mother, was strengthened, when I read Freud's statement that the apparently innocent memory he presented, served as a screen (hence *screen memory*) for "the two most powerful motive forces—*hunger and love*" (p. 316, my italics). I was struck by the fact that in the course of analysing one of his dreams in *The Interpretation of Dreams* (the dream of the *Three Fates*) Freud binds the very same words, love and hunger, to motherhood (1900a, p. 204). (It should be noted that in all likelihood Freud analysed that dream prior to writing his paper).[10] Thus, whereas in his "Screen memories" article Freud's associations and interpretations focus on his unconscious *adolescent* wishful fantasies regarding these two most powerful motives, the analysis of his dream focuses on his *earliest experiences* of these motives, at his mother's breast. Freud interprets the relevant section of the dream saying, "the inn-hostess of the dream [one of three women appearing in the dream] was the mother who gives life, and furthermore (*as in my case*) gives the living creature his first nourishment. Love and hunger, I reflect, meet at a woman's breast" (1900a, p. 204, my italics). In the same sequence—even though, of course, not connecting it directly to himself—Freud then adds the following anecdote: a young man, a great admirer of feminine beauty, who was suckled as a baby by a good-looking wet-nurse, had once remarked "I'm sorry that I didn't make better use of my opportunity" (p. 204).

My view that the two women of the meadow memory are closely connected with the two most significant female figures of his early life, further leans on the fact that each of the women appears in the by-now-familiar "list" of personae and events from Freud's early life. While Freud refers to "my nurse" directly, his mother is not mentioned explicitly. Yet she plays an essential role in "two small occurrences during the railway-journey" (1899a, p. 310) to which he refers. The lack of explicit mention of his mother, as well as the allusion to the occurrences on the train as having been "small"—which they by no means were—indicate the extent to which Freud's reluctance to go into issues concerning his mother went.

Even in his personal letter to Fliess in which he does reveal intimacies concerning his nurse and mother (altogether avoided in his disguised self-analysis), he introduces these experiences saying, "to put it in writing is more difficult than anything else for me" (Masson, 1985, p. 268). It is of significance for understanding the complex links between the two women in Freud's mind, that Freud describes an intimate situation that occurred when on the train with his mother, in the same letter in which he points to his nurse as having been his seducer. The sequential and thematic link between nurse and mother in his report is also unmistakable. For in the letter there follows immediately on the heels of the disclosure about the nurse—with only a semi-colon separating it from the words he had just put down—the following intimate memory involving his mother:

> that later (between two and two and a half years) my libido toward *matrem* was awakened, namely, on the occasion of a journey with her from Leipzig to Vienna, during which we must have spent the night together and there must have been an opportunity of seeing her *nudam* . . . . (p. 268)

Even though he writes to his closest friend and confessor, Freud needs to resort to Latin to depict the event, which occurred while "we must have spent the night together"; perhaps he needed to distance himself from that over stimulating, emotionally loaded, and confusing occasion (as well as to overcome some discomfort in relating it Fliess). Further support for these possibilities lie in Freud's immediately subsequent comment, again separated from the earlier one with a semi-colon only:

that I greeted my one-year-younger brother (who died after a few months) with adverse wishes and genuine childhood jealousy; and that his death left the germ of [self-]reproaches in me. (p. 268)

That night spent with his mother evoked an admixture of feelings—however rudimentary—among them of triumph (over his dead brother, ultimately his father), guilt, and reproach.

Thus it turns out that each, mother and nurse, were connected in Freud's mind with powerful, early sexual evocation or stimulation. (I here take the leap and add: presumably masturbation was involved in one way or another, as anyone who nowadays observes small children would agree). Yet the nurse remains "the '*prime* originator'" (1985, p. 268). This attribution of priority to the nurse seems to apply also, at least to some extent, to Freud's ways of regarding his early guilt, and accusatory feelings. While the above quotation suggests that Freud assumes that "the germ of [*self*-] reproaches" (my italics) was evoked in connection with his mother having given birth to his brother who then died, it is worth noting that unlike in Masson's interpretation, the original German text remains unspecific. Freud simply writes, "the germ of reproaches" (Keim zu Vorwürfen, Freud, 1896, p. 289) and thus, whether intentionally or not, leaves open the question of who is to be reproached. This may also be said, with some hesitation, about his nurse "who told me a great deal about God Almighty and hell" (Masson, 1985, p. 268), strongly suggesting that she instilled in him fantasies of hell and punishment for misdeeds—but who was the culprit who deserved punishment? One may speculate that simultaneously with fear of being punished for his own misdeeds, little Freud also harboured some vague fantasies, even at an early age, that his nurse was to be blamed and punished, that she was in fact "boxed up" because she had robbed him of his "innocence". In his references to his nurse, Freud repeats attributing cleverness to her; perhaps it is of some significance in connection with that attribution, that in his *Three Essays on the Theory of Sexuality* (1905d) he writes that children may be misled "by a clever seducer" (p. 191), or by an "uncultivated [peasant?]" women or by "unscrupulous nurses" (p. 180, f. 1)), at a time when the "mental dams against sexual excesses—shame, disgust and morality" do not exist, or are not secure as yet (p. 191).

Reluctance to expose mother

As for the second occurrence on the train, I suggest that fantasies attached to feelings of reproach, guilt, accusation, and punishment, however rudimentary, were evoked in the child Freud on his train journey, which was strongly linked in his mind to spending the night alone on the train with his mother. Whether such fantasies were conscious or not, one at least burst into consciousness, stimulated by a view he saw from the train. He describes in a letter to Fliess (December 3, 1897) that at the age of three years, when they moved from his birthplace to Leipzig, he passed through the station, "and the gas flames which I saw for the first time reminded me of spirits burning in hell. I know a little of the connections. My travel anxiety, now overcome, also is bound up with this" (Masson, 1985, p. 285). The threat of Hell—awaiting himself and, or, his mother, has become concretely alive on that train journey.

Why did Freud take a further two months before writing to Fliess about this occurrence, which was evidently strongly associated with the first event? I suggest the answer may lie in Freud's somewhat distant, more thoughtful comment that preceded letting Fliess know of the vision of Hell he confronted on his train journey, and its long-term effect on him (his train-phobia). He writes: "A pity that one always keeps one's mouth shut about the most intimate matters" (p. 285), adding a citation from Goethe's *Faust* (which also appears twice in *The Interpretation of Dreams*), "The best you know, you cannot tell the boys". Telling "the best" evokes most powerful emotions, as Freud has confessed to Fliess when about to "put it in writing" for him to read, two months earlier. It is as though Freud had to leave strong feelings behind in order to be able to share such intimate matters regarding his nurse, let alone his *matrem*, even with his closest friend and confessor who was, after all, also his critic (Eifermann, 2006).

To my mind this deep reluctance is more than evident in Freud's most restricted direct references to his mother throughout his magnum opus. So much more of interest, therefore, are the contexts in which she does openly appear. There is only one dream in which she appears explicitly in *The Interpretation of Dreams*, and it focuses on her. Moreover, it centres on the interweaving themes of sexuality, and of death. The dream contains a picture of his mother with a peculiar sleeping expression on her face. She is being carried out and lain upon a bed. Freud recognises the picture of his mother as one taken from an ancient Egyptian funeral relief familiar to him as a child. "I woke up in tears and screaming, and interrupted my parents' sleep" (1900a, p. 583). At the same time his associations to the dream led him to "an ill-mannered boy . . . who used to play with us in the *grass* in front of the house when we were children" (p. 583, my italics). Freud assumed that it was from this Philip (also the name of his half-brother) that he first heard "the vulgar term for sexual intercourse" (p. 583). His mother also appears in his associations to the dream of the *Three Fates* (1900a, pp. 204–208). One of these associations has already been presented (see p. 93 above), where I pointed out that in his interpretation of this dream Freud binds the words love and hunger to motherhood. Another association brings back to him how his mother convinced him of the reality of death. He relates in his associations how, as a child of six, doubtful of his mother's teachings—that we were all made of earth and to earth must return—she demonstrated to him, on her skin, the fact of her own mortality, as well as his own and all humanity's. She rubbed the palms of her hands together and showed him the blackish scales of epidermis produced by the friction.

Loss

As I have tried to show, the themes of loss, disappearance, and death, repeatedly emerge in Freud's associations in connection with his mother.

By comparison with his father's weighty presence in *The Interpretation of Dreams*—in Freud's own reported dreams, associations, and recollections—his mother's almost complete absence stands out even more. Freud's many disclosures regarding his father are, as he himself testifies, an expression of the personal significance *The Interpretation of Dreams* had for him. In his introduction to the second edition of the book (1908) Freud shares with his readers that only after completing it, did he grasp that it was "a portion of my own self-analysis, my reaction to my father's death" (1900a, p. xxvi).

The fact that Freud's mother lived a long life may well have hindered his revealing matters concerning her, but more importantly, her longevity probably limited his inner work on her. There is no evidence that Freud's systematic self-analysis touched this "weightiest of his attachments" (Gay, 1988, p. 505). The detrimental effect that this omission had on his understanding and theorising is evident in many of his works, for example, the minimal room he gave mothers in his case histories, and the general, lacunae in his attempts to come to grips with "the riddle of the nature of femininity" (Freud, 1933a, p. 113; Raphael-Leff, 2007).

Although Freud reflected as early as 1900, that "[L]ove and hunger meet at a woman's breast", it was only after his mother's death, in the unfinished *An Outline of Psycho-analysis* (Freud, 1940a), that the breakthrough to recognition of love for the pre-oedipal mother occurs (Raphael-Leff, 2007, p. 1355). This archaic mother is described there as the "first nourisher and *first* seducer", "first and strongest love-object for both sexes" (Freud, 1940a, p. 188, my italics). Had his mother died at an earlier age, he may not have concluded as he did, mourning his father's loss, that a father's death was "the most important event, the most poignant loss, of a man's life" (1900a, p. xxvi). While in the wake of her death, late in his own life, Freud was unaware of deep excitation in him, he mused, communicating to Jones, "[C]ertainly there is no saying what such an experience may do in deeper layers" (Gay, 1988, p. 573). Gay comments on Freud's musing that the phrase "there is no *saying*, is in English" (p. 712, my italics). I cannot help but wonder about the ambiguity of the phrase.

Freud's paper as a whole: an underlying preoccupation with father

Freud's interpretation of the meadow memory

In his preface to the 1908 second edition of *The Interpretation of Dreams* Freud reveals that the book has a "subjective significance for me personally—a significance which I have only grasped after I had completed it. It was, I found, a portion of my self-analysis, my reaction to may father's death" (1900a, p. xxvi). It is in this context that he writes of his father's death as the most important event in a man's life. I propose that it was not only in the domain of *The Interpretation of Dreams*, that Freud undertook his self-analysis as a reaction, in part, to his father's death. His father appears neither in his meadow memory, nor in any way on his "list". Yet in my understanding, his background preoccupation with his father lies at the heart of his interpretation of his screen memory.

Freud's associations to this memory, he says, are built around two fantasies. Both these fantasies are tied at their very core to his father. One of the fantasies related to what would have happened had his father's business not collapsed, a "catastrophe [that] had involved my whole existence" (p. 314): he would have stayed in his birth place and married the girl who grew up there. The other fantasy deals with what would have happened had he followed his father's plan for him to marry his niece. Freud assumes, that his father meant thereby "to make good the [catastrophic] loss" (p. 314) which he had brought upon his son following his financial collapse. Had he married his niece, a marriage of convenience rather than of love, a life of economic comfort, yet lacking in passion (sexual and intellectual), would have awaited him. Such a fantasy, Freud argues, of "Throwing away the flowers in exchange for bread" (p. 315), had its appeal for the young man in dire economic straits. Freud explains to his "patient", "You projected the two phantasies on to one another and made a childhood memory of them" (p. 315).

It is as though the meadow memory itself screened off that which the associations to it openly and strikingly reveal. Freud concludes that following his analysis of his "patient'" childhood memory it has become evident that its presentation in his article "is calculated to illustrate the most momentous turning-points in . . . [the "patient's"] life, the influence of the two most powerful motive forces—hunger and love [on his life]" (p. 316). Unlike in his dream of the *Three Fates*, in which Freud binds these words to the (his) archaic mother of infancy, hunger and love here represent the lasting effect that his *father* has had on the course of his life from early on. The first momentous turning-point of his life, parting from his birth place, has had a crucial and complex influence, one way or another, on his choice of his life-partner and profession. Freud's almost life-long preoccupation with making ends meet may also tally with his father's financial struggles, which had a restricting effect on him from early on.

Following his father's death, Freud wrote to his friend Fliess, on 2 November, 1896, that this death had affected him deeply. That "I valued him highly, understood him very well, and with his peculiar mixture of deep wisdom and fantastic light-heartedness he had a significant effect on my life" (Masson, 1985, p. 202). Freud goes on to say, "in my inner self *the whole past has been reawakened by this event*" (p. 202, my italics).

Transformations in Freud's "seduction theory"

Not only do the dreams and the variety of memories in *The Interpretation of Dreams*, which directly connect to his father, testify to this reawakening. Freud's ideas regarding his so-called "seduction theory", have their beginnings prior to his father's death on 23 October, 1896, in his "Project for a scientific psychology" (1895a), where he states that hysteria probably results from early sexual seduction by *a perverse father*. This theory regarding the aetiology of neurosis, evolved further prior to his father's death. The theory underwent many transformations, as evidenced in a number of his letters to Fliess (Blass & Simon, 1992; Schimeck, 1987). Two months following his father's death Freud revised his theory significantly. In a letter to Fliess of 2 December, he for the first time introduces the idea that the early seduction involves the father. He writes: "It seems to me more and more that the essential point of hysteria is that it results from *perversion* on the part of the seducer, and *more* and *more* that heredity is seduction by the father." (Freud, 1895, p. 212). Presumably his gradually reawakened memories had a part in the conclusions he reached—about one year following his father's death—specified in his letter to Fliess of 21 September, 1897. These conclusions showed the "seduction theory" specifically with regard to its incestuous aspect, to be most implausible. One of his arguments states that the theory assumes, "that in all cases, the *father*, not excluding my own, had to be excused of being perverse" (Masson, 1985, p. 264, original italics). Apparently unable to drop the theory entirely, yet deeply troubled by its shocking implication with regard to his own father, there emerged further memories in his ongoing self-analysis, which he revealed in a letter to Fliess on 3 October, 1897—written *following* his rejection of the theory. These memories absolved fathers, including his own, from necessarily having been the perpetrators when seduction has occurred. Freud says in his letter (already quoted) that he has discovered that "the old man took no active part in *my* case" (Masson, 1985, p. 268, my italics): in his case it was his *nurse* who had been the perpetrator. This revelation, it may be assumed, supported his shift away from his (inconsistent) belief that seduction is a product of paternal perversion. It also, presumably, lent support to his view, that its damaging effect occurred only *nachträglich*, as "delayed", or "deferred action", and only on condition that further abuse has taken place at a later age. As a consequence, his own case of early seduction by his *father* was, at all events, excluded. As has been demonstrated in the course of this paper, there is evidence that Freud did not altogether abandon his seduction theory, even as late as 1989. Indeed, traces of it are still to be found in the Dora case (1905e), where her uncle (father, in fact) is regarded as having been the seducer.

In the course of his preoccupations with memories of his whole past life, Freud began to doubt their validity and reliability. As I have pointed out, he already questioned the authenticity of his memories in the course of analysing his meadow memory. His doubts emerge again in the final paragraphs of his paper, where in a sense, he pulls the rug out from under the case he put forward for his new notion of screen memories and states that the distinction between these memories and other memories drawn from our childhood must diminish. Freud first questions "whether we have any memories at all *from* our childhood: memories *relating to* our childhood may be all that we possess" (1899a, p. 322, original italics). He goes on to say, even more assertively, that "childhood memories did not, as people are accustomed to say, *emerge*; they were *formed* at that time" (p. 322, original italics), that is, at the time of their re-emergence. Not only are the original events as experienced for ever lost, memories too are lost, since they undergo recurring transformations as they repeatedly re-emerge into consciousness.

Such reflections led Freud to partly relinquish the assumption that memories represent real past events, and to regard them instead as fantasies expressing unconscious infantile wishes. This fundamental shift in Freud's theorising was, however, never clearly settled by him, and remains a ground for controversy among analysts even to this day (Schimek, 1975).

Transience—a theme underlying the "Screen memory" paper

Undoubtedly, Freud's early life experiences of separation, disappearance, and death, as they have come to light in the course of this paper, effected his reaction to his father's death, and gave added meaning to the experiences of the past as recalled. Common to all the events described, not least his father's death, is the experience of loss. Memory, its distortion and loss, is the overall theme of Freud's paper from beginning to end. Freud opens his paper with loss through childhood amnesia, loss of that which has been known and experienced early in life, of which nothing remains. He further observes that one can never recapture an event as lived and experienced, since the recalled situation has forever lost its immediacy. Turning to the Henris' research Freud opens up the question, why some trivial childhood experiences are retained whereas others, of high significance, are lost to memory. The bulk of his article is then devoted to demonstrating that whatever is remembered is only apparently trivial, yet he raises questions regarding the very "genuineness" of memories that emerge, and doubts that they are being preserved in their original form. Freud ends with the conclusion that all memory is dynamic, hence transient: never lasting, forever subject to transformations.

As a final comment, I wish to return to the point I made at the beginning of my chapter, regarding the subjective nature of the interaction between reader and text. The present chapter is, of course, also subject to such subjectivity. I have become aware of the fact that the particular motif of loss and transience that I have unravelled as underlying the paper as a whole, is doubtless related to the fact that I have recently turned eighty. In my view, however, the fact that this personal reality has contributed to my discovery, in no way—in and by itself—undermines its validity.

Notes

1. Freud's concept, *Deckerinnerungen*, brings to my mind "tighter", and more "sealed-off" associations than Strachey's "Screen" does (unless I think of its modern, computer-related meaning). Yet his translation may be fitting. Freud knew, after all, that if he successfully handed over to us his method of listening, he inevitably would thereby provide us with the tools that would make his own screening somewhat transparent.

2. The complex issue of the nature of memory itself is beyond the scope of this chapter, except in the context of Freud's own concern with it in his "Screen memories" paper.

3. In his interpretation Freud furthermore links "by antithesis", by means of the symbolic representation of stiffness, between death (which "makes things stiff and cold") and sexuality ("like a penis—in heat") (1901b, p. 51, n. 2). I wonder whether there is any way of knowing whether Freud had this interpretation in mind already when writing his paper. I shall return to the connection he makes in his footnote between death and sexuality.

4. I would prefer the term *nanny* for such an early care-taker, but this is not how Freud refers to her (*Kinderfrau*).

5. No less relevant are Freud's anxieties concerning his own death strongly presented in his dreams of the year following the publication of his paper (Anzieu, 1986; Raphael-leff, 2007). Anzieu points out in this connection, that the one early childhood event missing from Freud's recapitulated "list", presented in his "Screen memories" paper, is the birth and premature death of his brother Julius, which he refers to only once, in a letter to Fliess of 3 October, 1897 (Anzieu, 1986, p. 410).

6. While sexual symbolism was as yet not systematised in Freud's work, such meanings were not far from his mind, as is evident from his equation of branch with penis, his use of "deflowering" etc. indicate. His very definition of the kind of screen memory with which his paper deals also testifies to his interpretation by means of symbols: "[A] recollection . . . whose value lies in the fact that it represents in the memory impressions and thoughts of a later date whose content is connected with its own by symbolic and similar links" (1899a, p. 316).

7. These other events, which left a deep and lasting impression on him, involved his *father*, as does the event described herein. The one is a memory of his father's reaction to him urinating in his parent's bedroom, at age seven or eight; the other, a memory of his father telling him of the experience of his hat having been knock off by a Christian, when he was ten or twelve.

8. In his analysis he regards this memory as a distortion of the original experience, "exaggerated in an almost hallucinatory fashion" (1899a, p. 312). He comments thereupon, that he "cannot help being reminded" in this connection, of a burlesque exhibition he once saw, in which the most inappropriate parts of some of the pictures "were built up [blown up] in three dimensions—for instance, the ladies' bustles" (p. 312). This odd, semi-comical sexually coloured insertion may be understood as a denial of the threat to masculinity the recalled situation still held for Freud.

9. Freud refers on various occasions to the scar on his chin, a life-long reminder and proof of the event (e.g., 1900a, p. 17). I wonder how far the same thought, conscious or not, continued to live in him in later years, when he suffered from cancer of the jaw, and even whether it played a role in his inability to give up his addiction to cigars which aggravated his illness. One may regard the thought as countering Freud's ambition—considered by Lear (2005) as the driving force in Freud's life.

10. Freud informed Fliess that he was engaged in writing the paper in January 1899, the year in which it was published. At that time Freud was already further into his book than its middle, engaged in writing the last, theoretical chapter of his *The Interpretation on Dreams*, or the first, his review of the literature on dreams. The book was published late in late 1899 and was dated 1900.

5

The waning of screen memories: from the Age of Neuroses to an Autistoid Age

Jorge L. Ahumada

Upon receiving the kind invitation of Drs Gail S. Reed and Howard B. Levine to contribute to this book on "Screen memories" two diverse trains of thought crossed my mind.

The first was realising that my earliest, and yet fairly well remembered, recollection is, no doubt, a screen memory, to which I steadfastly clung—I might have been three or four years old at the time. It vividly depicted what I assumed to be my paternal grandfather on his deathbed, with a long white beard, reclining gravely and peacefully in his final adieu. I recalled insisting time and again, to the surprise and hilarity of whoever in the family happened to listen, that I remembered my grandfather—who died when I was eight months old. Only when slightly older, most likely at five years of age, while contemplating the portraits of my two grandfathers that hung beside each other, did it dawn upon me that not only had I conflated and confused my grandfathers in my mind—the dignified bearded image in my vivid memory was that of my *maternal* grandfather who had died nearly two decades before I was born—but it was this portrait that was the source of the visual image in my purported memory. From that moment on I discreetly dropped the subject of my remembering my grandfather. Such contact in my childhood with the illusory nature of screen memories brought a shocked awareness of the tricky powers of psychic processes quite beyond my ken: an insight that likely nourished my later interest in the workings of the mind and may have helped lead me to a career in psychoanalysis.

My second train of thought, arising shortly thereafter, came up at cross purposes. I found myself pondering that the screen memory about my grandfather's death had played little or no role in my three different personal analyses, my training analysis included, and that in over four decades of analytic practice work on screen memories had found little place in my work with patients. In fact, in neither of my two books published in English, *The Logics of the Mind. A Clinical View* (Ahumada, 2001) and *Insight. Essays on Psychoanalytic Knowing* (Ahumada, 2011a), did the cases there presented, mostly in the form of extended vignettes on the ongoing psychoanalytic clinical processes, describe work on the elucidation of patients' screen memories. How was I to understand this?

The most obvious reason, that the patients did not volunteer screen memories so that the opportunity to analyse them was not the norm in my clinical experience, itself raised the question of the how and why of this lack. Two different though compatible possibilities opened up: first, that I did not help to make sufficient place for their emergence; second, that my patients might differ significantly from those on which the literature on screen memories was built a century ago.

Concerning the first possibility, my formal psychoanalytic training in the 1970s in Buenos Aires took place in a Freudian–Kleinian conceptual frame, with Racker's, Bion's, and Meltzer's developments being at the intellectual forefront. In contrast to psychoanalysis in the US, where for many analysts the reconstruction of patients' early history kept a relevant place, the psychoanalytic conceptual and technical frame in which I trained gave precedence to transference analysis in the here and now, with the emergence of the patients' early history being seen as its by-product. That is, in the Argentine context, work on early memories was taken up when they emerged spontaneously in the course of analysing the transference in the here and now, rather than being something to be actively sought after or inquired about. The second possibility, that the patients I worked with were different from those on which the psychoanalytic literature on screen memories had been built, is difficult to prove conclusively, but as we shall see, is one that has been considered by other authors. As I pondered the invitation to contribute to this volume further, I decided that it would be useful and of interest to pursue this question and reflect upon the impact of the changes in the psychopathologies upon what, as seen from the lens of my practice, came up as a waning of screen memories—and of childhood memories generally.

An inspired recent paper on the subject by a US psychoanalyst, Lucy LaFarge (2012), highlights that while the concept of screen memories has been broadened since Freud's time to include the screen memories that arise in response to trauma throughout the life-cycle and the screen-like memories that may be newly formed during analysis, the narrower group of childhood screen memories described by Freud had, by the 1960s, ceased to be a significant subject in psychoanalytic writing. This was evidenced by the fact that the term was not included in Moore and Fine's *A Glossary of Psychoanalytic Terms and Concepts* (1968). Most significantly, LaFarge added that contrary to Freud's initial predictions (1899a, 1901b) screen memories do not yield to analytic work in the way in which dreams and symptoms do. Unlike dreams, patients will not easily associate to screen memories, and once analysed, the latter do not readily fade. She cites Greenacre (1980) who noted that loss of interest in screen memories is linked to a loss of interest in the broader area of reconstruction. Greenacre suggested that perhaps the reason for this loss was that both screen memories and reconstruction accentuated the importance of trauma and the link to external, historical reality, at a time when analysis had moved towards an interest in psychic reality, metapsychology, and the structure rather than the content of the neuroses.

As I understand the literature, however, loss of interest in reconstruction of the early history, and in screen memories as part of the process of reconstruction, is not true of all US analysts (I single out the US because as far as I can gather it is the region of the psychoanalytic universe in which the Freudian emphasis on the reconstruction of the patients' early history gained most prominence). Thus Mahon and Battin-Mahon (1983) consider the evolution of screen memories as a valid index for the termination of an analysis, while for Harold Blum (2005) Freud's 1937 assertion "What we are in search of is a picture of the patient's forgotten years that shall be alike trustworthy and in all essential respects complete" (Freud, 1937d, p. 258) still holds in the main, and it is precisely the attention to reconstruction of the early years that differentiates psychoanalysis from psychotherapy.

Despite those instances to the contrary, I have come to believe that the absence of screen memories in my clinical practice was not an isolated phenomenon. I could not attribute this lack to a disinterest in the subject of trauma, because early trauma has been of prime interest to me, and holds pride of place in my exploring current psychopathologies. In regard to the latter, both Greenacre and LaFarge attribute the current absence of interest in screen memories to the intrinsic difficulties inherent in the analysability of contemporary patients, without, however, taking into consideration the possibility that this difficulty reflects changes in the structure of the patients that we now commonly see, in contrast to those on whom Freud based his early paper.

True that as LaFarge mentions, Freud initially placed high hopes on the analysis of screen memories, which he saw as the gateway to grasping and reconstructing the totality of the patients' early history, a view that he repeatedly returned to and voiced till the end of his life. But it is also true that in the decade following publication of his "Screen memories" paper, in "Remembering, repeating and working-through" (1914g), while continuing to express huge expectations of the exploratory potential of screen memories for the clinical redressing of infantile amnesia, Freud opened up a much more complex picture that merits detailed consideration. There he compared two ways of proceeding in psychoanalysis: the first he linked to "the old hypnotic technique" (p. 148), while the second he called "the new technique" (p. 149).

In regard to the former, Freud expressed gratitude for its having brought his attention to focus upon single psychical processes in isolated or schematic form, which encouraged him "to create more complicated situations in the analytic treatment and to keep them clear before us" (p. 148). In these hypnotic treatments, he held, remembering was simple:

> The patient put himself back in to an earlier situation, which he seemed never to confuse with the present one, and gave an account of the mental processes belonging to it, in so far as they had remained normal; he then added to this whatever was able to

emerge as a result of transforming the processes that had at the time been unconscious into conscious ones. (p. 148)

Further on, speaking of the patients' disappointment at the fact that not enough things come into their heads while attempting to free-associate, he says that even this desire is fulfilled, especially in conversion hysterias, and that

> "Forgetting" becomes still further restricted when we assess at their true value the screen memories which are so generally present. In some cases [he argues] I have had an impression that the familiar childhood amnesia, which is theoretically so important to us, is completely counterbalanced by screen memories. Not only *some* but *all* of what is essential from childhood has been retained in these memories. It is simply a question of knowing how to extract it out of them by analysis. They represent the forgotten years of childhood as adequately as the manifest content of a dream represents the dream-thoughts. (p. 148)

But thereafter, passing on to "the new technique", Freud acknowledged that under its aegis "very little, and often nothing, is left of this delightfully smooth course of events" (p. 149). And he goes on:

> There are some cases which behave like those under the hypnotic technique up to a point and only later cease to do so; but others behave differently from the beginning. If we confine ourselves to this second type in order to bring out the difference, we may say that the patient does not *remember* anything of what he has forgotten and repressed, but *acts* it out. He reproduces it not as a memory but as an action; he *repeats* it, without, of course, knowing that he is repeating it. (pp. 149–150)

It is to be highlighted that beyond speaking of two procedures, "the old hypnotic technique" and thereafter "the new technique", Freud refers also to two quite different ways of proceeding on the part of the patients in the psychoanalytic session, which involves two different kinds of cases that use the analytic situation differently—though it happens that some patients may behave in both ways at different times. He separates those patients—whom he explicitly links to the neuroses, namely to hysteria and to obsessional neurosis—who are able to use the psychoanalytic situation mainly for remembering in a fashion resembling the hypnotic procedure, from those patients who are unable (or unwilling) to remember and who are prone to enact their unconscious conflicts in the transference link to the analyst as the only alternative the psychoanalytic method opens to them. Significantly, he adds that "The greater the resistance, the more extensively will acting out (repetition) replace remembering", and furthermore that "if, as the analysis proceeds, the transference becomes hostile or unduly intense and therefore in need of repression, remembering at once gives way to acting out. From then onwards the resistances determine the sequence of the material which is to be repeated" (p. 151). In such instances, he maintains, "we must treat his illness, not as an event of the past, but as a present day force" (p. 151), and in this case it is important for the analyst to seek that the patient obtains "the courage to *direct his attention* to the phenomena of his illness" (p. 152, my italics) in order to gain his collaboration towards "a reconciliation with the repressed material". The new technique, Freud argues, "implies conjuring up a piece of real life", by which he means the *transference as a real experience in a particular context*, that of the transference as playground because, as he pointedly puts it, "one cannot overcome an enemy who is absent or not within range" (p. 152).

This passage from the memories-centred and recollection-centred method in relevant ways akin to "the old hypnotic technique", on to a transference-centred and enactment-centred method, the "new technique", reflects in all likeness an expansion in the scope of the indications of the psychoanalytic method. It is hardly by chance that Freud wrote "Remembering, repeating and working-through" in the same year in which another landmark paper, addressing a new theory meant to deal with psychopathologies beyond the classical neuroses, saw the light of day: "On narcissism: an introduction" (1914c). While the more restricted technical scope of the method dealing with recollection could encompass those patients whose psychic functioning had evolved to the point of each being able, as did patients under hypnosis, to "put himself back in an earlier situation, which he seemed never to confuse with the present one, and gave an account of the mental processes belonging to it" (1914g, p. 148), the much more difficult and complex "new technique" offered a wider scope. This made a place for patients unable to nimbly put themselves back in an earlier situation and who, contrarily, tended to act out because, being unable to recollect, they went on to live the present situation with the analyst concretely in terms of—that is, superimposed or confused with—the earlier, childhood scenes.

In other words, patients that could work along the restricted, recollection-centred method were able to recover and direct their attention to what had happened in earlier scenes discriminated as such, while those in the "new method" needed to be prompted on in order to direct their attention to—and to reconcile themselves with—the phenomena of their unconscious psychic dynamics as put into action in the relationship with the analyst. The latter was necessary in order to place themselves in the position to gradually gain conscious ostensiveness about the hitherto repressed events.

Still another way of stating this is that patients suitable to use the recollection technique were able to *direct their attention* in order to access the sought-after repressed, hitherto unconscious, infantile scenes without getting confused with them: while in patients who required the road of action in the "new technique", the unconscious infantile situations (be these repressed or as yet unrepresented) need first to be turned into "a real experience" in the transference in order to become accessible. One might, of course, want to ask whether the "real experience" is a veridical repetition or a transformation of and a stand in for as yet unrepresented traumatic scenes, but such question is not answerable abstractly. The further unfolding of the clinical process might help set the place of the emerging material. As happened in the case of the screen memory of my dying paternal grandfather when contemplating the portraits of both grandfathers, ostensiveness of evidences of *error* are usually more accessible than ever elusive "truths". Truth-evaluation is not primarily a function of the analyst, but of the analysand's evolving sense of reality. Truth-evaluation is central to meaning-change and meaning-creation and is part of the psycho-synthesis, not of the psycho-analysis. As expanded elsewhere (Ahumada, 1994) I fully agree with Freud that rearrangement of meanings should be left to the analysand "without our intervention, automatically and inevitably" (Freud, 1919a, p. 161), such abstinence being a central component of the analyst's neutrality. In other words, the creation of new meanings is a function of the process, not of the analyst.

It can be surmised from the discussion above that what Freud calls the "delightfully smooth course of events" (p. 149) of the recollection-technique is a sort of ideal-type model fit in the main for work with the more sophisticated psychic resources found in the classical neuroses—he mentions hysteria and obsessional neuroses—while the "new technique" of transference enactment, transference analysis, and working through reflects the change in the method, forced by contact with patients pertaining to the admittedly quite diverse field of narcissism he is introducing at the time.

Similar to the way in which a century ago Freud found it necessary to distinguish two types of cases, those accessing memories directly and those needing enactment as the road to a "real experience" in session, a third type of case must nowadays be considered to account for the current "autistoid" shift. Winnicott's advice that "Our patients, more and more, turn out to be needing to feel real, and if they don't then understanding is of extremely secondary importance" (1967b, p. 582) applies fully to "autistoid" patients in which the attentional deficit blocks the access to "real experience" in and out of session.

What I am proposing is that screen memories as Freud brought them up in 1899 and 1901 might likely be grasped as a vicissitude of psychic conflict as it expresses itself in the case of attentive, inquiring, observationally keen, and intellectually evolved oedipal child minds belonging at the healthier pole of the neuroses—starting, not casually, with its prime example: Freud's mind in his childhood. My conjecture on the waning of screen memories is that the changes in child psychopathologies have for decades mitigated against the kind of keen attention to one's mind and to one's own milieu that the build-up of screen memories requires.

Before turning to a too brief consideration of what some relevant authors in and out of psychoanalysis have said about the current changes in psychopathology, let me offer a representative clinical example (Ahumada, 1997).

The fifteen-year-old boy—let us call him Tom—was brought to analysis by his parents when their idea that despite his deftness in handling quite complex mechanical objects he was intellectually subnormal was shaken by the finding of an IQ of 131 in a test prompted by his paediatrician. He had no relationships outside his family except for a sole, disturbed friend he would contact occasionally, and lived in the main in what to his parents was a state of distraction, truly of mindlessness. He did not pay attention at school and was able to read just a few lines at a time; he fell asleep in class as soon as the teacher started speaking. At school he was two years behind his age level, and he was only able to attain this level of accomplishment because his mother would read volumes to him as examinations approached that, when he managed to pay attention, he would remember phonographically. Unconscious terror made itself obvious only in relation to the maternal grandparent, of whom he was in dread; his inhibition of play and aggression lifted only in a peculiar context: he was an excellent marksman and an enthusiastic hunter. The analytic process was painfully slow and consisted mostly of silence that demanded the uttermost patience on my part. It took him years in a four times a week analysis to contact, and then acknowledge, feelings of anger or rivalry.

We came gradually to grasp a basic split in his universe: on one side the world of adults, the annihilating "Big Ones" he avoided or submitted to, the place of excitements he cannot "think"; on the other side his own place, the no-place of the submitting-child-subject-to-annihilation, a place allowing neither pleasure nor any success. This became strikingly clear whenever he gained a very good grade at school: he would panic and the following day he would get the lowest grade, which calmed him immediately. The world of adults he felt as a combined-parental–couple locus and it came as a major relief, which he expressed himself, when he came to feel mother and father as people distinct from each other, as this allowed him to handle his relationship to each parent in distinct ways. This capacity was acquired only after years in analysis, after gaining some social life outside his family, and his emerging, for the most part, out of his post-autistic state. By that time he had gained private spaces for himself where he did not feel intruded upon by adults. This had begun—or was reflected by—his sailing alone in a small boat for hours on end in a relaxed vital mood. After a time he started taking his small brother or his cousins for a sail as passengers, enjoying it as long as it was clear that he, and no one other than he, was the captain on board.

An incident while hunting throws light on the quite covert rivalry and violence underlining his basic split of the universe. Targeting his telescopic sights on a big buck deer he was suddenly very emotionally struck by the thought that the buck was unaware of what was happening. When he mentioned this in session I told him—but this had become already clear to him on narrating the event—that what had struck him so much was getting in touch with the fact that this was the way *he* usually felt, both in life and in the session: as the one being targeted on the wrong side of the gun. This certainly happened whenever he approached the possibility of contact with pleasure or sexuality.

What matters in the present context is that as happens with post-autistic patients (or as I prefer now to call them, extending Bernd Nissen's (2008) term, "autistoid" ones) as distinct from neurotic cases, Tom brought no dreams and no daydreams, and in fact denied having any fantasies at all; early memories were non-existent and continued to be so throughout treatment. It was thus a momentous time when, several years into treatment, he did bring in a daydream, the only one that ever came into his analysis, but one, he said, he had entertained in many variants: he was the sole man in the universe, the only partner to the only girl, and the only possessor of a gun, car, boat, or plane in which his girl and he unendingly went on and on at his whim. By way of a highly ideal contrast, the analysis of this daydream provided him with some intellectual grasp of his intolerance to rivals, but produced no substantive change. It must be noted here that changes eventually leading to a broadening of an area of privacy in his mind started in quite a remote place, removed from adults (the analyst included), in his sailing by himself where no rivals disputed his being captain: it often took weeks or months before such progressions found their way to being mentioned in session. In fact, a capacity on my side to interpret without in so doing being equated with, or experienced as, an intruding annihilating adult from whom Tom must immediately become disconnected, was requisite to sustain an ongoing analytic process.

Now, does this clinical evolution fit the two technical models that Freud brought up in 1914, in "Remembering, repeating and working-through"? It is far indeed from the "delightfully smooth course of events" (p. 149) Freud proposed would happen in the recollection-centred ideal-type model that resembled the old hypnotic method. In my work with Tom there were no recollections, not only of remnants remaining in the area of the infantile amnesia, but also, initially and for a long period, of the ordinary course of events in his daily life. There is scant place for the search of screen memories when it happens that, amid the prevailing mindlessness, memory of affect is compromised to such point. Furthermore, it is only in a painfully limited and protracted sense that the second Freudian model—"the new technique" in which the patient does not remember, but enacts his infantile conflicts in the link to the analyst whereby the transference relationship as playground allows the unconscious infantile scenes to come up in the form of "a real experience" and in such way become accessible—can be said to apply.

In the emotional sense and for many years, instead of a link to the analyst it might fit better to speak of a *non-link*! We encounter here Tustin's description of autistic children, deemed to be a-symbolic, as having very little mind, a void of fantasies, and an "obstructed" transference (1988, p. 103–104). While Tustin's remarks refer to younger children and Tom is well into adolescence, both Leo Kanner (1943) and Bruno Bettelheim (1967) were aware that as autistic children grow up most of them remain to a greater or lesser extent autistically isolated. That official psychiatry, namely the *DSM-IV*, has not as yet found a taxonomical place for them should not trouble us.

How does Tom's sole fantasy, his daydream that he was the only man in the universe, the only partner to the only girl, and the only possessor of a gun or car, boat or plane in which he and his girl unendingly went on and on at his whim, compare with screen memories? While screen memories involve typically a fixed, hyperclear visual image, Tom's daydream was not fixed, and it undertook a number of variations. It was not a childhood memory nor was it an initial finding at the time his treatment started. It came about during the analysis and was both a result of it and a signal of its progress. A point of coincidence is that beyond being a wish-fulfilling fantasy it would seem to fulfil the traumatolytic screening-function that Glover (1929) ascribed to screen memories. It patently counter-balances—and in so doing serves to blot out—his long-standing unconscious phantasies of being annihilated by rivals, in part sibling rivals but mainly oedipal rivals most clearly embodied, at the time treatment started, in the figure of the grandfather of whom he was in terror.

What seems to me most relevant is that while screen memories appear by themselves, so to say, during infancy and childhood, Tom's daydream took years to take form within the frame of the emotional containment provided by the analyst in the session. Its emergence was the result of subtle, mostly undetectable and indescribable changes that increased his ability to bear and pay attention to his emotions: Winnicott's (1967a) "mirroring", the expanding affective and attentional double mirroring of the patient by the analyst and of the analyst by the patient, seems a central concept that helps us to formulate an idea of what went on. It would seem that a major difference between screen memories and the sort of daydream that emerged in Tom's analysis is that the affective background on which screen memories emerge has already evolved by traversing quite advanced stages of emotional containment, an achievement that characterises the neuroses.

In the case of *autistoid* patients such as Tom, Freud's recollection-technique does not find a place, while the gathering of "real experiences" in his "new technique" can only come to operate after, and as the result of, protracted work of affective mirroring by way of which the patient's *attentional disconnection from affect is repaired in the link to the analyst*, and the patient's psychic states attain the level of the neuroses (Busch de Ahumada & Ahumada, 2005). As Leo Kanner was well aware and put roundly in the title of his landmark paper, we are confronted with "Autistic disturbances of affective contact" (Kanner, 1943). His choice of phrase emphasised that in these circumstances and patients, attentional contact with whatever be felt as not-me is strenuously disavowed.

Now, can attentional disconnection be said to be currently reinforced by the wider society to the point that the "then" of the Age of Neuroses comes to be in good measure replaced by the "now" of an Autistoid Age? Far-fetched as this suggestion might sound in psychoanalytic quarters, the UN General Assembly has declared by a unanimous vote that 2 April would be the World Autism Awareness Day (United Nations, 2014). That on the subject of a societal turn to autistic dynamics the United Nations have far outdistanced our own awareness evidences a huge gap between what has been recognised at the level of the political scene and what we psychoanalysis have been able to muster.

Freud raised an early warning in *Civilization and Its Discontents* (1930a) when he stated that man risked becoming a "prosthetic god" by being assimilated to his technological gadgets. Helene Deutsch's (1942) description of the "as if" personalities documented the shift in pathology away from or "beyond" neurosis toward the mimetic dynamics that appeared to be a sign the times, and in the 1940s and 1950s there came an upsurge of attention to borderline and narcissistic disturbances. Is it possible then that the Age of Neuroses might be coming to a close?

Three decades ago, in 1980, André Green explicitly opined that classical neuroses were now in the minority, and that for most of our patients an attempt to understand them in terms of the theory of neuroses would require forcing our interpretations upon the material. Four years later Eugenio Gaddini (1984) traced the changing panorama of our patients along with the twentieth century, and concluded that in the course of the century the neuroses had been gradually giving way, first to character disorders and then to narcissistic and borderline states, while at the same time in the social scene people immersed themselves more and more into patterns of mimetic behaviours, in which individual identities became dissolved.

This mimetic dominance in the social and psychic dynamics of global society, inaugurating a tribal stage at the expense of individuation, was highlighted by Marshall McLuhan in his pioneering book on the impact of the media on the wider society, *Understanding Media* (1964). In my view (Ahumada, 2011b) perhaps the best evidence of attentional disconnection on the side of children raised in the context of our current media culture is found in the ever increasing difficulties at the educational level: mindless states, worldwide rather than local, usher in a "new illiteracy". As further evidence, consider that based on studies of the Swiss Federal Office of Statistics, in the editorial entitled "On course for the poorhouse" (Eckert, 2005) reports an alarming rise in modern "illiteracy". Despite having completed their education, over a fifth of the students could not master tasks requiring minimal reading skills, a deficit which leads to social marginalisation and virtually no chance of finding employment. This "new illiteracy" affects those who, having had the chance of a good education, cannot profit from it. A survey in Buenos Aires of youths contemplating university studies found out that only 15% of them had a clear notion of which career they will engage in. The rest were divided roughly equally between those having no idea of what they planned to study and those undecided about committing to further study (Parmat, 2010). Not much attentional endowment there!

Confusion is ample in the psychiatric scene, to the point that despite widespread references in the press to an "epidemic of autism" *only recently, in the* **DSM-V,** *it has set a taxonomical slot for adult* *autistic cases*. While the *DSM-IV* had subsumed four child categories under the title of autistic spectrum disorders (Kanner's, Asperger's, attention deficit hyperactivity disorder (ADHD), and attention deficit disorder (ADD)), now the *DSM-V* has folded them all into a single diagnosis of autistic spectrum disorder (ASD). Prevalence goes up and up as the years pass: an official US organisation, the Center for Disease Control (CDC) has recently estimated that autistic spectrum disorders impinge on one in 10 school-age boys (CDC, 2013).

Amid the society-wide "epidemic of autism" it should come as no surprise that screen memories have been on the wane. We have likely slid farther and farther from the kind of keen attention from early on to one's mind and milieu that the build-up of screen memories would seem to require.

6

"Screen memories" revisited

Shlomith Cohen

"If I tell all my memories will I get rid of them?" asked a patient who was tormented by flashes of traumatic memories, of a nature he was too anxious to reveal. He was not sure whether they were actual memories or figments of his imagination, but was nevertheless haunted by their almost magical power over him. His pressing plea was that they would be erased from his mind. Could therapy be directed towards erasing or carried out while bypassing those fragments of memories? Like many of our patients he was suffering from memories that were symptoms of his disturbance. Freud had discovered already, in his work on hysteria, the connection between disturbances in memory and psychopathology, and ever since memories have taken centre stage in psychoanalytic practice. The invitation to reread and comment on Freud's "Screen memories" offered me the opportunity to grapple with this topic and follow the vicissitudes of a major psychoanalytic discovery.

Prior to focusing on memory, Freud was preoccupied with its opposite—the act of forgetting. In his paper "The psychical mechanism of forgetfulness" (1898b), Freud presented the dynamics of a momentary loss of a memory. The process of bringing this memory to consciousness involved not only retrieving the forgotten name of the Italian artist Signorelli, but also revealed a rich network of threads that wove this element of memory into a rich unconscious stratum of sexual desires, death anxiety, anxieties and concern about his status and performance as a doctor. He concluded that the repression of the particular memory was a result of augmented unpleasure that was attached to it. Communication of the forgotten name "from an external quarter" brought resolution of the tension and enabled the work of revealing the censored unconscious connections that was essential in working through the momentary dysfunction as is expected of psychoanalytic therapy (1898b, p. 295).

Freud's analysis of the event of forgetting strived to reach through the gap that was opened in the function of memory to the unconscious layer of the psyche where the really meaningful psychic events took place. His approach at this point involved looking into the unconscious mechanisms of memory and forgetting, to expose through them the deeper layer of wishes and fantasies that are rejected from the conscious mind of the person according to the pleasure principle.

A year later, in his "Screen memories" (1899a), Freud took a significant step forward. This time he grappled with the issue of memory itself. He focused on some intriguing phenomena—early, bright memories of events that seem insignificant to the person who remembers them, appear to challenge the common-sense notion that connects the strength of a memory to the significance of the event that it refers to. The realisation of a discord in the relationship between a historical event and its memory initiated an exploration into the nature of a triangular relationship between the actual historical experiences of a person, its representations in memory, and the internal, unconscious processes that operate on these representations in his/her mind.

In this chapter I offer my reading of Freud's paper on screen memories, and discuss its innovative implications for psychoanalytic technique. I shall also address the issue of memory as an experience and as a process.

The discovery of screen memories

Investigating his own memories and those of others brought Freud to conclude that conscious memories that are known and can be told to others may actually conceal a complicated set of forces and processes that the remembering person acts to disguise. In his dialogical style, Freud involves his reader in his effort to follow these unconscious processes that operate in creating and shaping memories.

The idea of memory as a screen contained the meaning of covering—a secondary, relatively unimportant, yet conscious idea serves as a curtain behind which to hide an important idea that is not allowed to become known. In Freud's words: "Further investigation of these indifferent childhood memories has taught me . . . that an unsuspected wealth of meaning lies concealed behind their apparent innocence" (1899a, p. 309).

In discussing the nature of screen memories Freud confronted two puzzles: The first related to the ways in which memories are selected in the mind of the remembering person. Seemingly peripheral events that look meaningless may be remembered while obviously meaningful ones from his past are lost to his consciousness. Freud rejected the possibility that the cause of this phenomenon is related to the immaturity of the memory apparatus of the child, as children show an impressive capacity for learning and retaining very complicated tasks. The intricate connection between the importance of past events and their availability to memory brought Freud to see these phenomena in the context of neurosis. He came to understand that memories are the result of unconscious processes of conflict, repression, and substitution which involve compromises that create and shape them (1899a, pp. 305–308). Thus, he concluded, memories cannot be considered as simple testimonies of past experiences as they occurred in the objective history of the remembering person, even when that person believes whole heartedly in their validity. Psychoanalytic investigation shows memories to be complex mental events whose double function is to both reveal and conceal the historical and psychological truth of the past at the same time.

The second puzzle that intrigued Freud was even greater—memories, it appears, may contain details and events that do not agree with the objective reality that took place at the time indicated by that memory. It may even be that a memory contains details that happened at another place or at another time, or may not have even happened at all except in the imagination of the remembering person. From this conclusion, it was only a short step to claim that what is experienced as a memory is not the veridical event that it appears to be. It can in fact be a complicated creation of the unconscious mental process—an experience is worked through and shaped according to the mental state of the individual, and projected on to the past as a memory to enhance the person's sense of self as consolation, as a wish fulfilment etc. (1899a, pp. 314–318). Understood in this way, the work of memory seems close to the work of dreams, a comparison that Freud took up much later (Freud, 1937d).

In his analysis of screen memories Freud suggested flexibility in the relationship between the historical experience and the memory that represents it—childhood experiences may be represented in a more recent memory, but it could also be that the recent past will be represented as a childhood memory. Although this second possibility was the one that engaged Freud in the present paper, it is interesting to note that it has hardly been referred to subsequently by Freud himself or by later writings on this matter. Indeed, viewing later memories as concealing earlier truth better concurred with the archaeological metaphor of the psychoanalytic work, wherein the analyst is portrayed as if he were digging in the later layers of defensive structures to reach fragments of the lost truth of the ancient past.

The concept "screen memory" assumes the existence of two layers of memory: the layer of psychic truth where conflicts between drives and inhibitions are located, where they have to be concealed from consciousness, and a layer that is aimed to conceal it. Entailed in the concept "screen memory" is the assumption that the psychic truth can be revealed, while the function of memory as an agent of that truth is put into question. Freud concluded his article by going even further. He wrote:

> Our childhood memories show us our earliest years not as they were but as they appeared at the later periods when the memories were aroused. In these periods of arousal, the childhood memories did not, as people are accustomed to say, *emerge*; they were *formed* at that time. And a number of motives, with no concern for historical accuracy, had a part in forming them, as well as in the selection of the memories themselves. (1899a, p. 322, original italics)

Herein lies the radical essence of the paper: it claims that one's memories and the stories they reveal cannot be considered objective historical truths. Freud did not see memory as a process of documentation or even a distortion of experience. Rather he saw it as a result of a dynamic creative process of the mental apparatus. This radical idea, that memory is not "as it appears", but rather encompasses deep and wide psychic processes has been difficult to accept and internalise. This realisation clashes with our intuitive sense of memory as an anchor in the objective reality, an anchor needed to feel a clear sense of oneself in relation to others and to the world. The idea that we cannot expect to know what really has happened in the past would appear to dislodge memory from the basis of psychoanalytic treatment. But a thorough study of Freud's papers on psychoanalytic technique shows that Freud never gave up, neither his belief in the centrality of working with memories in the psychoanalytic treatment, nor his belief that memories contain elements of historical truth.

In his preface to his translation of Freud's article in 1950, James Strachey noted that the "intrinsic interest of this paper has been rather undeservedly overshadowed . . ." and that overriding attention was given to its references to elements of Freud's biography. Attempting to relate the findings concerning his biography to the newly developed theoretical model, authors gave more attention to this aspect when discussing the paper. Indeed, Freud's biography understandably aroused immense curiosity, and his self-analysis has continued to serve as a key to understanding his theory. Generations of students of psychoanalysis learned from Freud's unique personal study about memory details that are worth pursuing for understanding and treating psychopathological cases. But beyond that, it may be that by focusing on the personal life of Freud in this paper, attention was diverted from the unsettling theoretical discussion that presented the account of the patient's past as a complicated source for psychoanalytic investigation.

From the perspective of more than one hundred years of inquiry into memory, both within psychoanalytic thought and in other related fields of research, we have gained a fresh look at Freud's ideas about memory that can both sharpen and expand our understanding of the meaning of memory in the psychoanalytic process. A contemporary perspective also suggests a new interpretation of the concept of screen in relation to memory.

Freud's account of the role of memory in the clinical practice of psychoanalysis

From the beginning of his inquiry into the mechanism of hysteria, Freud recognised the connection between the failed memory of the hysteric patient and her symptoms. He gradually expanded this view to all types of neuroses, even to the area of psychoses. Following his understanding of the central place of memory in the patient's mental life, Freud viewed the task of the psychoanalyst to help uncover it. He continued over the years to elaborate on this issue in his writings, two of which deserve a particular notice. In "Remembering, repeating and working-through" (1914g), he described the evolution of his ideas on the central role of memory in the psyche. He wrote:

> In the first phase . . . it consisted in bringing directly into focus the moment at which the symptom was formed and in persistently endeavouring to produce the mental processes involved in that situation . . . Remembering and abreacting . . . were what was at that time aimed at. . . . Next, when hypnosis had been given up, the task became one of discovering from the patient's free associations what he failed to remember . . . Finally, there evolved, the consistent technique used today in which the analyst gives up the attempt to bring a particular moment or problem into focus. He contents himself with studying whatever is present for the time being on the surface of the patient's mind . . . The aims of these different techniques has, of course remained the same. Descriptively speaking, it is to fill in gaps in memory; dynamically speaking, it is to overcome resistance due to repression. (1914g, p. 147)

Freud presented two other ideas in this paper that are also important to the present discussion. He maintained that one can remember in more than one way, such as by retrieving through action or through the compulsion to repeat. Furthermore, he claimed that memory of the past has privilege over the experience of the present. Again, in his own words: "while the patient experiences [his illness] as something real and contemporary, we have to do our therapeutic work on it, which consists in a large measure in tracing it back to the past" (1914g, p. 152).

In one of his later works "Constructions in analysis" (1937d) Freud added yet another dimension to the work of memory in the psychoanalytic relations. His point of departure was an argument with a sceptic, who challenged the ability of psychoanalytic interpretations to uncover the historical truth of the patient. Freud wrote:

> But at this point we are reminded that the work of analysis consists of two quite different portions, that it is carried on in two separate localities, that it involves two people, to each of whom a distinct task is assigned. It may for a moment seem strange that such a fundamental fact should not have been pointed out long ago; but it will immediately be perceived that there was nothing being kept back in this, that it is a fact which is universally known and, as it were, self-evident and is merely being brought into relief here and separately examined for a particular purpose. We all know that the person who is being analysed has to be induced to remember something that has been experienced by him and repressed; and the dynamic determinants of this process are so interesting that the other portion of the work, the task performed by the analyst, has been pushed into the background. The analyst has neither experienced nor repressed any of the material under consideration; his task cannot be to remember anything. What then is his task? His task is to make out what has been forgotten from the traces which it has left behind or, more correctly, to construct it. The time and manner in which he conveys his constructions to the person who is being analysed, as well as the explanations with which he accompanies them, constitute the link between the two portions of the work of analysis, between his own part and that of the patient. (1937d, pp. 258–259)

These ideas have far reaching ramifications in the therapeutic relationship. They allude once more to the influence of the therapeutic relationship in shaping memories that are aroused by the treatment process. Freud encouraged the psychoanalyst to recognise that even delusions, fantasies, and hallucinations contain a kernel of objective historical truth. The role of the therapy is to sort out the psychic truth from all the distorting defensive processes, and reach that truth. In this respect memory has an advantage over a dream, as it contains a fragment of a reality that the remembering person has to reject. For this reason we can say that the suffering person is suffering from his memories (1937d, p. 268). Freud never gave up the idea that as a result of the psychoanalyst's work of reconstruction her patient will be able to recall her memories of the past, but he recognised this to be at best a long continuous process.

Freud's insights into the nature of memory penetrated widely beyond the scope of psychoanalytic theory and practice. Investigating into a person's memories to find evidence of the historical truth of his life became a hallmark of psychoanalytic thinking. One of its more popular applications can be seen in several of Alfred Hitchcock's mystery films.

However, with the general advancement of the investigation into memory (Damasio, 1999; Pally, 1997a,b; Schacter, 1996), the question of abuse of the role of memory in psychotherapy by both patients and therapists began to surface (Shevrin, 1994). The phenomenon of false memories cast a shadow on the validity of memories that were told by patients to their therapists. It turned out that patient and therapists may collude in creating narratives about the patient's past that appear as memories of real historical events. The issue even reached the court rooms (Loftus, 1994). Psychoanalysts felt a certain urgency to re-evaluate their assessment of the validity of memories that emerge during the psychoanalytic process in order to secure the psycho-analytic endeavour that was aided by memory to understand and alleviate psychic distress (Brooks Brenneis, 1994; Fónagy, 1999; Spector Person & Klar, 1994).

Prominent psychoanalysts felt that it was necessary to free psychoanalytic treatment from an over reliance on memory as a source of validation of experience. This revision resulted in the devaluation of the role memory in the psychoanalytic treatment down to the point of rendering it almost superfluous (Fonagy & Target, 1997; Sandler & Fonagy, 1997; Fonagy, 1999).

Grappling with the value of the psychological and historical truth of memory in the work of psychoanalysts pushed aside the place of memory processes as an important element of experience. Yet, one cannot deny the significance of memory as an experience that motivated Freud more than a hundred years ago, and that has become all the more present in our culture today.

I shall re-evaluate the role of memory in the psychoanalytic process via a discussion of two clinical vignettes.

The role of memory in psychoanalysis of an adopted child

In the first vignette I will discuss the appearance of memory as a significant experience in the therapeutic relationship.

Danny started psychoanalysis when he was five and a half. Having been adopted at the age of two and a half by a childless couple, he suffered from developmental delay and severe behaviour disorders. I shall concentrate here on an experience of memory that took place about a half a year into the analysis. (A fuller account was given in Cohen, 1996.)

> A powerful moment of encounter with memory from the past occurred before my intended vacation. Danny had by this time of the analysis allowed himself more pleasurable regressive experiences. He was exploring many aspects of water: its power and sense of fullness and boundlessness, its power of fertility and sensual qualities of heat, cold, and wetness. He was drawn to water as a place where he could come closer to actualise his wish to be physically close to me. He wanted to take a bath, wash his hair, undress, wet me, and so make me participate in his wish to be born from me. It was my task to enable the pleasure of regression but within the boundaries of "as if" quality of play. In the midst of that came my vacation.
>
> Danny came in with his mother, very excited. He ran away from me to be near to her. When I approached him he oscillated between running away and attacking me. I said: "You are telling me—I have my mother, I don't need you. You are not my mother. Mother does not leave her child." Danny stopped his actions and sat quietly on the carpet between his mother and me and was absorbed in a state of contemplation, very much unlike him. His look was concentrated on a point in the air. In the quiet that ensued I could listen to what I had just said, surprised by my own blatant words, about a mother who does not leave her child. I said: "Maybe what I just said reminded you of the mother that you had and left you." Danny held his mother very tightly, came to sit on her lap and started to play with her like a baby. He wanted to poke into her purse, to open her blouse and suck her breast. He wanted her to undress, to feel her skin against his. It was an intensive moment of embarrassment, and his mother was confused and helpless. I sat near mother and child and said to Danny: "If you will be without clothes, then you will feel very close to mother, you can then feel her body. You want so much to get inside her body, so you can really know that you are her

baby." Mother, who until then was very embarrassed and hesitant in her reactions, pulled herself together, gently restrained Danny and calmed him.

It should be mentioned here that Danny's adoptive mother had difficulties in the early phase of her relationship with him precisely in the area of primitive physical contact and that she had demanded that he behave himself and keep his distance like a grown child. If we look at the event in the analytic session, we should ask what past experience was reconstructed at this particular moment—the anticipation of my leaving for vacation—was it the abandonment by his biological mother, or the rejection by the adoptive mother of the internal baby in Danny's mind at the time of adoption? A complex view of memory allows us to refrain from deciding which layer of experience was reconstructed here. Rather, we can say that at this moment a telescopic experience was created that enveloped several memories from various layers of experience with abandonment and loss in that child. We may claim that from Danny's perspective, in anticipating my approaching vacation, his task was to live in this moment in the present, the unfolding experience of separation that confronted him with previous experiences of rejection and abandonment. Here memory did not function to sort out evidence and testimony about that which had really happened in a particular moment in his past. Rather, remembering had an important function of binding and granting meaning to the moment in the present. I viewed my task as Danny's psychoanalyst to join him at that moment in his quest to contain his anxiety of the present separation, through better containing the painful past traumatic separations. Here past and present were intertwined in a rather complex way and not as a straightforward reconstruction of an earlier historical event.

On returning from my vacation, Danny phoned me to ask whether I had brought him a present. In the beginning of the session Danny sat on his father's lap, unwilling to let him go. I said that he was worried that I had not thought about him, and thus he wanted to know whether I had brought him a present. He wanted to be sure that I remembered him. Father asked astonishingly: "Is this true, what Shlomith said?": Danny nodded his head. It seemed that Father was surprised to realise the extent to which worry and rage can be related to being forgotten, and surprised at Danny's demand to exist in my mind.

How does the analytic couple—patient and analyst—live with memory in the treatment? The case of the adopted child shows that memory and remembering was attached to the sense of existence and continuity of being. I suggest that his moment of remembering was one of connecting a past experience with his present one, despite the ruptures in his life. As such, it was a powerful mode of experiencing himself in relation to significant others who cared for him. Danny needed to know that I remembered him, that he existed in my mind not only in the present, but also when he was not with me. For the adopted child and for post traumatic people in general, memory is affected by distorting the function of remembering, leaving the post traumatic person with either no memories, or obsessed by repeated memories that exist outside the sense of ownership of the internal experience.

On the creation of memories within the psychoanalytic process in an adult patient

The second vignette demonstrates the process of creating a memory from fragments of traumatic impressions in the psychoanalytic dialogue.

The question whether memories are formed or aroused in the psychoanalytic discourse came to the fore in the psychoanalysis of Mr T in the second year of his four times a week analysis. The background of this vignette was also my approaching vacation. During a period of two weeks we dealt with present events and with flashes from the past in an associative process of remembering.

> T told me about a child who got hurt while playing with an adult who was with him. T was not sure who was responsible for hurting the child, either the adult or the child himself. The mother of the child thought that this adult is dangerous to children, and T, who is a close friend, felt himself accused by the mother. Maybe, he thought, the child had to be better protected.
>
> (As T was talking the atmosphere became heavily loaded with anxiety and guilt that grew out of proportion to the actual event with the child.)

T said they played together and it is unfair to blame the adult.

There was a pause, and T was absorbed in himself. The sense of danger rose even higher. I wondered if he was getting into a psychotic state—a thought that was not alien to me about T, or whether he was responding to a traumatic memory. I asked him if what he was just telling me reminded him of anything. He shook his head. But the anxiety turned into an acute fear of me in the room. T searched for a place to actually hide from me. In my thoughts I wandered from the adult that was accused unjustly to the frightened child that was sitting beside/within him.

I looked for an anchor in the events of his life history. T was a little child who had been caught in a harsh divorce between his parents. He had certainly lost a sense of security and was afraid that a terrible thing could happen. I imagined that he had witnessed episodes of outburst that he was not able to understand, but only had a speechless sense of danger.

I was aware that this construction of mine was mostly triggered by my guilt over the approaching vacation, and was my way to contain my own anxiety. Thus, I refrained from offering it to T. Instead, I chose to relate to the immediate experience in the room—a strong fear of something unexpected that might happen.

In the next session T hardly spoke. He took out of his bag a very personal object from his childhood and showed it to me. He had found it years ago in a drawer of his mother, with whom he lived after his parent's divorce. At the end of the session he asked me to keep it for him. He had in the past already given me things to keep, but obviously this object had a special value at this moment.

At the next session T was very suspicious. I felt as if I was threatening by my sheer presence. I also felt threatened by him, sensing him to be possibly psychotic, even violent. I spoke to him about the change that I had gone through in his mind from a trusting caring person to a very threatening one. I added: "I think about that little child that you gave me to keep safe in a secure place, and also to keep safe from that violent process that can happen inside you that turns a trusting relationship into a bad and dangerous one."

At the end of the session reality impinged upon us unexpectedly by a door that was slammed somewhere, and raised T's fright even higher.

In the next session, after a weekend, T came more frightened than usual. I asked what had happened. He replied: "Don't you remember?" I thought about the slammed door but waited quietly. After a few minutes he asked: "aren't you angry?" I did not know what I was supposed to be angry about, I only remembered the fright. I said: "I am thinking of the anger here that turned into fear."

T corrected me: "In my view it is the fear that turns into anger."

I accepted his correction, but still did not know what was at the basis of this experience. I asked: "the door that was slammed?"

T said: "It was not that. It was what broke and was scattered on the floor." His fear was rising once more, as if it was happening right now. Was this a hallucination? I knew that I had not heard that kind of noise. It felt as if T was somewhere else, maybe absorbed in a traumatic memory, and I asked if he could tell me more.

T said: "When I was a little child, I do not remember how old or where, my baby brother was still crawling. There were all sorts of things scattered on the floor. Father would leave such things that are dangerous for a baby. Mother said that he was doing that on purpose. She could not take it anymore and left home."

Impressed by the acute sense of danger that this memory evoked, I felt an urgent need to clarify the objective dimension of the traumatic past experience. Driven by my own countertransference I asked if someone was wounded and T did not remember anything of that sort. I learned that he had heard this story from his mother years later, maybe as part of her battle against his father. At this point I realised that reconstructing the past was not the essence of the communication. It seemed to be T's way of communicating his present sense of danger in his life in the context of my approaching vacation. Intrigued by my need to hang on to the details of the past I came to see it as my countertransference reaction aimed at diverting the attention from the accusation of abandonment by my enraged and frightened patient. It was my way of trying to evaluate the actual danger in the immediate situation, projecting my anxiety on the patient's past.

I said how difficult it was to absorb all that was there—the dangerous pieces, the fright, the mother's leaving, fear of the father. I added that we will need time to deal with everything, but it is not easy due to my imminent vacation. I felt an urge to stress that I will return.

In the session before the vacation T said: "I feel lost in the middle of the sea. There is nothing, nothing."

I said: "I am going on vacation."

T said: "It is not that you are leaving. You do not exist."

I spoke about my vanishing as an object. Not distancing but being erased. I vanish and the memory of me is vanishing too. It is not only that I am gone, but that part of him that remembers is gone, erased.

My words touched T and he relaxed.

We checked the dates of the vacation and there was a moment of silence.

T said that he felt sad, afraid of what might be during this time. He understands that what he is afraid of are his own feelings.

I said that he was afraid that his feeling angry, envious, and vengeful about my going on my vacation, can destroy everything, even his memory of me. And then, without his memory he can lose himself in an empty space like in a sea where there is nothing and nobody.

Reflecting on the object that Mr T gave me from his childhood that survived from his broken home, I did not know how this object was important, but I could think of it as evidence of his memories. The anxiety that accompanied the act of depositing it in my hands testified to the risk of its destruction. T felt that he could not protect it, and I added to his thoughts my understanding that he could not protect it from his own rage, envy, and retaliation that could destroy that child (I referred in my mind to his child within). The attack on the child entailed a present attack on the capacity to feel loss and longing. In the period of two weeks that I described the sense of danger started as an actual event in the external world—the child that was hurt while playing with an adult who was with him. But it turned into an overwhelming wordless internal experience. The memory of a little lost child appeared first as a concrete object, not as a psychic experience. Hallucinations, bizarre objects (Bion, 1967) appeared, and frightened both T and his analyst. Through a process of projective identification with the analyst, influenced by present experiences (the coming vacation, the slammed door), those elements were transformed into fragments of memory, gathered meaning, and slowly began to become part of his self-experience. Months passed before they became contents that could be told as memories and could appear in dreams.

Mr T was tormented by traumatic childhood memories that were connected to the fear of closeness and of surrender to a maternal object. The fear of remembering became fear of thoughts and even more of fantasies and dreams. Language itself became dangerous. Realising the connection between that fear and the attempt to eradicate feelings and thoughts was central at this stage of the analysis.

The analytic relationship was vital to the process of working through the fragments of memories and overwhelming emotions into a meaningful experience of the past. Beyond understanding the particular causes for arrest in the capacity to remember those experiences, we could feel that reliving the flashes of memories from the past and sharing them within a meaningful relationship with a living person in the present enabled them to become creative elements in the mind.

In both clinical vignettes we could see the emotional impact of remembering on the present moments in the analytic process. I suggest this is an expression of a need for memory that stems from the need to bind fragments of impressions and experiences to create a sense of a whole person, an experiencing subject who knows herself as a distinctive person in the world. Losing oneself as an experiencing subject is a major source of distress to the post traumatic person who has lost her memory in this experiential function (Shengold, 1989). Traumatic experience affects memory by inhibiting the process of linking elements of experience into a meaningful whole. Such distortions of the function of remembering leave the post traumatic person either without memories, or obsessed by repeated memories that exist outside of the sense of ownership of the internal experience. It is not a matter of one memory or another that must be retrieved, but *the general need to be a remembering person that owns her mental life*. Thus, Freud's assertion that the past is not a fixed entity waiting to be discovered. It is rather continuously recreated through the ever evolving process of remembering. From this perspective, the stubborn insistence of obsessive–compulsive thoughts and behaviours seem to be efforts to reclaim through lost memories lost parts of the self.

The capacity to remember is central to the experience of subjectivity, whether or not the remembered impressions are accurate in objective standards. The original impressions of the historical experience are subjected to incessant elaborations, and to continuous influences of the interaction with others and with external reality. As Freud taught us in his groundbreaking insights, only a small part of these processes reaches consciousness. Focusing our attention on searching for traumatic memories of past episodes to amend their impact and compensation, may grant memory false validity and stability. This thrust may result in overlooking the power of memory as a lived experience, thus denying the human subject a basic subjective experience of continuity and ability to communicate internal experience with another. Here it is appropriate to cite the words of the distinguished neuropsychologist Daniel Schacter, who claimed that memory results in the subtle interplay between past and present. "The subjective sense of pastness that makes our memories feel as though they belong to us . . . is a fundamental and perhaps singular feature of human memory" (Schacter, 1996, p. 38). Psychoanalytic work has a unique contribution to this endeavour.

Concluding remarks

In the psychoanalytic encounter, transference and countertransference comprise the meeting ground between past and present, between construction and reconstruction, and where a new relationship is shaped in the light of memory of old relationships. As we enter into the patient's experience, we are located on the border between past and present. We witness in the present the patient who tells us about other times and other places. The patient gives us pieces of memory. But these pieces are more than stories about another time and place. They are communications about present internal events. We can ask why this piece of memory is told to us now. I want to suggest that the difficulty of realising that we can never fully know our patients, as they carry with them memories to which we have only partial access, may bias us to downplay the weight of the elements of memory in the psychoanalytic encounter that are beyond our reach, and bring us instead to focus on the here and now of the encounter that seems more within our grasp.

The mutative power of the transference lies in its potential to transform old memories into internal events that can be open to a new experience with the analyst in the present time when therapy takes place. Here memory, or the lack of it, appears in the act of remembering, as a mental activity of the mind aimed to create and enhance the sense of self.

The psychoanalytic process creates a unique opportunity to pursue the remembering processes in endless circles of deconstruction, construction, and reconstruction of the self and external reality. These processes are saturated with anxiety, for the deconstruction of memory structures may shatter the basis of familiar structures of the ego. The role of the psychoanalyst as a benevolent person is to support these processes. The task of the psychoanalyst is not to support and strengthen any particular memory structure over others that might be created in the continuing analytic process. Rather, he may encourage the flow of consciousness in free associations in the endless motion from the known and familiar to the unknown and surprising that will allow the evolution of a new unthought known (Bollas, 1987).

7

Reading Freud's semiotic passion

John P. Muller

In his 1899 New Year's greeting to Fliess, Freud wrote: "In the first place, a small bit of my self-analysis has forced its way through and confirmed that fantasies are products of later periods and are projected back from what was then the present into earliest childhood; the manner in which this occurs also emerged—once again by a verbal link" (the last phrase in German is *wieder eine Wortverbindung*, Masson, 1985, p. 338; Masson, 1986, p. 370). It is generally accepted that in this letter Freud is referring to his "Screen memories" paper of 1899 (Masson, 1985, p. 339) and that the paper itself is autobiographical (Bernfeld, 1946). The latter point led Strachey to write that the "intrinsic interest of this paper has been rather undeservedly overshadowed by an extraneous fact" (Strachey, 1950, p. 302). The "extraneous fact" is the paper's autobiographical relevance, which, to the extent it has "overshadowed" Freud's ideas, may be said to cover them. My primary interest here is not in the autobiographical relevance of Freud's memories as such, but rather in the semiotic features of his conceptualisations and clinical interventions.

Freud's self-analysis of his childhood memories indicated that details associated with an adolescent erotic passion were "translated back" into an innocuous early childhood memory of yellow flowers and tasty bread, leading him to the generalisation that this process of retention and disguise is governed by semiotic rules of transformation. Such rules not only determine the formation and meaning of "screen memories", Freud tells us, but also account for how dreams are formed as well as the structure of neurotic symptoms. Regarding childhood memories, Freud states that "people often construct such things unconsciously—almost like works of fiction" (1899a, p. 315); Freud's German states: "*dass man solche Dinge . . . unbewusst macht, gleichsam dichtet*" (1952, p. 546). The verb *dichten* means to compose, to write—a *Dichter* is a poet or writer; every educated German speaker knows of Goethe's autobiographical *Dichtung und Wahrheit* [*Poetry and Truth*]. Before Jacques Lacan's birth in 1901, Freud is here suggesting that the mechanism of the unconscious construction of screen memories is a linguistic one, that in some way, "so to speak", the unconscious *writes*, it composes a text that tightens and condenses meaning. As we review Freud's paper, it will become evident that for Freud screen memories are products of unconscious working-over ("*Überarbeitung*", Freud will tell us), and that a general semiotic framework can be discerned in Freud's formulations.

What Freud offers in this paper ("once again", as he tells Fliess above) overlaps with what he articulated in his paper on "The psychical mechanism of forgetfulness" (1898b), in a letter to Fliess in 1896 (Masson, 1985, pp. 207–209), in his examples of the formation of hysterical symptoms (1895d), and in what he will demonstrate in *The Interpretation of Dreams* (1900a) and *The Psychopathology of Everyday Life* (1901b).

For example, in his 1898 paper on forgetting the name of the painter Signorelli, Freud wrote: "The translation of 'Signor' into 'Herr' was therefore the means by which the story that I had suppressed had drawn after it into repression the name I was looking for" (1898b, p. 292). Translation and inscription are central to Freud's theory of unconscious functions, as he wrote to Fliess in 1896:

> As you know, I am working on the assumption that our psychic mechanism has come into being by a process of stratification: the material present in the form of memory traces being subjected from time to time to a *rearrangement* in accordance with fresh circumstances—to a *retranscription*. (Masson, 1985, p. 207)

This re-writing marks a transition from one developmental epoch to another: "At the boundary between two such epochs a translation of the psychic material must take place . . . A failure of translation—this is what is known clinically as 'repression' " (p. 208). The failure is a failure in conscious translation, while the translation that takes place unconsciously is a brilliant success. Among others, Mahony (2001) has called our attention to the central role of translation in Freud's conceptualisations of psychic processes, in Freud's own work as a translator and writer, and in how translations of Freud's writings have assisted or impeded the transmission of Freud's ideas. For these reasons I will try to pay close attention to the translation of Freud's 1899 paper in an effort to achieve some degree of precision in understanding the "overshadowed" ideas in his paper.

The process of translation had already played a role for Freud in the constitution of hysterical symptoms. In 1895 he wrote:

> It is my opinion, however, that when a hysteric creates a somatic expression for an emotionally-coloured idea by symbolization, this depends less than one would imagine on personal or voluntary factors. In taking a verbal expression literally and in feeling the "stab in the heart" or the "slap in the face" after some slighting remark as a real event, the hysteric is not taking liberties with words, but is simply reviving once more the sensations to which the verbal expression owes its justification. (1895d, pp. 180–181)

The verbal expression is being translated into the somatic symptom. "The fact", Freud writes, "that somatic symptoms of hysteria can be brought about by symbolization of this kind was already asserted in [the] 'Preliminary Communication' " (1895d, p. 152).

Reading Freud's text

Freud's title for his paper is *"Über Deckerinnerungen"*, which Strachey translates as "Screen memories". The word *Über*, meaning "over", "above", but also "on" or "about", suggests Freud is here engaging in an exploratory rather than definitive examination of his topic. The German noun *Decke* means "cover" and the verb *decken* means "to cover". The noun *Erinnerung* means "reminiscence", or "recollection", or "memory". The verb *erinnern* means "to remember". No less a figure than Hegel (Verene, 1985) has worked over the German term as *"Er-inner-ung"*, to establish an inner life, to interiorise, to internalise. Freud's title would then declare a dual purpose: (1) to discuss the process of constituting an interiority or "subjectivity"; (2) to examine the ways in which a "cover" operates to cover up, to at once retain and disguise what is experienced.

At the start Freud tells us that in his clinical work he has to deal with his patients' "fragmentary recollections" from childhood, broken bits of memories ("*Bruchstücke von Erinnerungen*", 1952, p. 531). These "isolated recollections" ("*vereinzelt stehender Erinnerungen*", p. 531) are not available in memory "as a connected chain" of events ("*als zusammenhängende Kette*", p. 531) (1899a, p. 303). He goes on to describe a normal developmental transition from the fragmentary subjectivity of early childhood to a sense of narrative coherence emerging by age ten. This transition is made possible through a semiotic process that makes meaningful links in our experience by means of signs as they substitute for one another or are placed one after the other in narrative sequence. In neurotic pathology fragmented memories and discontinuous self-narratives also resemble childhood fragmentation, requiring a range of semiotic interventions in order to restore narrative coherence.

In this first paragraph Freud marks a distinction between what is of "psychological interest" (1899a, p. 303)—"*Ein psychologisches Interesse*" (1952, p. 531)—and what pertains to "psychical functioning" (1899a, p. 303)—"*dem psychischen Verhalten*" (1952, p. 531). He calls attention to the "fundamental difference between the psychical functioning of children and of adults" (1899a, p. 303). "Psychical" is here understood to be different from "psychological", which appears to bear on normative discipline-specific issues such as cognition, development, and psychopathology as objective referents. What is of "psychical importance" (*psychischer Wichtigkeit*) is the "psychical meaning" (*psychischen Bedeutung*) of an experience as it is processed through "psychical functioning". In my view the "psychical" refers to the meaning-making processes and outcomes whereby, once again, "our lives can be reproduced in memory as a connected chain of events", for, Freud explains, from that time on "there is also a direct relation between the psychical significance of an experience and its retention in the memory" (p. 303).

Freud repeats the word *psychische* as if struggling to persuade the reader of its meaning by sheer repetition. In the first three paragraphs of his paper he applies it to "functioning", "significance", "importance", "content", and "acts". For the next three pages, in laying out the research findings of the Henris, he does not use it at all, but instead refers to "psychological" problems and the "psychology" of adults. Freud then notes that childhood memories appear to be incomplete, but rather than accepting the claim that some details are "forgotten", he prefers to consider them "omitted" (*"weggelassene"*, "left off", 1952, p. 535). He then asks a key question: "We must first enquire why it should be that precisely what is important is suppressed and what is indifferent retained" (1899a, p. 306).

The German word translated here by Strachey as "important" is more specific: *Das Bedeutsame*, "the meaningful", that is, "important" precisely because of its meaning. The omitted content is not "forgotten" in some random manner but rather suppressed because its meaning is disturbing. Freud proposes that "two psychical [*psychische*] forces are concerned in bringing about memories of this sort" in which the meaningful is omitted and the "indifferent" retained (p. 306). One force seeks to retain the meaningful while the other seeks to omit it, the resulting outcome being a compromise substitution, namely "another psychical [i.e., semiotic] element closely associated with the objectionable one". "It is a case of displacement on to something associated by continuity " (p. 307). (*"Kontiguitätsassoziation"* (1952, p. 537)—the Strachey translation has an unfortunate misprint here, the word should be "contiguity"), or it is a case of a repression "accompanied by the substitution of something in the neighbourhood (whether in space or time)" (1899a, p. 308). For this reason Freud advises us to look for the significance of a screen memory detail not in its own content but in "the relation holding between its own content and a different one which has been suppressed" (p. 307). Hence the pertinence of the saying that the sham is not made of gold but has lain with something that is—namely, that the substitute has a contiguous relation (in space or time) with the original. Freud then makes his first generalisation:

> The process which we here see at work—*conflict, repression, substitution involving a compromise*—returns in all psychoneurotic symptoms and gives us the key to understanding their formation. Thus it is not without importance if we are able to show the same process operating in the mental [Strachey's word for "psychischen" (1952, p. 537)] life of normal individuals. (p. 308; italics in German text are omitted by Strachey)

After this generalisation, the word "psychische" now cascades across the next half-page as Freud refers to psychical material, psychical activity, psychical life, psychical operations, and psychical intensity, all leading up to his detailed clinical example.

Hearing Freud's address

Freud now moves into reporting his dialogue with his patient (himself). As in his case of Katharina (1895d), Freud's use of dialogue facilitates the text's performance of its content, primarily through the addressivity of the text. Addressivity includes the use of deictic indicators (I-you-here-now), emphasising the present tense, asking questions, and expressing affect, all serving to include the reader in the investigative process as an ongoing concern. Midway into a two-page ("objective") self-report of life history, the patient tells Freud of his railroad memories, saying "as you will recollect" (1899a, p. 310), and thereby reminding us that this is a dialogue. The dialogue-form then quickly takes on the features of addressivity, as the next paragraph opens with "Now" (*nun*, meaning "now" or "well now") and a question: "Now [taking stock from where we are] what is there in this occurrence to justify the expenditure of memory which it has occasioned me?" (p. 311). The paragraph ends with a repetition of the question and again the conjunction *nun* as the patient addresses Freud: "Well [*nun*, taking stock from where we are at *this* point], can you point out any way ["*einen Weg zeigen*", 1952, p. 542] of finding an explanation or interpretation of this redundant memory [of the yellow and of the bread] of my childhood?" (1899a, p. 312).

With this suggestion of a momentary impasse, of having no marked path on which to proceed, we await Freud's response with interest: "I thought it advisable to ask him since when he had been occupied with this recollection . . ." (p. 312). Freud is here proposing a temporal index for the recollection, to mark it in the patient's history and thereby structure continuity. This temporal index, framed as a question, "was all that it was necessary for me to contribute to the solution of the problem" (p. 312)—but this is not so, for Freud will make several additional effective interventions. The patient now makes use of the temporal index as the dialogue intensifies and the indicators of addressivity multiply. He acknowledges that Freud's intervention fills a gap: "I have not yet considered that point ... Now that you have raised the question, it seems to me almost a certainty" that the "childhood memory" did not occur to him in his earlier years. The use of the personal pronoun "I" proliferates: "But I can also recall ...When I was seventeen ... I know quite well ... But I see now [*"nun,"*] that I shall have to tell you ... So listen. I was the child of people who were originally well-to-do ..." (p. 312). Here Strachey changes the present into the past tense, translating "I was the child of people ..." for *"Ich bin das Kind ..."* ("I am the child...") (1952, p. 542). The emphasis remains on the present tense: "I believe now [*"jetzt"*] that I was never free from a longing for the beautiful woods ..." (1899a, p. 312)—and there was another longing. Strachey again diminishes the text's addressivity when he translates: "But it is no use evading the subject any longer: I must admit that there was something else that excited me powerfully" (p. 313). The German reads: *"Nun nützt wohl kein ausweichen mehr; ich muss Ihnen gestehen ..."* (1952, p. 543), "Now it is no use to keep evading; I must confess to you ...", with the stress on the "now" and the "you" of the confession. The patient ends his account, "For when I see her now [*"jetzt"*] ..." he feels indifferent to the girl he loved. (1899a, p. 313). I, you, now, present tense of the verb, questions: these are the tools Freud the writer uses to bring us into the address of the text, not as a recollected past event but as repeated in the present, with us, his readers, as his addressees.

Freud now makes his second intervention (his first was to propose a temporal index for the screen memory) as he proposes a set of iconic relationships, based on similarity. He says the patient's indifference to the girl "sounds very much like" (*"Das klingt ja ganz ähnlich wie"*, 1952, p. 544) his indifference to the common dandelion (similarity of attitude) and that "there may be a connection between the yellow of the girl's dress and the ultra-clear yellow of the flowers" in the childhood scene (1899a, p. 313). This simple iconic relationship based on perceptual similarity does not convince the patient, who responds with a display of some resistance: "Possibly. But it was not the same yellow" (p. 314), but then goes on to use the temporal index proposed by Freud by noting that at a later date he was in the Alps, offering this to Freud as a link ("I can at least let you have an intermediate idea"; p. 314). He then continues to offer new material, saying: "But I have not finished yet. I now come to a second occasion which stirred up in me the impressions of my childhood" (p. 314), and he discloses his father's plan to have him marry his cousin and make his life more comfortable, thereby compensating for the family's economic catastrophe.

Freud now makes his third intervention in which he offers a verbal (symbolic) formula based on conventional German: "Then I am inclined to believe that the childhood scene we are considering emerged at this time, when you were struggling for your daily bread"—at the time of the alpine hikes. The verbal symbol "bread" now dominates the interpretive field: ". . . or, in symbolic language, of how sweet the bread would have tasted for which you had to struggle so hard in your later years" (pp. 314–315). Such unconscious use of symbolic-verbal phrases appears to be language-specific. For example, when Freud later re-considers an example from the Henris, he wonders if a Frenchman would recognise an allusion to masturbation in the phrase, "to break a branch off a tree", the verbal equivalent for the German phrase used in the text.

In each of his interventions Freud makes use of different types of signs, distinguished from each other by the way they represent their objects, as specified by the American philosopher and semiotician Charles Sanders Peirce (1998; see also Muller, 2005). Icons are signs that represent their objects by being similar to them in some way (yellow flowers, yellow dress); indexes are related to their objects through having a contiguous association with them (alpine yellow marking Freud's late adolescence); symbols represent according to conventional codes, language being the primary locus of symbols ("to earn one's bread", "bread and butter occupations"). The working of signs, their impact on the sign's receiver, is called by Peirce "semiosis", an endless process whereby signs produce their effects which become new signs producing their effects. Their effects in this case are evident in how the patient continues to produce more details of his recollections and shows less resistance to their possible meanings.

Freud sums up the unconscious process that joined three separate experiences: elements of childhood, the first visit back (passion for the girl in the yellow dress), and the second visit back (father's plan for him to marry his cousin and have a comfortable life):

> Yes. You projected the two phantasies on to one another and made a childhood memory of them. The element about the alpine flowers is as it were a stamp [*"die Marke"*, also a "brand"]

giving the date of manufacture. I can assure you that people often construct such things unconsciously—almost like works of fiction ["*unbewusst macht, gleichsam dichtet*"] (1899a, p. 315)

Like Lacan, who stated the unconscious is constructed *like* a language (not as language), Freud states this unconscious composition is *like* writing.

Freud then defines what he means by a screen memory:

> [A] recollection of this kind, whose value lies in the fact that it represents in the memory impressions and thoughts of a later date whose content is connected with its own by symbolic or similar links, may appropriately be called a *"screen memory"*. (1899a, p. 316)

When Freud tells his patient that the screen memory represents the basic motives of hunger and love, he says love seems under-represented. Freud the patient responds, again with the intensity of address in the present: "No. You are mistaken. The essence of it is its representation of love. Now I understand for the first time. Think for a moment! Taking flowers away from a girl means to deflower her". (p. 316). The German word for representation here is *Darstellung*, meaning "the staging" of love, presenting the sexual act (unconsciously) through an iconic figuration (as in charades) of the verbal (symbolic) convention, "to deflower". Freud explains that the unconscious thoughts continue (*fortsetzen*) conscious ones in the impulse to picture the marriage night. The dialogue now speeds up: "I can go on with it [continue it, "*fortsetzen*"] now myself", says the patient, and Freud completes his thought as his patient says, "So it remains unconscious—" and Freud adds "And slips away into a childhood memory. You are quite right" (pp. 316–317). As Freud stages this dialogue, the oedipal-rival resonances can't be missed: "No. You are mistaken", "I can go on with it myself." Such oedipal resonances may well constitute the motivation for the screen memory itself—the adolescent leaving home and moving toward independence, in tension with childhood oral gratification.

Thinking Freud's model

In discussing his early childhood Freud tells us of his longing for the beautiful woods near home where "I used to run off from my father, almost before I had learnt to walk" (p. 312–313). I take this as a lovely metaphor for the semiotic process of displacement, of retention and disguise through the use of substitute contiguous signs. As children do, Freud runs off (when he is barely able to walk) in order to get his father to chase and catch him. The affection is palpable, as is Freud's later gratitude in acknowledging how his father did try to "catch" him by the proposed arranged marriage to his cousin. Displacement, the role of the indexical substitute, and the compromise formation sustaining the wish and waiting to be read, all of this is addressed by Freud in spelling out a dynamic model of semiosis.

The bare outline of the elements can be summarised as follows: 1) The yellow flowers represent iconically Gisela's yellow dress, which itself is an index of Gisela by contiguity with her body; 2) "Taking away" the girl's (yellow) flowers represents symbolically removing her dress and "deflowering" her; 3) The tasty bread represents symbolically the "comfortable life" with his cousin as his father proposed. But stating this much does not adequately show Freud's complex thinking at this point. How does the unconscious thought "prolong" the conscious thought? "You think to yourself, 'If I had married so-and-so', and behind the thought there is an impulse to form a picture of what this 'being married' really is" (p. 316). But the picture is expressed allusively, disguised as a childhood scene: "In accordance, as you say, with a general law ["*Gesetz*"]" that transforms the sentence ("*Satz*") into, in short, "If I had married her, I would be comfortable now."

The word *Satz* lends itself to confusion here because it can mean both "sentence" as well as "clause" (or "phrase"). Strachey's text is confusing at first, because instead of translating *Satz* as "sentence" (with two clauses), he translates *Satz* as "clause". But the German distinguishes *Satz* from the two component clauses, the *Vordersatz* and the *Nachsatz*. Freud the patient goes on:

> ... the clause ["sentence", "*Satz*", 1952, p. 548)] that had remained unconscious sought to transform itself into a childhood scene which, on account of its innocence, would be able to become conscious. With this end in view it had to undergo a fresh transformation, or rather two fresh transformations. One of these removed the objectionable element from the protasis ["*Vordersatz*" (1952, p. 548), the first, conditional clause: "If I had married . . ."] by expressing it figuratively; the second forced the

apodosis ["*Nachsatz*" (1952, p. 548), the second, consequential clause, "then I would be . . ."] into a shape capable of visual representation—using for the purpose the intermediary ideas of "bread" and "bread-and-butter occupations". I see that by producing a phantasy like this I was providing, as it were, a fulfilment of the two suppressed wishes—for deflowering a girl and for material comfort. (1899a, p. 317–318)

In the protasis the "suppressed" ["*unterdrückten*", 1952, p. 548] wish to deflower is expressed "figuratively" ["*bildlich ausdrückt*", 1952, p. 548] through "picturing" the taking of the yellow flowers, mediated by the function of the iconic yellow colour together with the verbal formula "to deflower". The suppressed wish for material comfort, the apodosis, is "pressed into a form" which is "capable of a visual staging" ("*der visuellen Darstellung fähig ist*", 1952, p. 548), mediated not by the icon but by the verbal symbols "bread" and "bread-and-butter occupation". These "fresh transformations" are a re-coding into images (with disguised meaning) of what had been formerly coded unconsciously as a conditional sentence ("If . . ., then . . ."). Freud's claim here is astonishing in its assertion of the complexity of unconscious linguistic activity, unconscious reading that discerns meaning and unconscious writing that crafts alternative semiotic expressions.

Freud now elaborates his model. Memory traces from childhood offer points of contact for the later phantasy: "you know how easily our ingenuity can build connecting-bridges from any one point to any other" (1899a, p. 318) ("*wie leicht es unserem Witz wird, Verbindungsbrücken von überallher überallhin zu schlagen*" (1952, p. 549) in constituting the screen memory. Hence the key to decoding it: ". . . what provides the intermediate step [or the connection, "*die Verbindung*" (1952, p. 550)] between a screen memory and what it conceals is likely to be a verbal expression" (1899a, p. 319), which will enable us to make sense of the details, "*einen Sinn verbinden*" (1952, p. 549), "to connect [to] or bind a meaning". Verbal-phonetic material provides a bridge between conscious and unconscious processes by binding details and offering a translatable meaning.

Freud ends up suggesting that all memories are screen memories whose features may be summarised as follows: 1) Memory traces from childhood are not available to consciousness. 2) At a later date, marking when the memory first emerges, the trace is translated back into a visual-plastic form which then becomes conscious for the first time. 3) This translation takes place unconsciously via the intermediate step of language ("symbolic or similar links", i.e., verbal symbols as well as icons and indexes). Freud concludes:

> ... the raw material of memory-traces out of which it [the screen memory] was forged remains unknown to us in its original form ... It may indeed be questioned whether we have any memories at all *from* our childhood: memories *relating to* our childhood may be all that we possess. (1899a, p. 322)

So again: the memory-trace is not able to become conscious until translated unconsciously via a semiotic or verbal formula into an unconscious visual form, which can become conscious. This requires a complex, systematic, and precise act of reading, writing, and translating. Freud is telling us that there is no staging of an impulse without unconscious stage directions. Since traces in their original form remain unavailable for conscious thought, childhood memories are formed after childhood, following a process of translation/transformation. Ordinary self-consciousness, a "sense of identity" through time, is necessarily a continuously modified compromise formation. Toward the end of his paper Freud writes:

> The whole subject deserves a more thorough examination; but I must content myself with pointing out what complicated processes—processes, incidentally, which are altogether analogous to the formation of hysterical symptoms—are involved in the building up of our store of memories. (p. 320–321)

Among the complex issues requiring further examination, we note that Freud makes recurrent mention of how "indifferent events" are "recollected (*too* clearly, one is inclined to say) in every detail" (p. 305–306). In his memories the yellow of the flowers "is a disproportionately prominent element" and the taste of the bread is "exaggerated in an almost hallucinatory fashion" (p. 312). He again notes "the ultra-clear yellow of the flowers" (p. 313) and the taste "which amounted almost to a hallucination" (p. 315). He makes the same point in his analysis of how he forgot the name of the Italian painter Luca Signorelli: "For example, in the Signorelli case, so long as the painter's name remained inaccessible, the visual memory that I had of the series of frescoes and of the self-portrait which is introduced into the corner of one of the pictures was *ultra-clear*" (1901b, p. 13). After hearing the lost name, Freud states: "I was myself able to add the artist's *first* name, *Luca*. Soon my ultra-clear memory of the master's features, as depicted in his portrait, faded away" (1898b, p. 291). As Molnar (1994) succinctly puts it, "The ultra-clarity of the unnamed portrait marks the absence of the word" (p. 86).

The tension, even perhaps opposition, between the sensory presentation of the image and the verbal construction was noted by Freud earlier:

> Once a picture has emerged from the patient's memory, we may hear him say that it becomes fragmentary and obscure in proportion as he proceeds with his description of it. *The patient is, as it were, getting rid of it by turning it into words* (Freud, 1895d, p. 280).

This may be related to what Freud says about "an impulse to form a picture" of the wedding night, a forbidden impulse that unconsciously "continues" the conscious thought, "If I had married so-and-so" (1899a, p. 316). Once the picture is installed as a screen memory (after its formation as an unconscious translation with the help of traces), it remains fixed and fixed to its impulse. Details are ultra-clear in inverse proportion to their meaning, or, as Barthes (1984) puts it, "cleared utopianically of its connotations, the image would become radically objective, or, in the last analysis, innocent" (p. 42).

The visual image is, in itself, fixed and non-linear, whose ultra-clear details serve to deny ambiguity, in contrast to the verbal construction, always linear, fluid, and ambiguous because it is context-dependent. We see this with the word "flower" as it forms part of two different verbal chains. When Freud provides the symbolic formula for the bread, he tells the patient: "Throwing away the flowers in exchange for bread strikes me as not a bad disguise for the scheme your father had for you" (Freud, 1899a, p. 315), while a page later the patient says, "Taking flowers away from a girl means to deflower her" (p. 316). There is no fixed meaning to the term "flowers", beyond its general denotative botanical significance. Here its connotative status shifts depending on its verbal/affective context, as a representation for love/sex when "taken away" from a girl, or as a representation of frivolous work when "thrown away" and "exchanged" for bread: ". . . you were to give up your unpractical ideals and take on a 'bread-and-butter' occupation" (p. 315). There is even a third use of the term by Freud when he states that the sexual picture "does not develop into a *conscious* phantasy but must be content to find its way allusively and under a *flowery* disguise into a childhood scene" (p. 317, italics around "flowery" omitted by Strachey). Here "flowery" perhaps means something like "elaborate", or "gaudy", or "innocent", or, literally, "full of flowers". The point is that while images are fixed, words shift meaning depending on context. In the imagistic presentation of the screen memory, words are perhaps resisted because they are the stepping stones to consciousness of the pictured content, words always being at risk of making too much conscious.

Freud's thinking about the centrality of language for consciousness persists well beyond this early period, for in "Formulations on the two principles of mental functioning" (1911b), Freud continued to link consciousness and language:

> It is probable that thinking was originally unconscious, in so far as it went beyond mere ideational presentations ["*Vorstellungen*"] and directed itself to the relations between impressions of objects, and it acquired further qualities, perceptible to consciousness, first by means of the binding to verbal residues ["*durch die Bindung an die Wortreste*", 1952, p. 234]. (1911b, p. 221, translation modified)

Freud is making three important claims here:

1. The earliest psychic activity is the "ideational presentation", which is not about the presentation of an idea but rather a picture, or more specifically a sensible quality, that is "placed in front of", (a *vor-stellung*), a sort of stream of images. These "ideational presentations" are not representations, they are not icons. For an image to serve as an iconic sign it must be taken *as* a sign of what it resembles. At this primitive level there are no representations, simply presentations.

2. There then follows unconscious thinking, an act that goes beyond the streaming images by directing itself to the relations between impressions of objects, to qualitative differences, to compare them.

3. Thinking becomes perceptible to consciousness when its subject matter is bound to/by verbal residues, phonetic bits, semiotic indicators.

This third step does not mean that all verbally bound experience is conscious, but rather capable of becoming conscious. Freud makes this explicit in his paper on the unconscious when he states: "As we can see, being linked with word-presentations is not yet the same thing as becoming conscious, but only makes it possible to become so" (1915e, pp. 202–203). Moreover, as discussed earlier, the psychic act of repression, which for Freud is a "failure of translation" for consciousness, indeed requires that linguistic functions of translation operate unconsciously. Analysis is effective when the vocalised articulation (whose full meaning cannot be present to consciousness) resonates with an unconscious articulation that, in fashioning the unconscious fantasy, at once structures neurotic behaviour and also binds together experience so that it can become conscious as a connected chain of events.

8

Phyllis Greenacre: screen memories and reconstruction

Nellie Thompson

> Not only *some* but *all* of what is essential from childhood has been retained in [screen] memories. It is simply a question of knowing how to extract it out of them by analysis.
>
> Freud, 1914g, p. 148

The aim of Freud's paper on "Screen memories" (1899a) was to clarify the concept of a "screen memory" as one that owes its value not to its own content but to the relation between that content and some other that has been suppressed. Screen memories are predominantly visual: the witness seems detached, and to be watching him or herself as a child. A screen memory may seize on a past event, or a past event may be moved forward. In contrast to their relatively indifferent or patently distorted content, screen memories are characterised by special luminosity or intensity. Freud drew on autobiographical memories to illustrate his description of screen memories.

Freud made further observations on screen memories in *The Psychopathology of Everyday Life* (1901b edition), "Recollection, repetition, and working-through" (1914g), and *A Childhood Recollection from Dichtung und Wahrheit* (1917b).

Screen memories played an integral role in the clinical work of Phyllis Greenacre (1894–1989). She wrote two papers on them, and observations on them are found throughout her writings. The first paper, "A contribution to the study of screen memories" (1949) linked their intensity and visual quality to five psychodynamic sources. The second paper, " 'It is my own intervention.' A special screen memory of Mr. Lewis Carroll: its form and history." (1955b), traced the origin and reworking of a recurring screen memory in the writings of Charles Dodgson–Lewis Carroll.

This paper has two parts. The first reviews Greenacre's two papers on screen memories, and the second discusses her four papers on reconstruction (Greenacre, 1975, 1979, 1980, 1981) in which they figure prominently. Greenacre's clinical approach rested upon her conviction of the importance of reconstruction. In particular she points to Freud's late paper, "Constructions in analysis" (1937d), and identifies with his estimation of the therapeutic value of constructions as affording a pathway by which early, pre-verbal and pre-oedipal experiences could be glimpsed and recovered. Why reconstruction, and the work of construction, fell out of favour with analysts is also addressed in these papers. Finally, I draw attention to a neglected autobiographical dimension of these papers, Greenacre's evocative description of her inner psychological world during clinical work with patients. The contemporary resonances of her experience of clinical work is a useful caution against the assumption that in relationship to their patients' past analysts adopted a position of austere neutrality and abstinence.

"A contribution to the study of screen memories" (1949)

Greenacre's interest in screen memories was precipitated by clinical findings, which she described in "Vision, headache and the halo" (1947), a paper that explored the impact on childhood superego formation of stressful experiences accompanied by overwhelming visual stimulation. She described a group of patients, each of whom as a young child

> . . . receive[d] a stunning psychic blow, usually an overwhelming visual experience which has the effect of dazing and bewildering it. There is generally the sensation of lights, flashes of lightning,

> bright colors or of some sort of aurora. . . . The initial experience always produces the most intense emotions, whether of awe, fear, rage or horror. Extremely severe lancinating pain may be part of the disturbing experience. (Greenacre, 1947, p. 177)

Greenacre was struck by finding that similar situations of stress could "reactivate" the original experience and the visual components of the superego in these adult patients. She was also impressed by Ernst Kris's suggestion that "that these light effects—halo or aurora—might be related to the peculiar peripheral luminosity and general intensity of screen memories" (Greenacre, 1947, p. 193).

Greenacre's 1949 paper begins, however, with her finding that there is "a special form of screen memory in which there is an intensity of stubborn persistence but *without brightness*, and in which the content appears factually disturbing and very little elaborated" (Greenacre, 1949, p. 74, my italics).

In extreme situations the memory is "an insistent unpleasant scene" that is readily related by the patient with a "marked degree of isolation being achieved by an almost complete withdrawal of affect" (1949). In her experience such memories are related to the central theme of the neurosis, are rigidly defended, and only recovered by the patient at the end of the analysis.

The paper includes a very detailed clinical report of such a screen memory reported early in the analysis of a thirty-five-year-old nurse. She had sought treatment because she found her sexual feelings towards both men and women intolerable, resulting in feelings of guilt, anger, and severe panic (Greenacre, 1949, p. 77). The patient claimed that her sexual "enlightenment" had been "extraordinarily delayed", and that she had not seen a male genital until she was in nurse's training. On the fifth day of the analysis, however, the patient recounted that when she was eight or nine she had got up in the night, passed her parents' bedroom, which was dimly light, and had observed them having intercourse. The scene had a *"dreary clarity"* in her mind and she recalled her father's face as looking cruel and unattractive although in fact he was a good-looking man. The patient would neither discuss nor elaborate on this screen memory. It soon emerged, however, that she had in fact slept in her parent's bedroom until she was four years old. Thus her screen memory used "reality" to cover earlier reality, illustrating Freud's point that a screen memory may seize on a later experience to mask an earlier one.

Phyllis Greenacre: screen memories and reconstruction

During the patient's analysis several deeply traumatic experiences condensed in the screen memory appeared in her dreams, symptoms, and defensive structure. As a young child, the patient witnessed a man exposed and masturbating (most likely a schizophrenic cousin of her father's with whom he shared a likeness); and the further sexual trauma of an attempted rape. Although the patient had a strong ego and was well loved by both parents, the traumatic experiences of her childhood were *"unusually severe"* (original italics). The events preserved in the patient's screen memory were eventually recovered through an analysis of her sadomasochistic character structure and her libidinal development.

After further careful study of the structure of a number of screen memories Greenacre proposes that their special intensity and visual quality corresponds to varying pressures from five sources:

a) The strength of the sense of reality dependent on the stage of ego development: The stronger the ego and the firmer the sense of reality, the better can the young individual tolerate frustration and anxiety and the less need he has for the compromise involved in displacement and screening.

b) The intensity of the disturbing experience which provokes the screening. In general . . . [the] psychic traumata of childhood do involve vision directly in greater proportion than in the adult years. The brightness accompanying screen memories may be a displacement from the shock of a horrific experience accompanied by focusing on a trivial detail.

c) The stage of libidinal development of the child and the degree of general erotic arousal at the time with resultant frustration and anxiety. Thus the utilization of a traumatic experience or event may be markedly different dependent on whether it occurs in the oedipal phase or during the latency period, i.e., whether in the ascendency or relative quiescence of erotic feeling and interest . . . not only the stage of libido development but the specific concatenation of recent experience of the child may determine his point of saturation for frustration and anxiety after which he must resort to displacement and denial as defensive measures.

d) Screen memories are also influenced by "the genetic stage of the superego development" and "by the special vicissitudes of the individual's superego formation . . . It seems, however, that the detached onlooker quality characteristic of the typical screen memory may be due not only to the paralysis and temporary depersonalization caused by fright . . . and carried over to the substitute remembered experience, but further . . . to the arousal of the superego functions whose force influences decisively the need to deny and the feeling of general intensity, and which are represented by an actual watchfulness in the screen memory."

e) The form and degree of sadomasochistic character structure which has already been built up in the person at the time of the event(s) for which the screen memory is substituted . . . where there is no severe degree of sado-masochistic character, simple, pleasant or tepid events may be used as the screen, whereas in severely morbid personalities really traumatic events may be seized upon as representations of the earliest anxious fantasies or experiences of the child . . . (Greenacre, 1949, pp. 75–77)

In enumerating these five sources Greenacre builds on Freud's observations on screen memories by providing a dynamic framework for understanding the intensity and visual quality of screen memories within the context of the complex interplay between psychosexual development and the child's significant relationships. Screen memories are continually modified by "new and less disturbing experiences" that mask or screen the original experiences they preserve. For this reason it is especially important to explore the patient's environment and emotional relationships that form the setting for the experience(s) that give rise to screen memories. Without this the analyst may only see the genetic background and not the "uniquely individual elements bound together and hidden by the screen" (Greenacre, 1975, p. 710).

While acknowledging Freud's observation that repression, displacement, condensation, symbolisation, and secondary elaboration are found in both dreams and screen memories, Greenacre draws a firm distinction between dreams and screen memories. This differentiation is linked to their respective visual qualities, which reflect their perceptual origins, and in the case of screen memories strengthened by the superego.

. . . in general the screen memory is isolated, bright-edged, whereas the dream does not have so clear a periphery and, as Lewin has shown (Lewin, 1949), many have curled edges that roll under or back. I believe that this difference is on a rather simple basis. According to Lewin the deepest dream screen is the breast and the nursing experience. Here the mouth rather than the eye is the primary receptive organ. The dream occurs during sleep and has as its base the earliest twilight and sleepy states at the end of feeding. The screen memory on the other hand arises in consciousness and seeming alertness, utilizing experiences then in which vision has the primary role and is generally reinforced by the all-seeing function of the superego. (Greenacre, 1949, pp. 83–84).

Later in her paper "On reconstruction" (1975), she will further argue that unlike dreams, screen memories cannot be understood by asking for free associations.

" 'It's my own invention'. A special screen memory of Mr. Lewis Carroll: its form and history." (1955b)

Greenacre's second paper on screen memories is a *tour de force* of applied analysis. It links the stresses and experiences of Charles Dodgson–Lewis Carroll's early life to the themes and literary forms of his stories and poems, which preserved the history of his childhood. Her study of Lewis Carroll's screen memories followed from the publication of the book, *Swift and Carroll: a Psychoanalytic Study of Two Lives* (1955a). Greenacre's interest in these two men followed from her papers on fetishism (1953a, 1955c), which surmised that fetishism originated when individuals were subjected at,

> certain critical periods in early life to external stresses of a nature that upset the integrity of the self-perception and the assimilation of the sensations of their own bodies . . . One way in which this impairment of secure self-awareness of the body appeared was in disturbed subjective sensations of changing size of the total body or of certain body parts. (Greenacre, 1955a, pp. 10–11).

Aware that Alice and Gulliver presented exactly those sensations that her patients complained of, Greenacre determined to study the relationship between the lives of Carroll and Swift and their remarkable stories. Her aim was not to account for the creativity of either man, but rather to understand how the stresses of their early lives found expression in their writings. In addition to her dual biography of

Swift and Carroll, she wrote individual papers on each man. (The paper on Swift was titled "The mutual adventure of Jonathan Swift and Lemeul Gulliver—a study in pathography" (Greenacre, 1955d)).

The narrative of "'It's my own invention'" that describes a screen memory within a screen memory of Lewis Carroll, is driven by an intricate interweaving of the details of Carroll's childhood with the recurring themes of his stories and poems whose literary forms are parody, nonsense, caricature, and satire (Carroll, 1933). Carroll, born Charles Dodgson, was one of eleven children, the oldest boy and third child, whose birth was followed by eight more babies, born at approximately eighteen month intervals. His father was a clergyman. The family lived in a small parsonage, with a garden where the children played and where Charles invented games and gadgets, made toys, and wrote rhymes for his three brothers and seven sisters. Although Carroll appears to have been his mother's favourite, he nonetheless lost her attention (and her lap) to the babies that followed him. Certainly the experience of observing the transformation of his mother's pregnant body, followed by the birth of a new baby, confronted Carroll with puzzles he could not solve and feelings he could not resolve. (Greenacre observes that these births are commemorated in *The Hunting of the Snark*, a poem in eight fits which each climax in a grand explosion [Greenacre, 1955b, p. 240].) It is not surprising that as a child he is reported to have often asked "please explain".

In a bow to Lewis Carroll I will begin with Greenacre's solution to the screen memory and the childhood experience it preserves, which is the subject of her paper:

> ... [it] is one of a series of interlocking, overlapping and telescoping screen memories and dreams, which appeared with obsessional repetitiveness throughout the writer's entire life. The themes which appear time and again are the primal scene, fused with the sight of an older and degraded man, perhaps a gardener, in a state of sexual excitement which produced a counter excitement in a small boy onlooker; all this in turn fused with the awareness of the birth of babies—of birth cries, and either the very clear fantasy of the event or the actual partial sight of it. The excitement aroused in the passive auditor is both sexualized and aggressive. (Greenacre, 1955b, pp. 242–243)

This "repetitive" and "perhaps compulsive" screen memory is first recorded in the writings of Charles Dodgson when he was twelve or thirteen, and surfaces as a screen memory within a screen memory in *Through the Looking Glass* when Alice recalls a "strange" afternoon scene:

> Of all the strange things that Alice saw in her journey through the Looking Glass, this is the one that she always remembered most clearly. Years afterward she could bring the whole scene back again, as if it had been only yesterday,—the blue eyes and the kindly smile of the Knight—the setting sun gleaming through his hair and shining on his armour in a blaze of light that dazzled her—the horse quietly moving about, with the reins hanging loose at the neck, cropping the grass at her feet—and the black shadows of the forest behind—all this she took in like a picture—as, with one hand shading her eyes, she leant against a tree watching the strange pair, and listening in a half-dream to the melancholy music of the [Knight's] song (Greenacre, 1955b, p. 211).

The White Knight on his horse is Alice's screen memory, but the White Knight's song ("a sitting on the Gate") is *his* screen memory, and both screen memories belong to Carroll as the creator of Alice and the White Knight, who represents Charles Dodgson, "the puzzler and inventive gadgeeter" who in his own way fell in love with Alice Liddell. Prior to this scene Alice is "haunted by dreamy memories of primal scene jousting" which, according to Greenacre, recur with "obsessional repetitiveness" in Carroll's writings (1955b, p. 213). In an effort to rescue Alice from her distress, the White Knight claims to have invented a new pudding, but it turns out to be only blotting paper, sealing wax, and gunpowder. To alleviate Alice's disappointment, he then offers her a song of his own invention, and successively titles the song *Haddocks' Eyes*, *The Aged Aged Man*, *Ways and Means*, and, finally, *A-sitting on a Gate* (1955b, p. 451). Alice realises that, in fact, the song's tune is not the White Knight's invention, because it is taken from "I give thee all, I can no more" written by Thomas Moore. The song the White Knight has composed to this tune is too long to reproduce, but Greenacre noted that elements of it first appeared in *Useful and Instructive Poetry*, which Carroll published when he was twelve or thirteen, then again in a parody of Wordsworth's *The Storm*, written when he was nineteen. Resonances recur in *Upon a Lonely Moor*, when Lewis Carroll's persona was emerging in Dodgson's mid-twenties (1955b, pp. 215, 219).

The subject of the White Knight's song relates his encounter with an "aged, aged man" a-sitting on a gate. Towards the end of the song the aged, aged man recalls an old man he used to know. The stanza that follows is new having been added to the version of the poem published in 1856 when Carroll was twenty-four (Greenacre, 1955b, p. 218).

> I weep, for it reminds me so
> Of that old man I used to know—
> Whose look was mild, whose speech was slow,
> Whose hair was whiter than the snow,
> Whose face was very like a crow,
> With eyes, like cinders, all aglow,
> Who seemed distracted with his woe,
> Who rocked his body to and fro,
> And muttered mumblingly, and low,
> As if his mouth were full of dough,
> Who snorted like a buffalo—
> That summer evening long ago,
> A-sitting on a gate.

Greenacre argues that the new final stanza of the "aged, aged man" depicts Carroll's memory of witnessing an older man in a state of sexual excitement, a figure repeatedly found in Carroll's stories and writings:

> The figure appearing sometimes in one guise and sometimes in another, but with his acrobatic swaying, jigging and snorting rhythm, is ... a typical dream representation of sexual excitement. It is interesting, therefore, to realize that in the very structure of Carroll's stories, these figures all appear as memories which are represented in dreams. ... [this leads] to the conclusion that there was some actual event as the basis of a repressed memory of the author which was insistently recurring in this hidden form, an observation of excitement which also stirred him, the observer. (1955b, pp. 232–233)

In earlier versions of this poem Carroll had employed parody that allowed him to keep under control the impulses and intense, frightful feelings aroused by his memory.

In an undated, seven-page handwritten letter to Ernst Kris, Greenacre recounted her solution to the origins of Carroll's screen memory that is psychologically more suggestive than the interpretation offered in her published paper.

Dear Ernst,

In connection with Screen Memories you may be interested in what seems to me something like a screen memory within a screen memory of Lewis Carroll's. It appears in "Through the Looking Glass" the chapter concerning the White Knight, entitled "It is my own invention." This chapter I believe contains the secret of Carroll's wish to exhibit himself to little girls, whether or not he carried this out can hardly be as clearly told; but it stemmed from some experience of his own childhood, where he suffered from penis awe in seeing a gardener masturbate seems to me very probable. The garden and the gardener are of course ubiquitous in Carroll's stories and in his own childhood the actual garden with its play train called Love is noteworthy—a train by which one might be injured by the speed of the train and so a first aid station was set up,—with the first rule that anyone must lie quietly and allow the train to pass over the body three times, before asking for aid . . . (Greenacre, n.d., letter to Ernst Kris)[1]

Towards the end of her paper Greenacre noted that the screen memory within a screen memory, and the screen memory within a dream are analogous to the dream within the dream. In support of her argument that the screen memory within a screen memory in Lewis Carroll's *Through the Looking Glass* represents an autobiographical memory of Charles Dodgson, she cites Freud's observation that when an incident is represented by the dream work as a dream within a dream it signifies the strongest confirmation of the reality of the incident.

The relationship between Dodgson's screen memories and Carroll's stories illustrates another double emphasised by Greenacre: the author within the author—Lewis Carroll within Charles Dodgson. Lewis Carroll emerged in 1856–1857, when Dodgson was in his mid-twenties. Greenacre argued that when an author uses a pseudonym they are "expressing their deepest wishes, thoughts and conflicts". As an Oxford faculty member Dodgson produced rather pedestrian work in mathematics, kept a compulsive record of his correspondence, and meticulously cross-indexed his dinner menus. But as Lewis Carroll his writings are imbued with his fantastic imagination and employ nonsense and parody to pose intellectually sophisticated puzzles and questions, that embody a mature sublimation of his childhood plea "please explain".

Greenacre describes the Dodgson–Carroll relationship as mutual bondage. She notes, without fully exploring it, the fact that in 1897 forty years after the appearance of Lewis Carroll, Charles Dodgson began to refuse any correspondence addressed to Lewis Carroll. Mail was returned to the dead letter office marked "not known". Greenacre describes this as Dodgson "expelling" Carroll from Oxford. The relationship, if any, between this expulsion and Dodgson's death on 13 January, 1898, only months later, is not explored.

Finally, screen memories are not only ever-present in Carroll's stories and poems, but his reminiscence of the afternoon boating party that gave birth to the Alice stories has the quality of a screen memory.

> Full many a year has slipped away, since that "golden afternoon" that gave thee birth [i.e., the Alice story] but I can call it up almost as clearly as if it were yesterday—the cloudless blue above, the watery mirror below, the boat drifting idly on its way, the tinkle of the drops that fell from the oars, as they waved so sleepily to and fro, and (the one bright gleam of life in all the slumberous scene) the three eager faces, hungry for news of fairyland, and who would not be said "nay" to: from whose lips "Tell us a story please" had all the stern immutability of Fate! (Greenacre, 1955b, p. 207).

Two other members of the boating party, Alice Liddell and Canon Duckworth also recalled a "golden afternoon". Duckworth described a "beautiful summer afternoon", while Alice Liddell wrote of "the burning sun of that July afternoon". According to the meteorological record, however, the day was "cool and rather wet". This discrepancy between the actual weather and the memories of Alice, Duckworth, and Carroll is intriguing, suggesting that the memory of "insistent brightness served a screening function to all three of these main participants" (1955b, p. 208). Greenacre is silent on the screening function of Carroll's memory of the boating party. The Alice stories gave visual and literary expression to fantasies, anxieties, and questions aroused in Carroll's infancy and early childhood, that were disturbing and deeply puzzling. His reminiscence of an idyllic summer afternoon screens the troubling, perplexing, yet exciting memories and experiences they faithfully preserve.

Four papers on reconstruction and screen memories

> I believe that the ability to understand and utilize screen memories may be fundamental in the work of analyzing
>
> Greenacre, 1975, p. 708

Late in her career, when she was in her eighties, and concerned that reconstruction and work with screen memories had fallen into disuse, Greenacre wrote four papers: "On reconstruction" (1975); "Reconstruction and the process of individuation" (1979); "A historical sketch of the use and disuse of reconstruction" (1980); and "Reconstruction:its nature and therapeutic value" (1981). In the 1980 paper she blamed the "fading" of the traumatic theory of neurosis and the inadequacy of the cathartic method of treatment as factors responsible for the near-disappearance of reconstruction from psychoanalytic thinking and literature. The fact that some sexual trauma had not, in fact, taken place but was the "imaginative product of the patient's childhood" gave rise to a conviction about the primary importance of fantasy and childhood fantasies that were, in turn, linked to phases of genetic development.

Greenacre also linked the decline of reconstruction to the influx of émigré analysts to the US, and in particular to their influence within the New York Psychoanalytic Society, where by 1948 they constituted one third of the Society's membership (Thompson, 2012, p. 23). It would be a mistake, however, to read Greenacre's observations as a criticism of either ego psychology or the contributions of émigré analysts. She was especially close to Ernst Kris and admired Heinz Hartmann's "The ego and the problems of adaptation" (Greenacre, 1971, pp. xvi–xvii). Nonetheless, she noted that the enthusiasm with which many members of the second generation of psychoanalysts greeted Freud's metapsychological papers of the 1920s and 1930s contributed to the view that "the importance of trauma as well as of the traumatic theory of neurosis" was a thing of the past. She posited that mourning for Freud, accompanied by a 'clinging" to his final writings, had contributed to the minimisation of the technique of reconstruction:

> At the same time that there was an apparent expansion in the intellectual framework of psychoanalysis, there was a somewhat

reactionary tightening in the teaching of technique. The precise interpretation began to take the place of reconstructive interest. (Greenacre, 1980, p. 39)

Many of Greenacre's colleagues dismissed the idea that it was possible to access or recover pre-verbal and non-verbal experiences. Her paper has an accompanying counterpoint no less important than its stated purpose, a defence of her work as an analyst:

> ... some of my colleagues have regarded my reconstructions really as constructions, imaginative speculations which I had impressed on my patients. So this presentation may be something of an apologia for my work. (Greenacre, 1975, p. 694)

In "Reconstruction and the process of individuation" Greenacre contended that reconstruction enriched psychoanalytic theory through a deeper understanding of infancy and early childhood and, in particular, how object relatedness was hindered by disturbances of incorporation and primitive projection. Further, the analyst's greater understanding of the patient's problems may find expression in their therapeutic attitude and interpretive responses due to "the widening of *his* or *her* empathy" (Greenacre, 1979, p. 141, original italics). She described two clinical cases where "developmental patterns rooted in disturbances of the preverbal period later reappear—reshaped, augmented, or diminished at critical periods in later years." Screen memories were especially valuable in reconstructing these disturbances because they provide an avenue to infantile experiences that occurred before verbal language was firmly established, often finding expression in somatic or bodily symptoms. She reported that she watched patients as devotedly as she listened to them because non-verbal communications—weeping, sweating, muscle cramps, blushing, sudden hoarseness—constitute the body's reporting in its own language. In her view,

> ... such nonverbal communications may be representative of experiences which have never heretofore been verbalized ... or they may be repetitions of childhood experiences which were at such an emotional pitch as to preclude clear verbalized thinking, that is, communication with the self, even when speech had been reasonably established. (Greenacre, 1971, p. xxiv)

Greenacre notes that one of Freud's last papers, "Constructions in analysis" (1937d), was a "clear and succinct" statement of the value of assessing the role of trauma and the essential role of reconstructions in clinical work. Freud drew a contrast between an interpretation, which is "something one does to some single element of the material, such as an association or a parapraxis," and a "construction", which is a piece of the analysand's early history that he has forgotten and which the analyst lays before him (Greenacre, 1975, p. 695).

Greenacre was troubled by the fact that the recently published *A Glossary of Psychoanalytic Terms and Concepts* (Moore & Fine, 1968), placed reconstruction,

> under the broader heading of "interpretation" and described it "as a special form of genetic interpretation", with which, however, it is not identical: *events* are reconstructed and *meanings* are interpreted. (Moore & Fine, 1968, pp. 58, 85, original italics)

This definition creates the impression that reconstruction is concerned with genetic interpretations of *events* rather than of *meaning* thus conveying the impression that these two (events and meaning) could be separated in any significant way (Greenacre, 1975).

Greenacre pointed out that construction has been omitted from this definition. This reversed Freud's emphasis, which saw interpretation as involved with a single element in the total process of reconstruction, whereas the *Glossary* presented interpretation as possibly including a number of reconstructions of individual events, that are now brought together in some significant way. In Greenacre's view this definition of reconstruction is so broad as to include "*any* clarification of connections between past and present mental states" (Greenacre, 1975, p. 696, original italics).[2] She also noted that the entry on reconstruction did not mention the function or significance of screen memories or the transitory somatic symptoms associated with early experiences (Greenacre, 1975). In Greenacre's view reconstructions that deal only with events are a kind of intellectual scaffolding holding together constructive speculations, which the analyst imposes on his analysand through a kind but authoritative transference.

> The fact that this definition seems to represent current accepted thinking by able and prominent colleagues has impressed me greatly. They are wont then to refer to constructions pejoratively as "mere speculations". (Greenacre, 1975, p. 708)

In offering her own description of construction Greenacre noted that her usage is close to Freud's but not "completely in accord" with it. She emphasises that constructions may emerge from the analysand too.

> Constructions may arise either in the mind of the analysand or in that of the analyst. Coming from the analysand, they may or may not be true glimmers of incipient insight . . . Constructions on the part of the analyst are inferences or tentative deductions which come into his mind as he listens and observes his patients . . . In contrast to construction . . . reconstructions are based on constructions that are gradually verified and accepted by the patient, and are the *joint work of the analysand and analyst*. (Greenacre, 1975, p. 697, my italics)

I will return later to Greenacre's point that reconstructions are the joint work of the analyst and analysand.

When Greenacre presented "On reconstruction" at the New York Psychoanalytic Society on 24 January, 1975, Norman Margolis, MD, discussed the paper. He acknowledged her concern that interest in reconstruction had declined, but pointed to a recent Kris Study Group monograph that reported the findings of two study groups, under the direction of Rudolph Loewenstein, pertaining to reconstruction: "Recollection and reconstruction and reconstruction in psychoanalysis" (Fine, Joseph, & Waldhorn, 1971). Margolis notes that in contrast to the restricted definition of reconstruction in Moore and Fine, there is a more complete definition in "Recollection and reconstruction":

> *One interprets the meaning of a dream or a symptom, but reconstructs the existence of a conflict, a fantasy, a phase of life or a traumatic event.* (Margolis, 1975, p. 63, original italics)

But Margolis notes that two pages later this definition is further condensed:

> . . . a reconstruction is a genetic interpretation which hypothesizes the existence of a certain not remembered event, which in turn forms the basis of an explanatory statement. It utilizes the background information, unconscious memory traces and affects to establish correct causal connections or provide new connections. (Margolis, 1975, p. 65)

Margolis observes that neither of these definitions reflects the richness of the discussions reported in "Recollection and reconstruction", and surmises that the introduction of the structural hypothesis with its appreciation of the role of ego defences shifted analytic technique to an emphasis on working with structure, patterns of defence, and general development. In doing so there occurred an "unwitting" diminution of the content that characterises the unique development of each individual. In this context interpretation was viewed as a more therapeutically effective intervention than reconstruction.

Margolis's observation is borne out by the conclusions of the study group "Reconstruction in psychoanalysis". In January 1961 Greenacre was invited to discuss with the group her paper, "Re-evaluation of the process of working through" (1956), which addressed the question of how to distinguish real trauma from fantasy. The discussion was clinically rich, and she emphasised her belief that real trauma creates more guilt than fantasy. Her paper is focused on a group of patients whose traumatic experiences occurred in latency but were repressed and "screened by *earlier* infantile fantasies on which they were projected" (Fine, Joseph, & Waldhorn, 1971, p. 115). In these cases "the decisive aspect of working through is the reconstruction and recovery of real, traumatic, organizing experiences in development" (p. 115). In this work screen memories are important because they "always contain important, though distorted and hidden elements of actual events" (p. 116).

In their conclusions the members of the Kris Study Group without actually dismissing Greenacre's position, gave more credence to the position on reconstruction they attributed to Ernst Kris and Anna Freud. Thus, while recognising that environmental influences were important (acknowledging Greenacre's position) they "doubted the necessity for, or the possibility of, ordinarily reconstructing and recovering real, discrete traumatic experiences from childhood because such events become molded into vastly complex, constantly transformed dynamic patterns". They cited Kris's opinion that the analyst works with these patterns rather than with individual events (Fine, Joseph, & Waldhorn, 1971, pp. 124–125). While Greenacre's response to the group's conclusion regarding the possibility of the reconstruction of real infantile and childhood events is unknown, their position may very well have reinforced her conviction that reconstruction of individual events, and hence work with screen memories, had been set aside and an essential part of analytic work was thereby lost. As a result that there was, in Margolis's words, "an 'unwitting" diminution of the content that characterizes the unique development of each individual" (Margolis, 1975).

Reconstruction, screen memories, and the analyst

In "Constructions in analysis" Freud pointed out that while the analysand's task in analysis has been described, the analyst's task has been pushed into the background. Margolis singles out this observation and finds that Greenacre's paper goes a long way towards correcting this imbalance with its description of the emotional requirements and the position of the analyst while analysing. His astute observation aside, this aspect of Greenacre's paper has been under-appreciated (Margolis, 1975).

As a prelude to describing Greenacre's account of what is required of the analyst and her accompanying emotional experience, her account of the analyst's task in working with screen memories, written several years later, is appropriate.

> As screen memories have evolved through years, they commonly have considerable stability as part of their defensive function, thus lacking the rich fluidity in symbolism so characteristic of dreams. The analyst must carry in mind the many events and landmarks of development in the analysand's life, somewhat as one follows the development of a character in literature. Then the full significance of the events of later childhood and adulthood becomes more readily apparent while *the patient's awareness of the analyst's presence and participation adds depth and naturalness to interpretations.* (Greenacre, 1979, p. 140, original italics)

In the passage above Greenacre described the analyst's role in reconstructing screen memories as one that required her to continually hold in mind the patient's unique development. In the last sentence, however, there is a subtle shift when she underscores that for the analysand, it is the *relationship* between the analyst and analysand that facilitates and authenticates the reconstruction of screen memories. This process, however, involves distress for the patient, and it is the "relationship between analyst and analysand that makes the nearly absolute truth tolerable and in some way acts as a catalyst for healing to take place" (Greenacre, 1975, p. 701).

Greenacre's description of the analyst's role challenged the idea, exaggerated in her view, that the analyst's role is a passive one. "Although the analyst's position is one of relative passivity, his mental job is one of complex incessant and orchestrated responsiveness" (p. 697). The analyst's mind "is generally in a state of special, intense, and complex activity, through in a peculiarly low key—a condition which, I believe, does not exist under other circumstances, *but is more allied to that of listening to music than to any other I can think of*" (p. 702, my italics).

The analyst's responsiveness within the transference depends on the nature of her empathy and freedom from any constricting neurotic interferences. The empathy of the analyst facilitates the gradual emergence of emotional themes with their unique individual ingredients. The experience of doing analysis increases the range and depth of the analyst's empathy, but is also,

> influenced by the nature of his own early experiences and the degree to which they have been assimilated, either through the push of regular maturational development or through his own personal analysis, supplemented by his experience in analyzing patients. (Greenacre, 1975, p. 705)

The timing of reconstructive interpretations depends on both "a subtle but decisive interaction between patient and analyst", and the analyst's internal psychic state. "Verbal communication may be the most important channel", since it is the "medium through which a final step in understanding—the real *knowing*—can be achieved. But there are many occasions when nonverbal and preverbal communications may be aroused and thus available to both analyst and analysand" (p. 703, original italics). These communications manifest themselves physically and the anxiety expressed represents a regressive pull to "preverbal troubled conditions in the early period between the total dependence on preverbal body language and the acquisition of speech" (p. 704). Unstated, but implicit here, is the suggestion that the analyst's capacity for regression and contact with primary process thinking is important.

Greenacre emphasises that the analyst's reconstructions depend on:

the completion, in the analyst's own *internal imagery*, of some special area of the patient's conflictual life, which has already been presented in fragments. Such an understanding is dependent on the interaction of the analyst's preconscious fusion of his own experiences with those of the analysand, and must occur in a way that allows him to make sense out of the fragments that had seemed puzzling. It is the feeling of 'this is it" that determines the timing. Such a significant interpretation generally includes some reconstruction, which rests on the verifications or the correction of earlier constructions, whether or not these have been communicated to the analysand . . . I believe that some preconscious self-analysis may go on in the analyst as he interacts with his patient. If he is not open to this, there is the risk of progressive rigidity and stereotypy in his analytic work and a retreat into formal theory. (Greenacre, 1975, p. 705)

The emotional and psychological intimacy of Greenacre's description is a compelling reminder that past analysts have written with honesty, insight, and sensitivity about their experience of doing analysis, the analytic relationship, and the impact that patients have had on them and their understanding of what impairs, hinders, or facilitates their analytic work. Greenacre's conception of the analyst's role in relationship to the analysand challenges the now prevailing caricature of early analysts as silent, rigidly passive, strictly adhering to abstinence, and only occasionally bestowing authoritative interpretations to their patients. Undoubtedly there were analysts who conducted analysis in this fashion. But the reflexive custom current today that draws a distinction between contemporary psychoanalysis as a "two person" psychology in contrast to yesterday's "one person" psychology has had the unfortunate effect of perpetuating the view that earlier analysts have little or nothing to offer when it comes to understanding the psychoanalytic process. The precise and yet poetic nature of her description is a much-needed reminder that it is possible to write aesthetically about the analyst's experience without sacrificing its technical requirements.

Conclusion

Greenacre's first paper on screen memories built on Freud's observations about their character by outlining a dynamic framework for understanding their intensity and visual quality within the context of the complex structural interplay between psychosexual development and the child's significant relationships. Her paper on Lewis Carroll illustrated how his screen memories of childhood influenced the literary forms and themes of his stories and poems. His writings provide layered and fantastic illustrations of two observations of clinical import made by Freud: screen memories contain an "unsuspected wealth of meaning" (Freud, 1899a, p. 309), and "*all* of what is essential from childhood has been retained in these memories" (Freud, 1914g, p. 148, original italics). The unforgettable, and iconic images that permeate his stories are also a testament to Freud's observation that "reproducible mnemic images" illustrate the strength of the wish to fix and remember important impressions (Freud, 1899a, p. 307).

The four papers on reconstruction are a reflection of Greenacre's "deep and enduring interest in the first years of infancy" (Greenacre, 1971, p. xxiv). They are a firm defence of the value of reconstruction for enriching psychoanalytic thinking on the myriad ways very early experiences continue to reverberate and shape later development. Screen memories were essential to reconstruction and Greenacre's ability to work with them is rooted in, I believe, an unusual capacity to "read" pre-verbal development and the patient's non-verbal and somatic communications. An important legacy of these papers is Greenacre's description of the internal psychological states she experienced while working with patients.

Greenacre's self-awareness of her inner states during clinical work is paralleled by a conscious narrative in her writings that constitutes a commentary, a reconstruction, of how she came to find herself pursing the clinical or theoretical problems that have captured her interest and curiosity.

She often revisits, from a different perspective, earlier clinical problems or theoretical questions she has written on or examines the same group of patients from different perspectives.[3] Her writings are characterised by a kind of "psychoanalytic" free association. The theoretical and clinical questions explored in one paper generate another paper, and then another, that are linked by her singular analytic intelligence and powers of expression with the result that her papers are imbued, as Jacob Arlow once noted, with an aesthetic and scientific integrity (Arlow, 1975).

Greenacre once observed that clinical observations, like memories, may act as a "screen". Clinical observations which are nascent rather than hidden may be screened by other clinical observations. Similarly, the analyst's conviction of their validity resonates with the feeling of intensity that accompanies a screen memory. Twenty years after writing "Vision, headache and halo" she discussed L. Bryce Boyer's "Vision, headache and the halo: further data" (Boyer, 1971).[4] In her remarks she commented on her state of mind when writing the paper and how she came to see the paper as a reverse of a screen memory.

> I wrote the paper with a sense of conviction of its clinical validity, and in the next few years I began to see how *condensed* it had been, as it lead over to further studies of penis envy and penis awe [Greenacre, 1953b], and later to various other attempts to understand the different forms of introjection and incorporation, e.g. respiratory incorporation which is often much associated with visual and tactile response (Greenacre, 1951). I have come to think of my paper on vision, headache and the halo as a kind of reverse of screen memory, i.e. as a condensed nodal representation which drew on many observations of which I was not yet thoroughly aware. *But in formulating it, various related topics emerged and began to develop in their own right. It is, incidentally, one of the delights of clinical research, that it leads inevitably to further exploration if one is not too quick to tie it up overly neatly and tightly with premature conceptualization.* (Greenacre, Discussion, 1967).

It is perhaps fitting that a chapter devoted to an exposition of Greenacre's papers on screen memories and reconstruction, should conclude with a passage wherein she describes how looking back at an early paper generated the insight that not only memories may be screened but also clinical observations whose pursuit enriched her work as a psychoanalyst.

Notes

1. The letter then continued to analyse the Knight's song. Greenacre and Kris were close colleagues and friends and in the early 1950s Kris was preoccupied with the problem of memory (Thompson, 2011). His 1956 paper, "The personal myth" is subtitled "The autobiography as screen". Greenacre's letter was probably written in early 1956.

2. The third edition (1990) of *Psychoanalytic Terms and Concepts* (edited by Moore and Fine) has an entry for screen memory, and construction is described as it relates to reconstruction. In my view, Greenacre probably would not have been satisfied with this definition because it does not present reconstruction as the mutual work of the analysand and analyst (see below p. 25). The 2012 revised edition (edited by E. Auchincloss and E. Samberg), screen memories are mentioned in passing in the entries for memory and reconstruction.

3. A trilogy of papers, "Vision, headache and halo" (Greenacre, 1947), "A contribution to the study of screen memories" (Greenacre, 1949), and "Prepuberty trauma in girls" (Greenacre, 1950) used the same group of patients to examine superego development from different perspectives.

4. Boyer gave this paper at the 1967 winter meeting of APsaA. The published version has a different title (see Boyer, 1971).

9

Screen memories today: a neuropsychoanalytic essay of definition

Florence Guignard

Introduction

Screen memories must today be seen in the larger context of the neuroscientific investigation of memory. In proposing that psychoanalysts consider the contemporary clinical importance of screen memories, Gail S. Reed and Howard Levine have offered those of us brave enough to respond a stimulating challenge.

At first glance, the term "screen memory" might appear to be only a description, obvious and barely metapsychological: a memory that presents itself as a conscious recollection of an ordinary event that hides another event, the latter being repressed by the subject, because it reflects a conflict or trauma. However, this rather straightforward appearance is deceptive: a screen memory is not the recollection of a real fact, and its temporality is completely imaginary.

If we return to Freud's 1899 paper on the subject, we can observe that Freud explored all the details of the screen memory as if they were part of a dream. He also tried to understand the false chronology of the screen memory.

I propose that we begin with a clinical example:

A little girl of four is strongly convinced she was present at the wedding ceremony of her parents where she was holding the train of her mother's wedding dress. One day, as she continued to insist on the veridicality of this memory in front of family friends, she was taken aback when her mother accused her of lying and punished her. Later on, she took a better look at a photo of her parents' wedding and discovered she had been wrong: she was definitely not on the picture! Needless to say, the photo had always been in the living room, and the little girl knew both her date of birth and the date of her parents' wedding.

Psychoanalytic understanding of such a conviction might seem evident: with this screen memory, the little girl fulfils her oedipal wish to participate closely in the emotional and sexual relationship of her parents. However, the strength of her conviction raises a question: she is a bright and skilled child, she generally behaves in accordance with the reality principle, she does not hallucinate, and, indeed, she is developing quite well. Some thirty years later, when she is in analysis, she will be able to link that screen memory to an atmosphere of passionate love for each other of her very young parents, and to her frequent experience of having been "forgotten" or put aside unknowingly by them.

So much for the visible part of the iceberg. We have to find out why such ordinary oedipal material takes the shape of a screen memory and why this little girl grasps the opportunity of the presence of strangers to make her spectacular declaration? We may see in this incident the opportunity for this young child's omnipotent self to cut short any need to elaborate the difference of generations that would oblige her to acknowledge the reality principle: she could definitely not exist before she is conceived and born, and she cannot take the place of either parent and evict the other to be part of the parental couple. We may also see how she thus avoids acknowledging the frustration of the unaccomplished wish of being constantly part of her parents' intimacy.

However, there still remains one other emotional quality to be taken into account: *the absence of any feeling of guilt*. I believe that this absence of guilt is linked to the strength of her conviction in her belief. I contend it is this belief that gives this screen memory such a deep emotional quality that it will be remembered long enough to become material to be analysed some thirty years later.

How then would such an absence of guilt be possible? Should both the desire to be part of the primal scene and the desire to get rid of one or the other parent not inevitably give way to a great amount of guilt—although not necessary conscious?

Here is the answer: feelings of guilt *do exist* of course, in the part of the well know mental functioning, first described by Freud, which deals with the drive conflicts between *symbolised* wishes—particularly oedipal desires—and the superego that leads them to be repressed. However, there exists also a *non-symbolised* part of the oedipal situation that contains the archaic love for the primal object that is also the basic object of a primary identification and of a safe identity feeling. As neuropsychoanalysts discovered it, this non-symbolised part, which contains very primitive emotions, does not need to undergo repression, precisely because it is not symbolised (Mancia, 2004). I shall develop further the neurological ground of such a discovery.

My hypothesis is that a screen memory is made of these very early emotional contents, that allow them to express an emotional situation without bringing with it all the conflictual background that is attached to its verbal, symbolic expression. In other words, screen memories are a product of an unrepressed, not a conflictual, unconscious.

In the example of the little girl who misremembers herself as present at her parents' wedding, a potential repetition of the oedipal situation has occurred, due to the connection of a well-known photograph with the arrival of strangers (the family friends). And it is that new situation that gave way to a screen memory.

Where are screen memories situated in the mental functioning?

I shall now develop how screen memories stem from another part of the unconscious functioning, in relation to another neurological locus than the one that relates to the *explicit memory* of symbolised events, which is potentially subject to being *repressed*. What I wish to emphasise is that *mnemic traces* dispatched towards each of these loci do not come from the same source.

Before going into details of these two ways of functioning of the memory traces, we have to examine further the status of screen memories as grounded in an *unconscious* part of psychic functioning and situated at the crossroad of several major functions:

- Day and night dreaming.
- Memory in relation to the unconscious.
- Defense mechanisms and organisation of a chronology for external and internal events.
- Symbolisation and language.

Dreaming—night and day

Freud first described screen memories in 1899. His important discovery was one of many within the vast field of *dreams* that he was studying with passion and fruitful results at about the same time (Freud, 1900a). Today findings by later psychoanalysts such as Bion (1962b), Meltzer (1984), and Ogden (1997), as well as important discoveries in the field of neuropsychoanalysis (Mancia, 2004) allow us to advance still further, and thus to consider night and day dreaming activity as stemming from the same psychic functions that underlie the fundamental basis of our capacity to think, to communicate, and to create. Bion's findings about transformations of psychic contents by the capacity to think also reduce the gap between dream and hallucination, as far as their functioning is concerned. A screen memory can be considered another in this series.

Freud gives screen memories a considerable importance when he writes some years later about their relation to repression of our infantile experiences during the latency period (Freud, 1914g):

> "Forgetting" becomes still further restricted when we assess at their true value the screen memories which are so generally present. In some cases I have had an impression that the familiar childhood amnesia, which is theoretically so important to us, is completely counterbalanced by screen memories. (p. 148)

In this last quotation, Freud shows his fundamental intuition about the mobility of psychic phenomena and their capacity to extend and overlap one another in normal psychic functioning. However, he did not continue to explore this phenomenon in his later writings. Had he reconsidered further the problem of childhood amnesia, would it have ruined his model of neurosis with its twofold development—oedipal phase and puberty—separated by a latency period that is less and less noticeable nowadays (Guignard, 2010)?

Contemporary metapsychology no longer restricts the role of dreaming to the satisfaction of a wish—a "wish" that would anyway need to be redefined with all its defences and disguises. From being "the guardian of sleep", *dreaming has become the guardian of psychic development*. When W. R. Bion designated the "capacity for reverie" as the prototype of the capacity for thinking—that is, the *alpha function*—he confirmed the developments made by Melanie Klein and her followers about the importance of unconscious phantasy and emotional activity in the process of symbolisation. Moreover, Bion erased the potential for rigid boundaries between nocturnal dreaming and daydreaming. He also illuminated the importance of unconscious functioning in human relationships—particularly in the psychoanalytical situation—as well as in the development of the capacity to think.

Memory in relation to the unconscious

Since Freud's *A Project for a Scientific Psychology* (Freud, 1895a) exploration of dream activity has been tightly linked to the question of the role of the *unconscious* in our mental activity. Freud's 1915 paper on the unconscious (Freud, 1915e) clarified this field of exploration and is still accepted today. Elaborating on Freud's thinking, several psychoanalysts, among them Jean Laplanche (Guignard, 2006; Laplanche, 2007), have postulated the existence of a "second unconscious". For them, the unconscious cannot be reduced to the repressed, especially when the latter is equated to that which has once been symbolised and verbalised (see Levine, Reed, & Scarfone, 2013).

First perinatal observations, then neurophysiologic discoveries have enhanced Laplanche's postulate that the unconscious functions in two distinct and identifiable ways, that there are in fact two unconsciouses. Such a development in our thinking takes into account the recent research on memory in the field of neuropsychoanalysis.

Today, we distinguish between two different types of memory. Neuropsychoanalysts have named them "explicit memory" and "implicit memory" (Mancia, 2004).

- *Explicit memory* matures once the child has reached the age of two and is able to speak and symbolise. It is fit for being repressed and then recovered, either spontaneously or through psychoanalytic working through.

- *Implicit memory* is the storehouse of affective and emotional experiences. These start much earlier—definitely before birth.

Studies in neurophysiology have determined how long the *amygdala* and the *hippocampus*, respectively, take to mature. It was discovered that the amygdala develops earlier—around the last weeks of uterine life—than the hippocampus, which develops during the first two years of life. The amygdala is the area where emotions and implicit memory come into the neuronal circuit, while the hippocampus selects and codifies information for the explicit memory. Hence, in terms of neuronal development, *implicit memory is available much earlier than explicit memory*.

Short-term memory still has its mysteries for the researchers, although one can assume that implicit memory should play an important part in it. In contrast, we can consider *long-term memory* as being made of *both* explicit—or declarative—*and* implicit—non-declarative—memory.

Implicit memory stores non-conscious and non-verbal experiences, such as *procedural and motor skills*, subliminal experiences of *priming* (meaning the capacity to identify an object only seen or heard subliminally); notably, it stores emotions and affects that are neither conscious nor linked to a specific, conscious recollection.

It seems obvious that *implicit memory* is part of the revolutionary function Freud describes in his paper on "Negation" (Freud, 1925h): an object has to be *qualified before it is acknowledged as being existent*. The prototype he gives of this way of functioning is: "good, to take in, bad, to spit out". Only a very primitive sensorial memory has necessarily to be taken into account here, in the absence of any higher, more sophisticated pattern of functioning, not yet ready to be put into action.

Recollection of *explicit memory* is selective and reconstructive; it can be put into words and gives a symbolic shape to the reconstruction of the history of the subject. It may include—or not include—a verbal elaboration of certain elements stored in the *implicit memory*. I would assume that most severe psychosomatic patients (Marty, 1991) are not in contact with their implicit memory.

This dual memory system brings with it the idea that the unconscious may function in two ways as well:

- *The unrepressed unconscious* would store emotional and cognitive experiences—starting before birth and going on during the whole of one's lifetime.
- *The repressed unconscious* would work at repressing *and* storing emotional and cognitive experiences that have already been symbolised and verbalised—from the age of two onwards.

Such a discovery is fundamental for the psychoanalyst, especially the clinician dealing with early trauma. Even though no one can have articulate memories of a traumatic event that occurred before language was acquired, it is now scientifically established that we keep memory traces of it in our implicit memory. Hence, such a traumatic event has inevitably an impact on our emotional, intellectual, and even somatic adaptation to the reality principle.

This discovery undermines Freud's hypothesis—in the *Project*—about the role of *Nachträglichkeit* in creating a trauma: contemporaneous research in genetics[1] and neurophysiology (see above, on *implicit memory*) no longer allows us to consider that, for example, a young child who was seduced did not experience a trauma at the moment of the seduction. It should be remembered what Freud named *Nachträglichkeit*: he believed that an event of seduction of a pre-latency child did *not* create a trauma in the child's mind. His argument was that there occurred a normal repression of the experience during the latency period, and that it was only *afterwards*, when a similar although less severe event occurred, from adolescence onwards, that the first event could be remembered "and *then* only would it acquire a traumatic meaning". In my opinion, partly symbolised and then repressed or only located in the *implicit memory* and hence, not subject to repression, the first event possesses a traumatic meaning at once.

In addition to the genetic importance of it, we may wonder if implicit memory draws towards itself perceptions of deeds and unspoken facts—or facts that are not allowed to be spoken of *on the same pattern used by Freud in his description of the "magnetic pull" that repressed instinctual derivatives have upon subsequent mnemic traces. One could also think here of what W. R. Bion described as "thoughts in search of a thinker"* (Bion, 1962b).

In regard to the unrepresented, the human mind has many opportunities to keep on working through various experiences all along one's life span. It meets Freud's developments of "Analysis terminable and interminable" (1937c), however, from another, more optimistic point of view. It fits with the modern idea that psychoanalytic work is devoted to helping the individual continuously work at *transforming* her experiences all throughout her life, with the action of constant instinctual pressure.

Defence mechanisms

How can we consider *screen memories* from the point of view of the ego's defence mechanisms?

In his 1915 essay on repression (1915d), Freud came to a point where he distinguished *primal repression* from *repression proper*. In his last writings, working on perversion (Freud, 1940e[1938]), he adopted the concept of "splitting", which Ferenczi had proposed quite a bit earlier (Ferenczi, 1949) and which Melanie Klein would later develop, when she conceptualised the "positions"—paranoid-schizoid and depressive—and the basic concept of "projective identification" (Klein, 1946).

We are used to linking *repression proper* to neurotic/normal psychic organisations, while *primal repression* and *splitting* are associated with psychotic pathologies and *confusion* as well as *borderline organisation*.

However, even if we were to accept the work of Klein about the superposition of the primary and the secondary system of defences, and that of Bion about the oscillation—normal or pathological—of the two Kleinian "positions" (SP↔D) in every human behaviour and state of mind, we would still have to investigate how these parameters work in the case of *screen memories*.

It seems obvious that no process of *repression proper* could be active in the field of *implicit memory*: such a conclusion would be a contradiction in terms. But what about more primitive mechanisms of defence, such as *splitting, denial, and/or foreclosure*?

I suggest that screen memories escape those mechanisms as well. In my view, a screen memory is not a split memory. Rather, a screen memory expresses a fantasy that has the quality of a dream narrative. The dream narrative is the appropriate vehicle for the unconscious construction of a screen memory. It plays the role of a link, not only between a wish and its fantasied realisation, but also between that wish and an attempt of *understanding* it, to give a sort of *explanation*, expressed through the false coherence of the screen memory.

Organisation of a chronology for external and internal events

We also have to take into account the special quality of *time distortion in a screen memory*. This distortion is different from the one we observe in the *dream*, as, contrary to what appears in a dream, there is always an apparent coherence in a *screen memory*.

This coherence seems to be due to the roles *displacement* and *condensation* play in screen memories, roles that are different from the ones they play in a dream. Although Freud described displacement and condensation as being very active in the construction of the dream, he also considered them as being generally used in the waking state. He particularly stressed their role in hysteria (Freud & Breuer 1895d) but he also kept describing them in his second, structural theory of the mind (Freud, 1923b), and Anna Freud confirmed their importance in her writings (Sandler, 1985). The human mind is continually seeking coherence in the subject's life, as well as in external events. When such coherence is missing, the first reaction is to deny the gap and to propose whatever explanation would seem to be plausible. The scientific way of reasoning trains us to accept *not to know* and *not to use* spontaneous mechanisms of displacement and/or condensation for the sake of our psychic comfort. Artists sometimes reach the same goal through their intuitive creativity. So did the poet Keats[2] when he invented the concept of "negative capability", enhanced later by Bion's work.[3]

Another clinical example will allow us to better explain the role of screen memories:

> A little boy of five enjoys making drawings and is quite successful in representing people in movement. As one compliments him about it, he goes on drawing while making the following comment:
>
> *Boy*: Before, I was making scribbles . . . I remember when I started to make a real drawing . . .
>
> *Analyst*: Oh! When was that?
>
> *Boy*: It was the day I stopped feeding from my feeding-bottle.

Needless to say, this little boy was much younger when he stopped being bottle-fed than when he started to draw "real drawings". But his screen memory condenses with great eloquence the necessity of losing the object to be able to have a representation of it. The quality of conviction in his explanation is striking. It appears to me as the expression of the importance of the natural working through that made it possible for him to have such a noticeable representation of movements for the figures he draws. He appears to have a solid ego nucleus: he can trust his external love objects to come back to him when they go away and, still more importantly, he is able to keep links with his internal objects in the absence of external ones, and has a dynamic representation of them.

Both the clinical examples of screen memory show the role of condensation and displacement. In the first one, the screen memory is based on an actual and present photo that gave way to a fantasy scenario with a displacement in time. In the second one, we observe a condensation of two periods of the child's life: the weaning and the ability to draw human representations in movement. Chronology was respected here, but in a shrunken way, so to speak, because of the role of condensation.

Clinical implications

Such discoveries about memory and the unconscious broaden the therapeutic hopes of psychoanalytic clinicians. They accept the necessity of hard work to refine their capacities for listening and for *feeling* in order to hear their patients' unspoken words as well as the unspeakable trauma and emotions they have experienced. These clinicians will also be confronted by the necessity of finding appropriate and tactful words to talk about these fragile and explosive matters with their patients. Analysts would commit an important clinical—and metapsychological—error, should they systematically wait for the patient to find the words without help: they would then be attributing to explicit memory what belongs to implicit memory, and would be considering the clinical material as repressed, when it is *unspoken* and *unspeakable*. The *narrative technique* elaborated by the Italian School of Psychoanalysis (Ferro, 2009) is proposing here a serious technical assistance, bringing into our everyday practice Bion's idea of "thoughts in search of a thinker" and proposing that it does not matter which member of the analytical pair is discovering a tiny particle of truth, as long as the psychoanalytical process goes on developing through the *narrative technique* (Ferro, 2009).

Screen memories propose here again to the clinician a "royal" opportunity to explore at more depth an unconscious material that succeeded in escaping—sometimes for a very long period of time—the painful work of psychic elaboration of any situation of psychic conflict and/or loss: pain, repression, guilt, and so on, are simply *avoided* by such a plausible compromise with reality as a screen memory. In my first clinical example, the little girl had simply "jumped" into the photograph of her parents—we might think of Lewis Carroll's *Alice in Wonderland* (1865). In the second example, the little boy had thoughtfully and philosophically put forward the fact that every loss of a beloved object contains a potentiality of development for a healthy self.

Conclusion

As Freud noticed, screen memories express precious psychic movements of the infantile (Guignard, 1996). They are not repressed because they do not need to be: their dreamy quality allows them to escape the guilt linked to a symbolised and acknowledged wish in the field of reality. In traumas, screen memories probably allow the person to escape the disaster of having been alone and helpless when the traumatic situation happened. Considering, as Freud did, the work on dreams as the "royal path" towards the unconscious, I would suggest that listening to a patient's screen memories is a valuable way of exploring the links between implicit and explicit memory. The analyst may try to understand the obstacles that prevent implicit memories from becoming symbolised and verbalised. Then she can explore how they have managed to undergo the fate of being linked to feelings of mourning and guilt, thus becoming candidates for repression.

Screen memories are an original expression born in the unrepressed part of the unconscious, that part containing implicit memory. They are a product of hybridisation, either between a real perception and the fantasy of an unfulfilled wish, or between two or more real experiences in life that did not happen simultaneously but have in common an episode of significant psychic work—for instance, the loss of an object. In any case, the time discrepancy between the two—or more—elements put together in a screen memory are the expression of important drive movements.

From the point of view of object relations, screen memories are tightly linked to situations of mourning. They could be welcomed as a momentary pause on the road of working through the loss of an object. They also express the strength of the life-drive in linking the loss of a love object to a personal ability newly acquired.

As in dreams and myths, the epistemophilic drive plays an important role in the constitution of screen memories. First, because such a shaping of a psychic content *escapes* repression and hence, is always at hand to think more about it—for example, within a psychoanalytic process. Second, because, like dreams and myths, it is in itself a permanent solicitation to explore further our psychic life, made of the hybridisation between fantasy and reality.

In trying to define screen memories, I would like to insist on their quality of being a tentative explanation of the world. Definitively, such an explanation can be but ephemeral, lasting only as long as the reality principle has not controlled the situation. But is it not the case of all the past discoveries? What would become of the domain of science without the powerful imagination of its most brilliant searchers?

Notes

1. For instance, the geneticist Dr Ariane Giacobino, member of Swiss, European, and American Societies of Genetics is studying the influence of environment on the fetus during gestation. She discovered that traumatic events occurring during gestation, especially when they are lasting or repeated for a long period of time, influenced the epigenetic data of the baby to be borne in the following way: normally, both parents' genetic imprint are "cleaned" by the fetus's original genome in the first weeks of gestation. Giacobino (2007) discovered that when a significant traumatic situation occurs for one parent or both during gestation, the "cleaning" operation does not function adequately and the child keeps traces of the parental epigenome in her own. She also discovered that such an external influence may last, although diminishing with each new generation over three or four generations in time.
2. Negative capability describes the capacity of human beings to transcend and revise their contexts. The term has been used by poets and philosophers to describe the ability of the individual to perceive, think, and operate beyond any presupposition of a predetermined capacity of the human being. It further captures the rejection of the constraints of any context, and the ability to experience phenomena free from epistemological bounds, as well as

to assert one's own will and individuality upon their activity. The term was first used by the Romantic poet John Keats to critique those who sought to categorise all experience and phenomena and turn them into a theory of knowledge.

3.   Wilfred Bion elaborated on Keats's term to illustrate an attitude of openness of mind, which he considered of central importance, not only in the psychoanalytic session, but in life itself. For Bion, negative capability was the ability to tolerate the pain and confusion of not knowing, rather than imposing ready-made or omnipotent certainties upon an ambiguous situation or emotional challenge.

10

Some final thoughts on memory and screen memory

Howard B. Levine and Gail S. Reed

We have chosen Freud's (1899a) "Screen memory" paper as the focus of this volume, not only because it offers us the opportunity to revisit and reinvigorate clinical thinking and debate about phenomena and technical issues that were important to classical psychoanalysis, but because it helps us to foreground Freud's thinking about memory and perception and highlight his anticipation of what we may now recognise as a radical post-modern formulation. Looking ahead to the future, we wish to emphasise this aspect of his paper along with some of the issues that remain to be further investigated and advanced.

One of the current controversies in our field involves contemporary psychoanalytic discussions and formulations concerning memories, including screen memories, and their place in therapeutic action. The controversy may follow at times from a failure to make and keep certain distinctions in mind. When we speak colloquially about "memory", we usually think of the recall of past experience or events. In this everyday sense, "memory" may be conscious or unconscious, historically accurate or not. Its form, however, is always either *pictorial* (e.g., "I remember an amazing mountain vista, whose peaks were covered with gleaming ice and snow.") and/or *narrative* (e.g., the memory of playing in the fields and stealing the little girl's flowers, which Freud (1899a) examines in his classic paper).

To the extent that memory is ideational, narrative, and/or pictorial, it is, however, *organised* and exists in a form that reflects an underlying psychic structure (mnemic traces, pictograms, representations, etc.). This is true even when that structure is a conflicted one (e.g., the childhood memory in Freud's (1899a) screen memory paper), or when the outline of the memory is vague or uncertain. For example, a patient reported a screen memory of swimming in a river as a child, being pulled inexorably down by a strong current towards a sewer pipe and struggling in a panic to resist the pull. He was unsure if this event had actually occurred, or was a dream, or phantasy image. Whatever its truth status or meaning, it was an ideationally based, psychic phenomenon accompanied by affect and cast in a relatively fixed narrative form.

In contrast to this colloquial understanding of memory, from the perspective of cognitive psychology, "memory" has been classified as explicit and implicit (Schacter, 1987), declarative and procedural (Cohen & Squire, 1980; Mandler 1984), and declarative and non-declarative (Zola-Morgan & Squire, 1990).

Bauer (1996, p. 30) has noted that:

> The precise distinctions captured by these classifications are not identical. Nevertheless, they overlap to a large extent, and they have in common a view that memory is best conceived not as a unitary trait, but as comprised of different systems, which serve distinct functions and are characterized by fundamentally different rules of operation. (Sherry and Schachter 1987; Squire 1992; Tulving 1985)

The latter can be characterized as follows:

> Explicit or declarative memory . . . involves the capacity for conscious recollection of names, places, dates, events and so on. In contrast, implicit, procedural, or nondeclarative [*sic*] memory represents a variety of non-conscious abilities, including the capacity for learning habits and skills, priming, and some form of classical conditioning. A defining feature of nondeclarative [*sic*] memory is that the impact of experience is made evident through a change in behavior or performance, but that the experience leading to the change is not consciously accessible (Zola-Morgan and Squire 1990). (Bauer, 1996, p. 30)

Bauer (1996) further notes:

> What tasks that tap declarative memory have in common is that they require recollection of a specific episode. In contrast, what tasks that tap non-declarative memory have in common is that recollection of a specific episode is not required, and in most cases . . . learning proceeds gradually, as a result of repeated practice. (Bauer, 1996, p. 31)

From this cognitive psychological perspective, which has been increasingly been imported into psychoanalytic discussions and formulations, we can say that there is a spectrum that exists between two broad categories or types of "memories". Unfortunately, the distinction between the two poles has not always been carefully or clearly maintained in psychoanalytic discourse. This can be seen in debates concerning the role of historical truth *vs.* psychic reality, insight *vs.* action, and whether interpretation and verbal understanding or positive emotional relationships are the leading factors in therapeutic action and analytic cure.

What is perhaps most unfortunate is that in cognitive psychology the term, memory, which in common parlance refers to something with a potentially articulable ideational content, is used to nominate something—implicit, procedural, or non-declarative "memory"—that reflects learning and experience, but by definition has an underlying psychic structure that is non-ideational.

For example, how do we understand the relationship between unconscious phantasy and "implicit relational knowing", as the latter is described in the work of the Boston Change Process Study Group (2010)? Their emphasis on implicit relational knowing seeks to replace what in other, more classically based formulations, would be ascribed to the effects of unconscious phantasy, with the latter assumed to be structured around an articulable, emotionally significant, imagined, or potentially imaginable transaction between an image of self and object.

In traditional psychoanalytic formulations, the unstated assumption has almost always been that what is implicit is organised, structured in an ideationally saturated, articulable form, but repressed or otherwise defended against by the ego. As such, there is always something potentially verbalisable but hidden—either because it is traumatic or unacceptably anxiety producing—there to be discovered. This is the essence of Freud's very powerful archaeological metaphor.

What analysts have become progressively aware of, however, is another distinct conceptual category: the possibility that action—for example, ways of being with or relating to—that reflects the implicit may follow from a deficit or discontinuity in the representational capacity of the psyche—that is, a de-cathexis, void, or disruption, rather than a defended against presence. (See Levine, Reed, & Scarfone, 2013 for extensive discussions of Freud's theory of representation, its implications for clinical practice, and its later adumbration in the work of Bion (1962a, 1970, 2005), Green (2005), Botella & Botella (2005)).

The work of the Boston Change Group calls attention to non-verbal interactions ("moments of meeting") that are therapeutic and operate without the necessity of insight, interpretation, or recollection of the past. While their perspective offers an important corrective to our overall understanding of non-interpretive curative factors and therapeutic action, it seems to underestimate the value of interpretation. In so doing, it inadvertently tends to confuse the movement towards a more comprehensive, complex, and finely nuanced understanding of curative factors by, in essence, blurring both the distinction and possible relationship between implicit and explicit, or declarative and procedural, memory through a kind of over focus on the one and failure to take the other sufficiently into account.

In contrast, although the conceptual language that Freud used was limited by that which was available to him, he seemed in some sense to be aware of the distinction and relationship between the two general categories of memory. In his General Introduction, for example, he characterised the absence of memories of the first years of life in adults as the "remarkable amnesia of childhood . . . the forgetting which veils our earliest youth from us and makes us strangers to it" (Freud, 1916–1917, p. 326). But earlier on, in the *Three Essays*, he

> proposed that the memories created by very young children are qualitatively different from those formed later in life. Early in development, children were thought to retain traces, fragments, or images of events, but not to retain coherent representations of past experiences (Freud, 1905d). Freud suggested that childhood amnesia exists because adults failed to reconstruct or "translate" these fragments to a coherent narrative. (Bauer, 1996, p. 30)

Some final thoughts on memory and screen memory

This useful contrast between repression of organised explicit memory, which, after Freud's introduction of the structural theory would be understood as motivated by conflict and the ego's need to protect itself from anxiety, *vs. failure of assembly of memory* due to insufficient narrative constructive capacity, captures and conceptualises the difference between represented and unrepresented states and may clarify some of the structural distinction between explicit and implicit, declarative and procedural.

Stepping back and looking at the problem across the full spectrum of Freud's work, this polarity can also be seen to be recognised very early on in his "Screen memory" paper (Freud, 1899a) and taken up again in the 1937 paper on constructions (1937d). In the former, he ends with the astonishing conclusion that:

> It may indeed be questioned whether we have any memories at all *from* our childhood: memories *relating to* our childhood may be all that we possess. Our childhood memories show us our earliest years not as they were but as they appeared at the later periods when the memories were aroused. In these periods of arousal, the childhood memories did not, as people are accustomed to say, *emerge*; they were *formed* at that time. And a number of motives, with no concern for historical accuracy, had a part in forming them, as well as in the selection of the memories themselves. (Freud, 1899a, p. 322, original italics)

In the latter, he proposes that a construction could serve the same dynamic function in the cure as the recall of an actual, previously repressed childhood memory.

If we connect the two assertions, we can see the emergence of a certain logic that has a distinctively post-modern, contemporary feel to it. If memory is not "immaculate" and veridical, if it is inscribed piecemeal and stored in and assembled from multiple brain systems, if it is assembled and created at each moment according to the exigencies of immediate psychological purposes and need, then the absolute historical veridicality of its content may not be as essential as its dynamic function—that might include conviction, coherence, and other psychological factors.[1] And from the perspective of implicit forms of knowledge, the importance of even an ideationally saturated construction may pale compared to a particular emotionally imbued relationship.

That said, however, the matter of screen memories takes us to a particular point on the spectrum between the implicit and explicit. Screen memories are ideationally saturated autobiographical memories, which may feel historically true to the subject who has them—"I remember that . . ."—or else may have something of the uncanny about them "I have this memory that . . ., but I don't really know if it happened or not."

Screens may not only defend against and hide, but also stand in for the recall of so-called "historically true" events and have a relationship to historically true experience that is analogous to that which exists between the manifest and latent content of a dream. That is: the screen is to the memory of the actual event as the manifest content of the dream is to the latent content.

Of course, this is all from the perspective of assuming that there is sufficient historical veridicality possible in what will be the recovered memory of the past experience that is being screened and thereby kept out of awareness. It is also possible that in some instances, the screen may reflect the fact that a potential memory—for example, of what may eventually be categorised as a traumatic event—has not yet achieved sufficient narrative form because it is weakly or unrepresented.

In regard to trauma, what is important in the process of therapeutic amelioration and working through is the historicisation and subjectivisation of the experience, which are important parts of its containment. These may require either making the implicit explicit or at least offering a construction that is plausible and can stand in for an explicit memory. So, for example, the question might be asked in regard to a patient's finding words to ask questions about a previously "untalkable about" traumatic event; did she now feel it was OK to ask questions because she had an accepting audience willing to listen or now knew the facts of what had happened? Or did she first have to be helped to develop the capacity to mentalize and therefore be able to think about the experience before she could then have questions to ask about it?

Another question that this raises is this; are all our so-called (emotionally significant) memories created at a specific moment in an intersubjective context with a specific, unconscious, psychodynamic purpose in mind, for and perhaps with a real or imagined significant other? Or is this the case more commonly seen initially and then as one develops autonomous capacities, one can provide the necessary work and observational presence needed to "create" or "assemble" memories on one's own?

We wish to end by thanking our contributors for taking us a long way into the re-examination and further development of Freud's seminal work and our readers for their patience and willingness to accompany them on the journey. We hope they will have found it worthwhile and we look forward to even further elaborations that we hope this volume will ignite.

Note

1. One of us (Levine, 2011) has discussed these matters at length in relation to Freud's (1937d) "Constructions" paper.

REFERENCES

Ahumada, J. L. (1994). Interpretation and creationism. *International Journal of Psychoanalysis*, 75: 695–707 [reprinted in *Insight. Essays on Psychoanalytic Knowing* (pp. 31–47). London: Routledge, 2011]

Ahumada, J. L. (1997). Counter-induction in psychoanalytic practice: epistemic and technical aspects. In: *Insight. Essays on Psychoanalytic Knowing* (p. 133–153). London: Routledge, 2011.

Ahumada, J. L. (2001). *The Logics of the Mind: A Clinical View*. London: Karnac.

Ahumada, J. L. (Ed.) (2011a). *Insight. Essays on Psychoanalytic Knowing*. London: Routledge.

Ahumada, J. L. (2011b). Postscript. What has God wrought? A plea for insight in media society. In: *Insight. Essays on Psychoanalytic Knowing* (pp. 201–207). London: Routledge.

Anzieu, D. (1986). Freud's self-analysis, P. Graham (Trans.). London: Hogarth.

Arlow, J. (1975). Unpublished. *Some Perspectives on the Writings of Dr. Phyllis Greenacre on the Occasion of her 80th Birthday Celebration*. Archives, A. A. Brill Library, New York Psychoanalytic Society and Institute.

Arlow, J. A. (1990). Methodology and reconstruction. *Psychoanalytic Quarterly*, 60: 539–563.

References

Auchincloss, E., & Samberg, E. (Eds.) (2012). *Psychoanalytic Terms and Concepts* (revised edn). New York: American Psychoanalytic Association.

Auerhahn, N. C., & Peskin, H. (2003). Action knowledge, acknowledgement, and interpretative action in work with Holocaust survivors. *Psychoanalytic Quarterly, 72*: 615–659.

Aulagnier, P. (1975). *The Violence of Interpretation*, A. Sheridan (Trans.). London: Routledge, 2001.

Baranger, M., Baranger, W., & Mom, J. M. (1988). The infantile psychic trauma from us to Freud: pure trauma retroactivity and reconstruction. *International Journal of Psychoanalysis, 69*: 113–128.

Barthes, R. (1984). *Image/Music/Text*, S. Heath (Trans.). New York: Hill & Wang.

Bauer, P. J. (1996). What do infants recall of their lives? Memory of specific events by one- to two-year-olds. *American Psychologist, 51*: 29–41.

Beebe, B., Lachmann, F., & Jaffe, J. (1997). Mother–infant interaction structures and presymbolic self- and object representations. *Psychoanaytic Dialogues, 7*: 133–182.

Bernfeld, S. (1946). An unknown autobiographical fragment by Freud. *American Imago, 4*: 3–19.

Bettelheim, B. (1967). *The Empty Fortress*. New York: Free Press.

Bion, W. R. (1957). On arrogance. In: *Second Thoughts* (pp. 43–64). London: Karnac, 1984.

Bion, W. R. (1959). Attacks on linking. In: *Second Thoughts* (pp. 93–109). London: Karnac, 1984.

Bion, W. R. (1962a). *Learning From Experience*. London: Heinemann.

Bion, W. R. (1962b). A theory of thinking. *International Journal of Psychoanalysis, 43*(4–5) [reprinted *Second Thoughts. Selected Papers on Psycho-analysis*. London: Heinemann, 1967; reprinted London: Karnac, 1984].

Bion, W. R. (1967). Commentary. *Second Thoughts* (pp. 120–166). Northvale, NJ: Jason Aronson.

Bion, W. R. (1970). *Attention and Interpretation*. London: Heinemann.

Bion, W. R. (2005). *The Italian Seminars*. London: Karnac.

Blass, R. B., & Simon, B. (1992). Freud on his own mistake(s): the role of seduction in the etiology of neurosis. In: J. H. Smith & H. Morris (Eds.), *Telling Facts: History and Narration in Psychoanalysis* (pp. 160–183). Baltimore, MD: Johns Hopkins University Press.

Blum, H. P. (1999). The reconstruction of reminiscence. *Journal of the American Psychoanalytic Association, 47*: 1125–1143.

Blum, H. P. (2003). Response to Peter Fonagy. *International Journal of Psychoanalysis*, *84*: 509–513.
Blum, H. P. (2005). Psychoanalytic reconstruction and reintegration. *Psychoanalytic Study of the Child*, *60*: 295–311.
Bollas, C. (1987). *The Shadow of the Object*: *Psychoanalysis of the Unthought Known*. London: Free Association
Boston Change Process Study Group (2010). *Change in Psychotherapy. A Unifying Paradigm*. New York: Norton.
Botella, C., & Botella, S. (2005). *The Work of Psychic Figurability. Mental States Without Representation*. New York: Brunner-Routledge.
Boyer, L. (1971). Technique in the treatment of characterological and schizophrenic disorders. *International Journal of Psychoanalysis*, *52*: 67–85.
Brenman, E. (2006). *Recovery of the Lost Good Object*. Hove: Routledge.
Brenneis, C. B. (2000). Evaluating the evidence: can we find authenticated recovered memory? *Psychoanalytic Psychology*, *17*: 61–77.
Breuer, J., & Freud, S. (1895d). On the psychical mechanism of hysterical phenomena: preliminary communication. In: *Studies on Hysteria*. *S.E.*, *2*: 1–17. London: Hogarth.
Brooks Brenneis, C. (1994). Belief and suggestion in the recovery of memories of childhood sexual abuse. *Journal of the American Psychoanalytical Association*, *42*: 1027–1053.
Brown, L. (1999). Review of: *Recovered memories of abuse: true or false?* J. Sandler & P. Fonagy (Eds.), Madison, CT: International Universities Press. *Psychoanalytic Quarterly*, *68*: 476–479.
Brown, L. (2006). Julie's museum: the evolution of thinking, dreaming and historicization in the treatment of traumatized patients. *International Journal of Psychoanalysis*, *87*: 1569–1585.
Busch de Ahumada, L. C., & Ahumada, J. L. (2005). From mimesis to agency: clinical steps in the work of psychic two-ness. *International Journal of Psychoanalysis*, *86*: 721–736.
Carroll, L. (1865). *Alice in Wonderland*. London: Macmillan.
Carroll, L. (1933). *Complete Works of Lewis Carroll*. New York: Random House.
CDC (2013). 1 in 10 US kids diagnosed with ADHD. www.webmd.com/childhood-adhd/news/20130401/
Cohen, N. J., & Squire, L. R. (1980). Preserved learning and retention of pattern analyzing skill in amnesia: dissociation of knowing how and knowing that. *Science*, *210*: 207–209.
Cohen, S. (1996). Trauma and the developmental process. *Psychoanalytic Study of the Child*, *51*: 287–302.

Damasio, A. (1999). *The Feeling of What Happens*. San Diego, CA: Harcourt.
De Masi, F. (2006). *Vulnerability to Psychosis. A Psychoanalytic Study of the Nature and Therapy of the Psychotic State*, P. Slotkin (Trans.). London: Karnac, 2009.
De Masi, F. (2007). The paedophile and his inner world: theoretical and clinical considerations on the analysis of a patient. *International Journal of Psychoanalysis, 88*: 147–165.
Deutsch, H. (1942). Some forms of emotional disturbances and their relationship to schizophrenia. *Psychoanalytic Quarterly, 11*: 301–321.
Eckert, H. (2005). Editorial: on course for the poorhouse. *Swiss Review*, No. 3, July, p. 1.
Eifermann, R. R. (1989). "It suddenly came to me"—on the "occurrence" of ideas and their sequel. *International Journal of Psychoanalysis, 70*: 115–126.
Eifermann, R. R. (1997). Countertransference in the relationship between reader and text. *Common Knowledge, 6*: 155–178.
Eifermann, R. R. (2006). Die Macht des Unbewussten: beschrieben und inszeniert, verdeckt und enthüllt in Freuds Traumdeutung und in ausgewählten Briefen an Fliess. *Jahrbuch der Psychoanalyse, 53*: 119–139.
Eifermann, R. R. (2007). On the inevitable neglect of the unconscious: a contemporary reminder. In: J. C. Calich & H. Hinz (Eds.), *The Unconscious: Further Reflections* (pp. 133–148). London: International Psychoanalytical Association.
Fenichel, O. (1927). The economic function of screen memories. In: *The Collected Papers of Otto Fenichel* (pp. 113–116). New York: Norton, 1953.
Ferenczi, S. (1949). Confusion of tongues between the adult and the child. (The language of tenderness and of passion). *International Journal of Psychoanalysis, 30*: 225–230. Also in: M. Balint (Ed.), *Final Contributions to the Problems and Methods of Psychoanalysis*. New York: Basic Books.
Ferro, A. (2009). *The Analytic Field: a Clinical Concept*. London: Karnac.
Fine, B., Joseph, E., & Waldhorn, H. (1971). Recollection and reconstruction and reconstruction in psychoanalysis. *Kris Study Group Monograph IV*. New York: International Universities Press.
Fónagy, I. (1999). The process of remembering: recovery and discovery. *International Journal of Psychoanalysis, 80*: 961–978.
Fonagy, P. (1999). Memory and therapeutic action. *International Journal of Psychoanalysis, 80*: 215–223.

Fonagy, P., & Target, M. (1997). Perspectives on recovered memories debate. In: J. Sandler & P. Fonagy (Eds.), *Recovered Memories of Abuse: True or False?* (pp. 183–216). London: Karnac.

Fonagy, P., Gergely, G., Jurist, E., & Target, M. (2002). *Affect Regulation, Mentalization, and the Development of Self.* New York: Other Press.

Freud, S. (1895). *The Complete Letters of Sigmund Freud to Wilhelm Fliess, 1887–1904*, J. M. Masson (Ed. & Trans.). Cambridge, MA: Harvard University Press, 1985.

Freud, S. (1895a). A Project for a Scientific Psychology. *S.E.*, *1*: 281–397. London: Hogarth.

Freud, S. (1895d). *Studies on Hysteria.* S.E., 2. London: Hogarth.

Freud, S. (1896). *Sigmund Freud Briefe an Wilhelm Fließ 1887–1904*, J. M. Masson (Ed.). Frankfurt am Mein: S. Fischer Verlag, 1986.

Freud, S. (1896b). Extracts from the Fliess papers (1892–1899). Letter 52. *S.E.*, *1*: 233–239. London: Hogarth.

Freud, S. (1898b). The psychical mechanism of forgetfulness. *S.E.*, *3*: 287–297. London: Hogarth.

Freud, S. (1899/1952). Über Deckerinnerungen. *G.W.*, *1*: 531–534. London: Imago.

Freud, S. (1899a). Screen memories. *S.E.*, *3*: 299–322. London: Hogarth.

Freud, S. (1900a). *The Interpretation of Dreams.* S.E., 4–5. London: Hogarth.

Freud, S. (1901b). *The Psychopathology of Everyday Life.* S.E., 6. London: Hogarth.

Freud, S. (1901b). Childhood memories and screen memories. In: *The Psychopathology of Everyday Life.* S.E., 6: 43–52. London: Hogarth.

Freud, S. (1905d). *Three Essays on the Theory of Sexuality.* S.E., 7: 135–245. London: Hogarth.

Freud, S. (1905e). *Fragment of an Analysis of a Case of Hysteria.* S.E., 7: 15–122. London: Hogarth.

Freud, S. (1908a). Hysterical phantasies and their relation to bisexuality. *S.E.*, *9*: 155–166. London: Hogarth.

Freud, S. (1908b). Character and anal erotism. *S.E.*, *9*: 167–176. London: Hogarth.

Freud, S. (1908c). On the sexual theories of children. *S.E.*, *9*: 207–226. London: Hogarth.

Freud, S. (1908e). Creative writers and daydreaming. *S.E.*, *9*: 141–153. London: Hogarth.

Freud, S. (1910c). *Leonardo da Vinci and a Memory of his Childhood.* S.E., 11: 63–137. London: Hogarth.

Freud, S. (1911b). Formulations on the two principles of mental functioning. *S.E.*, *12*: 218–226. London: Hogarth.

References

Freud, S. (1914c). On narcissism: an introduction. *S.E.*, *14*: 73–102. London: Hogarth.
Freud, S. (1914g). Remembering, repeating and working-through. *S.E.*, *12*: 147–156. London: Hogarth.
Freud, S. (1915d). Repression. *S.E.*, *14*: 141–158. London: Hogarth.
Freud, S. (1915e). The unconscious. *S.E.*, *14*: 159–215. London: Hogarth.
Freud, S. (1916–1917). *Introductory Lectures on Psychoanalysis*. *S.E.*, *15–16*: 1–496. London: Hogarth.
Freud, S. (1917b). *A Childhood Recollection from Dichtung und Wahrheit*. *S.E.*, *17*: 145–156. London: Hogarth.
Freud, S. (1918b). *From the History of an Infantile Neurosis*. *S.E.*, *17*: 7–122. London: Hogarth.
Freud, S. (1919a). Lines of advance of psycho-analytic therapy. *S.E.*, *17*: 157–168. London: Hogarth.
Freud, S. (1919e). "A child is being beaten". *S.E.*, *17*: 179–204. London: Hogarth.
Freud, S. (1923b). *The Ego and the Id*. *S.E.*, *19*: 1–66. London: Hogarth.
Freud, S. (1925h). Negation. *S.E.*, *19*: 223–239. London: Hogarth.
Freud, S. (1930a). *Civilization and Its Discontents*. *S.E.*, *21*: 64–145. London: Hogarth.
Freud, S. (1933a). Femininity. In: *New Lectures on Psycho-analysis*. *S.E.*, *22*: 112–135. London: Hogarth.
Freud, S. (1937c). Analysis terminable and interminable. *S.E.*, *23*: 209–253. London: Hogarth.
Freud, S. (1937d). Constructions in analysis. *S.E.*, *23*: 255–270. London: Hogarth.
Freud, S. (1939a). *Moses and Monotheism*. *S.E.*, *23*: 1–138. London: Hogarth.
Freud, S. (1940a). *An Outline of Psycho-analysis*. *S.E.*, *23*: 139–208. London: Hogarth.
Freud, S. (1940e[1938]). Splitting of the ego in the process of defence. *S.E.*, *23*: 271–278. London: Hogarth.
Freud, S. (1952). Über Deckerinnerungen. *Gesammelte Werke*, *1*: 531–554. London: Imago.
Freud, S., & Breuer, J. (1895d). *Studies on Hysteria*, *S.E.*, *2*: London: Hogarth.
Gaddini, E. (1984). Changes in psychoanalytic patients up to the present day. In: R. S. Wallerstein (Ed.), *Changes in Analysts and Their Training* (pp. 6–19). IPA Monograph No 4. London: International Psychoanalytic Association.
Gay, P. (1988). *Freud: A Life For Our Time*. London: J M Dent & Sons.

Giacobino, P. A. (2007). Epigenetics in reproductive medicine. *Pediatric Research: An International Journal of Clinical, Laboratory and Developmental Investigation*, *61*(5 Pt 2): 51–57.

Glover, E. (1929). The "screening" function of traumatic memories. *International Journal of Psychoanalysis*, *10*: 90–93.

Good, M. I. (1998). Screen reconstructions: traumatic memory, conviction, and the problem of verification. *Journal of the American Psychoanalytic Association*, *46*: 149–183.

Good, M. I. (1999). Review of: *Recovered memories of abuse: true or false?* J. Sandler & P. Fonagy (Eds.), Madison, CT; International Universities Press. *Journal of the American Psychoanalytic Association*, *47*: 237–240.

Good, M. I., Day, M., & Rowell, E. (2005). False memories, negative affects, and psychic reality: the role of extra-clinical data in psychoanalysis. *International Journal of Psychoanalysis*, *86*: 1573–1593.

Green, A. (1980). Passions and their vicissitudes. On the relation between madness and psychosis. In: *On Private Madness* (pp. 214–253). Madison, CT: International Universities Press, 1986.

Green, A. (2005). *Key Ideas for a Contemporary Psychoanalysis*. London: Routledge.

Greenacre, P. (n.d.). Letter to Ernst Kris. Papers of Ernst Kris. Manuscript Division, Library of Congress, Washington, DC.

Greenacre, P. (1947). Vision, headache and the halo: reactions to stress in the course of superego formation. *Psychoanalytic Quarterly*, *16*: 177–194.

Greenacre, P. (1949). A contribution to the study of screen memories. *Psychoanalytic Study of the Child*, *3*: 73–84.

Greenacre, P. (1950). The prepuberty trauma in girls. *Psychoanalytic Quarterly*, *19*: 298–317.

Greenacre, P. (1951). Respiratory incorporation and the phallic phase. *Psychoanalytic Study of the Child*, *6*: 180–205.

Greenacre, P. (1953a). Certain relationships between fetishism and faulty development of the body image. *Psychoanalytic Study of the Child*, *8*: 79–98.

Greenacre, P. (1953b). Penis awe and its relation to penis envy. In: R. Loewenstein (Ed.), *Drives, Affects, Behavior, Vol. 1* (pp. 176–190). New York: International Universities Press.

Greenacre, P. (1955a). *Swift and Carroll: A Psychoanalytic Study of Two Lives*. New York: International Universities Press.

Greenacre, P. (1955b). "It's my own intervention." A special screen memory of Mr. Lewis Carroll: its form and history. *Psychoanalytic Quarterly*, *24*: 200–244.

Greenacre, P. (1955c). Further considerations regarding fetishism. *Psychoanalytic Study of the Child*, *10*: 187–194.
Greenacre, P. (1955d). The mutual adventure of Jonathan Swift and Lemeul Gulliver—a study in pathography. *Psychoanalytic Quarterly*, *24*: 20–62.
Greenacre, P. (1956). Re-evaluation of the process of working through. *International Journal of Psychoanalysis*, *37*: 439–444.
Greenacre, P. (1958). Early physical determinants in the development of the sense of identity. In: *Emotional Growth, Volume I* (pp. 113–127). New York: International UP, 1971.
Greenacre, P. (1967). Discussion of Dr Boyer's Paper. Papers of Phyllis Greenacre. Manuscript Division, Library of Congress, Washington, DC.
Greenacre, P. (1971). *Emotional Growth: Psychoanalytic Studies of the Gifted and a Great Variety of Other Individuals, Vol. 1*. New York: International Universities Press.
Greenacre, P. (1975). On reconstruction. *Journal of the American Psychoanalytic Association*, *23*: 693–712.
Greenacre, P. (1979). Reconstruction and the process of individuation. *Psychoanalytic Study of the Child*, *34*: 121–141.
Greenacre, P. (1980). A historical sketch of the use and disuse of reconstruction. *Psychoanalytic Study of the Child*, *35*: 35–40.
Greenacre, P. (1981). Reconstruction: its nature and therapeutic value. *Journal of the American Psychoanalytic Association*, *29*: 27–46.
Greenson, R. (1958). On screen defenses, screen hunger and screen identity. *Journal of the American Psychoanalytic Association*, *6*: 242–262.
Grigsby, J., & Hartlaub, G. H. (1994). Procedural learning and the development and stability of character. *Perceptual & Motor Skills*, *79*: 355–370.
Guignard, F. (1996). *Au Vif de l'Infantile. Réflexions sur la situation analytique*. Lausanne: Delachaux, & Niestlé [out of print, please contact the author. First chapter translated in English: The infantile in the analytical relationship. *International Journal of Psychoanalysis*, *76*(6): 1083–1092].
Guignard, F. (2006). La pensée de Jean Laplanche. Convergences et apories. *Revue de Psychiatrie Française*, *37*(3): 90–109.
Guignard, F. (2010). Réflexions d'une psychanalyste sur l'enfant dans la société occidentale d'aujourd'hui. Ecoutes psychothérapiques – Dossier : Adieu Œdipe, bonjour Narcisse? *Filigrane*, *19*(1): 11–27.
Harris, A. (1996). False memory? False memory syndrome? The so-called false memory syndrome? *Psychoanalytic Dialogues*, *6*: 155–187.

Hoffman, I. Z. (1998). *Ritual and Spontaneity in the Psychoanalytic Process*. Hillsdale, NJ: Analytic Press.
Isaacs, S. (1948). The nature and function of phantasy. *International Journal of Psychoanalysis, 29*: 73–97.
James, H. (1881). *The Portrait of a Lady*. London: Penguin, 2003.
James, H. (1913). *A Small Boy and Others*. New York: Scribner.
Joseph, B. (1985). Transference: the total situation. *International Journal of Psychoanalysis, 66*: 447–454.
Joseph, R. (1996). *Neuropsychiatry, Neuropsychology and Clinical Neuroscience*. Baltimore, MD: Williams & Wilkins.
Kanner, L. (1943). Autistic disturbances of affective contact. *The Nervous Child, 2*: 217–250.
Klein, M. (1946). Notes on some schizoid mechanisms. In: *Writings of Melanie Klein Vol. 3* (pp. 1–24). London: Hogarth.
Kris, E. (1956). The recovery of childhood memories in psychoanalysis. *Psychoanalytic Study of the Child, 11*: 54–88.
Kulish, N., & Holtzman, D. (2008). *A Story of Her Own: The Female Oedipus Complex Re-examined and Renamed*. Lanham, MD: Rowman & Littlefield.
LaFarge, L. (2000). Interpretation and containment. *International Journal of Psychoanalysis, 81*: 67–84.
LaFarge, L. (2006). The wish for revenge. *Psychoanalytic Quarterly, 75*: 447–475.
LaFarge, L. (2008). On knowing oneself directly and through others. *Psychoanalytic Quarterly, 77*: 167–197.
LaFarge, L. (2011). Caught in the snare of deception: an exploration of the psychology of being deceived through two novels of Henry James. *Psychoanalytic Quarterly, 80*: 91–120.
LaFarge, L. (2012). The screen memory and the act of remembering. *International Journal of Psychoanalysis, 93*: 1249–1265.
Laplanche, J. (2003). Trois acceptions du mot "inconscient" dans le cadre de la théorie de la Séduction Généralisée. *Sexual. La sexualité élargie au sens freudien*. Paris: P.U.F. Quadrige, 2007.
Laub, D. (1998). The empty circle: children of survivors and the limits of reconstruction. *Journal of the American Psychoanalytic Association, 46*: 507–529.
Lear, J. (2005). *Freud*. New York and London: Routledge.
Levine, H. B. (2011). Construction then and now. In: S. Lewkowicz, T. Bokanowski & G. Pragier (Eds.), *On Freud's "Constructions in Analysis"* (pp. 87–100). London: Karnac.
Levine, H. B., Reed, G. S., & Scarfone, D. (2013). *Unrepresented States and the Construction of Meaning: Clinical and Theoretical Contributions*. London: Karnac.

Lewin, B. D. (1946). Sleep, the mouth, and the dream screen. *Psychoanalytic Quarterly*, *15*: 419–434.
Loftus, E. (1994), The truth that never happened. In: E. Loftus & K. Ketcham (Eds.), *The Myth of Repressed Memory* (pp. 38–72). New York: St. Martin Griffin.
Mahon, E., & Battin, D. (1981). Screen memories and termination of psychoanalysis: a preliminary communication. *Journal of the American Psychoanalytic Association*, *29*: 939–942.
Mahon, E., & Battin-Mahon, D. (1983). The fate of screen memories in psychoanalysis. *Psychoanalytic Study of the Child*, *38*: 459–489.
Mahony, P. (2001). Freud and translation. *American Imago*, *58*: 837–839.
Malcolm, R. (1970). The mirror: a perverse sexual phantasy in a woman seen as a defense against psychotic breakdown. In: E. B. Spillius (Ed.), *Melanie Klein Today, Vol. 2* (pp. 115–137). London: Routledge, 1998.
Mancia, M. (2004). *Sentire le parole* [reprinted in English: *Feeling the Words. Neuropsychoanalytic Understanding of Memory and Unconscious.* London: Routledge, 2007].
Mandler, J. M. (1984). Representation and recall in infancy. In: M. Moscovitch (Ed.), *Infant Memory: Its Relation to Normal and Pathological Memory in Humans and Other Animals* (pp. 75–101). New York: Plenum.
Margolis, N. (1975). Discussion. Archives and Special Collections. A. A. Brill Library, New York Psychoanalytic Society and Institute.
Marty, P. (1991). *Mentalisation et Psychosomatique*. Paris: Les empêcheurs de penser en rond.
Masson, J. M. (Ed. & Trans.) (1985). *The Complete Letters of Sigmund Freud to Wilhelm Fliess, 1887–1904*. Cambridge, MA: Harvard University Press.
Masson, J. M. (Ed.) (1986). *Sigmund Freud Briefe an Wilhelm Fließ 1887–1904*. Frankfurt am Mein: S. Fischer Verlag.
McLuhan, M. (1964). *Understanding Media. The Extensions of Man.* Oxford: Routledge and Kegan Paul.
Meltzer, D. (1973). *Sexual States of Mind.* Strathclyde: Clunie Press.
Meltzer, D. (1984). *Dream-Life. A Re-examination of the Psycho-analytical Theory and Technique.* Strathclyde: Clunie Press.
Molnar, M. (1994). Reading the look. In: S. Gilman, J. Birmele, J. Geller, & V. Greenberg (Eds.), *Reading Freud's Reading* (pp. 77–90). New York: New York University Press.
Moore, B., & Fine, B. (Eds.) (1968). *A Glossary of Psychoanalytic Terms and Concepts* (2nd edn). New York: American Psychoanalytic Assn.

Moore, B., & Fine, B. (Eds.) (1990). *Psychoanalytic Terms and Concepts* (3rd edn). New York: American Psychoanalytic Association.

Muller, J. (2005). Approaches to the semiotics of thought and feeling in Bion's work. *Canadian Journal of Psychoanalysis, 13*: 31–56.

Nadel, L., & Moskowitz, M. (1997). Memory consolidation, retrograde amnesia and the hippocampal complex. *Current Opinion in Neurobiology, 7*: 217–227.

Nissen, B. (2008). On the determination of autistoid organizations in non-autistic adults. *International Journal of Psychoanalysis, 89*: 261–277.

Novick, S. M. (1996). *Henry James: The Young Master*. New York: Random House.

Novick, S. M. (2007). *Henry James: The Mature Master*. New York: Random House.

Ogden, T. (1997). *Reverie and Interpretation: Sensing Something Human*. Northvale, NJ: Aronson.

Pally, R. (1997a). Developments in neuroscience. II: how the brain actively constructs perceptions. *International Journal of Psychoanalysis, 78*: 1021–1030.

Pally, R. (1997b). Memory: brain systems that link past, present and future. *International Journal of Psychoanalysis, 78*: 1223–1234.

Parmat, S. (2010). El difícil camino a la universidad. *La Nación*, 12 October 2010, p. 13.

Peirce, C. S. (1998). What is a sign? In: The Peirce Edition Project (Eds.), *The Essential Peirce, Vol. 2 (1893–1913)* (pp. 4–10). Bloomington, IN: Indiana University Press.

Racker, H. (1957). The meanings and uses of countertransference. *Psychoanalytic Quarterly, 26*: 303–337.

Raphael-Leff, J. (2007). Freud's prehistoric matrix—owing "nature" a death. *International Journal of Psychoanalysis, 88*: 1345–1373.

Reed, G. S. (1993). On the value of explicit reconstruction. *Psychoanalytic Quarterly, 62*: 52–73.

Reichbart, R. (2008). Screen memory: its importance to object relations and transference. *Journal of the American Psychoanalytic Association, 56*: 455–481.

Renik, O. (1993). Analytic interaction: conceptualizing technique in the light of the analyst's irreducible subjectivity. *Psychoanalytic Quarterly, 62*: 553–571.

Sandler, J. (1985). *The Analysis of Defense: The Ego and the Mechanism of Defense Revisited*. New York: International University Press.

Sandler, J., & Fonagy, P. (Eds.) (1997). *Recovered Memories of Abuse: True or False?* Madison, CT: International Universities Press.

References

Schachter, D. L. (1987). Implicit memory: history and current status. *Journal of Experimental Psychology: Learning, Memory and Cognition*, *13*: 501–518.

Schacter, D. L. (1996). *Searching for Memory*. New York: Basic Books.

Schacter, D. L., & Scarry, E. (Eds.) (2000). *Memory, Brain and Belief*. Cambridge, MA: Harvard University Press.

Schacter, D. L., Reiman, E., Curran, T., Yun, L. S., Bandy, D., McDermott, K. B., & Roediger III, H. D. (1996). Neuroanatomical correlates of veridical and illusory recognition memory: Evidence from positron emission tomography. *Neuron*, *17*: 267–274.

Schafer, R. (1983). *The Analytic Attitude*. London: Hogarth.

Schafer, R. (2000). Reflections on "thinking in the presence of the other". *International Journal of Psychoanalysis*, *81*: 85–96.

Schimek, J. G. (1975). The interpretation of the past: childhood trauma, psychical reality, and historical truth. *Journal of the American Psychoanalytic Association*, *23*: 845–865.

Schimek, J. G. (1987). Fact and fantasy in the seduction theory: a historical review. *Journal of the American Psychoanalytic Association*, *35*: 937–964.

Shapiro, T. (1993). On reminiscences. *Journal of the American Psychoanalytic Association*, *41*: 395–421.

Shengold, L. (1989). *Soul Murder*. New Haven, CT: Yale University Press.

Sherry, F., & Schacter, D. L. (1987). The evolution of multiple memory systems. *Psychological Review*, *94*: 439–454.

Shevrin, H. (1994). The uses and abuses of memory. *Journal of the American Psychoanalytic Association*, *42*(4): 991–996.

Siegel, D. J. (1996). Cognition, memory and dissociation. *Child and Adolescent Psychiatric Clinics of North America*, *5*: 509–536.

Spector Person, E., & Klar, H .(1994). Establishing trauma: the difficulty distinguishing between memories and fantasies. *Journal of the American Psychoanalytic Association*, *42*: 1055–1081.

Spence, D. P. (1982). *Narrative Truth and Historical Truth*. New York: Norton.

Spero, M. H. (1990). Portal aspects of memory overlay in psychoanalysis: an object relations contribution to screen memory phenomena. *Psychoanalytic Study of the Child*, *45*: 79–103.

Squire, L. R. (1992). Memory and the hippocampus: a synthesis from findings with rats, monkeys, and humans. *Psychological Review*, *99*: 195–231.

Steiner, J. (1993). *Psychic Retreats: Pathological Organizations of the Personality in Psychotic, Neurotic and Borderline Patients*. London: Routledge.

Stern, D. B. (1997). *Unformulated Experience: From Dissociation to Imagination in Psychoanalysis*. Hillsdale, NJ: Analytic Press.

Strachey, J. (1950). Editor's note to "Screen memories". *S.E.*, *3*: 301–302.

Target, M. (1998). The recovered memories controversy. *International Journal of Psychoanalysis*, *79*: 1015–1028.

Thompson, N. (2011). Ernst Kris: The objects of memory. *Journal of the American Psychoanalytic Association*, *59*: 1009–1022.

Thompson, N. (2012). The transformation of psychoanalysis in America: Émigré analysts and the New York Psychoanalytic Society and Institute, 1911–1961. *Journal of the American Psychoanalytic Association*, *60*: 9–44.

Tulving, E. (1985). How many memory systems are there? *American Psychologist*, *40*: 385–398.

Tustin, F. (1988). Psychotherapy with children who cannot play. *International Review of Psycho-Analysis*, *15*: 93–105.

United Nations (2014). World Autism Awareness Day. https://www.un.org/en/events/autismday.

Verene, D. (1985). *Hegel's Recollection: A Study of Images in the Phenomenology of Spirit*. Albany, NY: State University of New York Press.

Winnicott, D. W. (1967a). Mirror role of mother and family in child development. In: *Playing and Reality* (pp. 111–118). London: Tavistock, 1971.

Winnicott, D. W. (1967b). Postscript. D. W. W. on D. W. W. In: C. Winnicott, R. Shepherd, & M. Davies (Eds.), *Psychoanalytic Explorations* (pp. 569–582). London: Karnac, 1989.

Yovell, Y. (2000). From hysteria to posttraumatic stress disorder: psychoanalysis and the neurobiology of traumatic disorders. *Neuropsychoanalysis*, *2*: 171–181.

Zola-Morgan, S., & Squire, L. R. (1990). The primal hippocampal formation: evidence for a time-limited role in memory storage. *Science*, *250*: 288–290.

INDEX

absence, 32–34, 47, 50, 54, 97, 107, 147, 173–174, 177, 181, 188
abuse, 65, 67–68, 100, 125
  memories of, 65, 67–68, 78
  sexual, 65, 67
affect(ive), 69, 115, 140, 164, 177, 186
  background, 115
  contact, 115
  context, 147
  disconnection from, 115
  distressing, 10
  experience, 49, 177
  incompatible, 69
  memory of, 113–114
  mirroring, 115
  related, 32, 63
  symbolising, 71
  withdrawal of, 152
aggression, 42, 88–89, 112, 156
  reactive, 66
  sexual, 19
Ahumada, J. L., 27–28, 105, 110–111, 115–116
amnesia, 5–6, 60
  childhood, 102, 108, 188
  infantile, 37, 63, 107, 113, 175
  normal, 6
analysis (*passim*)
  applied, 155
  clinical, 58
  defence against, 75
  of children, 35, 60
  of dreams, 93
  of phobia, 12
  of screen memories, 34, 37–38
  personal, 167
  psycho-, 11, 98, 110
  resistance of, 29, 38
  self-, 3, 83, 87, 94, 97–98, 100, 122, 135
  termination of, 106
  training, 105
  transference, 105, 111
anger, 51, 53–54, 112, 130–131, 152
anxiety, 33, 46, 50, 53, 63, 67, 70, 74, 84, 103, 118, 127–129, 131, 134, 153, 160, 167, 187, 189
  castration, 91
  childhood, 47
  death, 119
  fantasy, 154
  -filled dream, 67
  great, 48

-provoking, 83
state, 67˙
travel, 96
Anzieu, D., 90, 93, 103
Arlow, J., 34, 169
Auchincloss, E., 171
Auerhahn, N. C., 43
Aulagnier, P., 43
autism
  epidemic of, 116–117
  World Awareness Day, 115
autistic
  cases, 117
  children, 114
  disturbances, 115
  dynamics, 115
  isolation, 114
  post-, 112–113
  spectrum disorder, 116–117
autistoid, 113
  age, 115
  patients, 111, 115
  shift, 111

Bandy, D., 68
Baranger, M., 41
Baranger, W., 41
Barthes, R., 147
Battin, D., 56
Battin-Mahon, D., 56, 106
Bauer, P. J., 186–188
Beebe, B., 69
behaviour, 108, 127, 133, 173
  change in, 186
  characteristic individual, 62
  disagreeable, 13
  disorders, 126
  human, 179
  mimetic, 116
  neurotic, 149
  routine, 62
Bernfeld, S., 80, 135
Bettelheim, B., 114
Bion, W. R., 40, 43, 69, 105, 132, 175–176, 178–181, 184, 188
  alpha function, 176
Blass, R. B., 100
Blum, H. P., 38–39, 72, 106
Bollas, C., 134
Boston Change Process Study Group, 187–188
Botella, C., 40, 188

205

Botella, S., 40, 188
Boyer, L., 170–171
Brenman, E., 72–73, 78
Brenneis, C. B., 65, 125
Breuer, J., 78, 180
Brooks Brenneis, C., 125
Brown, L., 40, 65
Busch de Ahumada, L. C., 115

Carroll, L., 42, 151, 155–160, 169, 182
case studies
   Chapter Nine
     five-year-old boy, 180–181
     four-year-old girl, 173
   Chapter One
     young woman, 29–33
   Danny, 126–128
   Miss S, 48–56
   Mr T, 128–132
   Tara, 67–68
   Tom, 111, 113–115
Center for Disease Control (CDC), 117
Cohen, N. J., 186
Cohen, S., 27, 34–35, 126
communication, 77, 119, 130, 134, 162, 167
   emotional, 69
   patient's, 76
   relational, 71, 77
   somatic, 169
   verbal, 70, 162, 167
     non-, 162
     -pre, 167
conscious(ness), 19–23, 59, 64, 69, 89, 91, 96, 101, 118, 120–121, 133, 145–146, 148–149, 155, 174, 177, 185–186
   account, 74
   altered states of, 64
   dynamics, 64–65
   effort, 63
   fantasy, 96
   flow of, 134
   idea, 120
   internal perception, 10
   memories, 18, 23, 59–60, 74, 120
   mind, 119
   narrative, 169
   non-, 69, 177, 186
   ostensiveness, 110
   phantasy, 19, 148
   pre-, 168
   processes, 108, 145
   recollection, 172, 177, 186
   self-, 146
   thoughts, 18, 103, 143–144, 146–147
   translation, 137
   version, 19
countertransference, 36–37, 39–41, 55–56, 75, 130, 133
   reaction, 130
Curran, T., 68

Damasio, A., 125
Day, M., 65
daydream, 86–87, 113–115, 175–176
De Masi, F., 66, 70
death, 7, 32, 46, 82, 84, 95, 99, 101–103
   anxiety, 119
   -bed, 104
   of father, 97–101
   of grandfather, 105
   of grandmother, 8, 21, 82
   of mother, 84, 98
   premature, 103
   reality of, 97
   theme of, 96–97
defence/defensive, 10, 20, 28, 36–37, 40, 42, 55, 59, 61, 71, 73–76, 162, 169, 176, 187–188, 190
   disguise, 28
   ego, 165
   function, 28–29, 38, 166
   measures, 153
   mechanisms, 175, 179
   operation, 34, 46
   pathological, 10
   patient's, 64
   patterns of, 165
   process, 34, 124
   purpose, 77
   rigid, 152
   screening, 29, 38
   second, 34
   structures, 121, 153
   system of, 179
Deutsch, H., 115
development(al), 35, 41, 62, 72–73, 81, 105, 138, 165, 176, 182, 188
   advanced level of, 75
   child's, 55
   course of, 39
   delay, 126
   disturbances of, 73
   early, 38
   ego, 153
     super-, 153, 171
   emotional, 73–74
   epoch, 136
   general, 165
   genetic, 161
   landmarks, 166
   later, 61, 169
   libidinal, 153
   maturational, 167
   mental, 60
   neuronal, 177
   of personality, 74
   of psychoanalytic thought, 58
   patterns, 162
   psychic, 75, 176
   psychosexual, 154, 169
   transference, 37, 39, 51, 70
   transition, 138

Index

twofold, 175
unique, 165–166
verbal, 168
displacement, 9–10, 21–22, 28, 32, 34, 59, 71, 89, 139, 144, 153–154, 180–181
dream(s), 21, 29, 33–34, 39, 51–54, 59, 67–68, 75, 85, 87, 93, 96–97, 99–100, 103, 106, 108, 113, 124, 132, 136, 153–156, 158–159, 172, 175–176, 180, 182–183, 186, 190
  activity, 176
  anxiety-filled, 67
  characteristic of, 166
  day-, 86–87, 113–115, 175–176
  field of, 175
  half-, 157
  meaning of a, 164
  memories, 157
  narrative, 179
  night, 175–176
  of nakedness, 21, 87
  quality, 182
  representation, 158
  screen, 42, 155
  thoughts, 28, 180
  within a dream, 54, 159
  work of, 121

Eckert, H., 116
ego, 153, 161, 187, 189
  defences, 165, 179
  development, 153
  immature, 42
  nucleus, 181
  powerful, 28
  psychology, 27, 161
  recollecting, 23
  split in the, 42
  strong, 153
  structures of the, 134
  super-, 42–43, 152, 154–155, 174
    childhood, 151
    development, 153, 171
    early, 43
    formation, 153
    functions, 153
Eifermann, R. R., 34–35, 81, 96
envy, 90, 131
  penis, 170

fantasy, 35–38, 43–47, 49–52, 55–56, 61, 84–85, 87, 95–96, 99, 101, 113–114, 119, 124, 132, 135, 156, 160–161, 164–165, 179, 182–183
  anxious, 154
  bodily, 73
  childhood, 161
  content, 45
  -creations, 87
  excited, 42
  infantile, 63, 165

original, 34
romantic, 87
scenario, 181
sexual, 86
sole, 114
unconscious, 32, 72, 85, 149
  unacceptable, 92
vague, 95
wishful, 93
wish-fulfilling, 114
world of, 54
Fenichel, O., 38
Ferenczi, S., 179
Ferro, A., 181
Fine, B., 38, 106, 163–165, 171
Fonagy, I., 70, 72, 125
Fonagy, P., 43, 65, 125
free association, 39, 123, 134, 155, 169
Freud, S. (*passim*)
  A child is being beaten, 60
  A Childhood Recollection from Dichtung und Wahrheit, 61, 150, 188
  A Project for a Scientific Psychology, 100, 176
  An Outline of Psycho-analysis, 98
  Analysis terminable and interminable, 179
  Character and anal erotism, 61
  Civilization and Its Discontents, 115, 161
  Constructions in analysis, 38, 40, 42, 59, 71, 77, 106–107, 121, 123–124, 151, 163, 189, 191
  Creative writers and daydreaming, 61
  Dora, 101
  Extracts from the Fliess papers (1892–1899). Letter, 52, 60
  Femininity, 98
  Formulations on the two principles of mental functioning, 148
  Fragment of an Analysis of a Case of Hysteria, 101
  From the History of an Infantile Neurosis, 24, 61
  Hysterical phantasies and their relation to bisexuality, 89
  Introductory Lectures on Psychoanalysis, 12, 24, 188
  Leonardo da Vinci and a Memory of his Childhood, 60
  Lines of advance of psycho-analytic therapy, 110
  Moses and Monotheism, 38
  Negation, 177
  On narcissism: an introduction, 109
  On the sexual theories of children, 90
  Rat Man, 4, 24
  Remembering, repeating and working-through, 38, 61, 107, 109, 113, 123, 150, 169, 175
  Repression, 179
  Screen memories, 28, 37, 39, 58–59, 61,

80, 82–85, 87, 89–92, 94, 101, 103, 106, 119–121, 135–136, 138–141, 143, 145–147, 150, 169, 172, 175, 185–186, 189
Sigmund Freud Briefe an Wilhelm Fließ 1887–1904, 95, 99, 136
Splitting of the ego in the process of defence, 179
Studies on Hysteria, 78, 136–137, 140, 147, 180
The aetiology of hysteria, 5
The Complete Letters of Sigmund Freud to Wilhelm Fliess, 1887–1904, 100, 137
The Ego and the Id, 180
The Interpretation of Dreams, 12, 21, 80, 87–89, 91, 93, 97–98, 103, 136, 175
The psychical mechanism of forgetfulness, 118–119, 136, 147
The Psychopathology of Everyday Life, 4, 38–39, 55, 61, 80, 82, 102, 106, 136, 147, 150
The unconscious, 149, 176
Three Essays on the Theory of Sexuality, 89, 95, 188
Über Deckerinnerungen, 85, 136, 138–141, 144–145, 148
Wolf Man, 24

Gaddini, E., 116
Gay, P., 98
Gergely, G., 43
Giacobino, P. A., 183
Glover, E., 38, 114
Good, M. I., 38, 65
Green, A., 116, 188
Greenacre, P., 28, 33, 38–43, 45, 56–57, 59, 65, 106–107, 151–171
Greenson, R., 38
Grigsby, J., 62
Guignard, F., 175–176, 182
guilt, 50, 65–67, 95–96, 128–129, 152, 165, 173–174, 182
-ridden, 32

Harris, A., 65
Hartlaub, G. H., 62
Hoffman, I. Z., 40
Holtzman, D., 54
hysteria/hysterical, 5, 100, 108, 111, 118, 137, 180
character, 66
essential point of, 100
mechanism of, 123
patients, 19, 123
symptoms, 23, 136–137, 146

identity, 47, 56, 73, 76
anchor, 39
genuine, 74
individual, 56

safe, 174
screen, 38
sense of, 146
impulse, 18, 143–144, 146–147, 158
forbidden, 147
sexual, 90
infantile, 44, 182
amnesia, 37, 63, 107, 113
conflicts, 114
events, 165
experience, 59, 71, 73, 76, 162, 175
fantasy, 63, 165
history, 75
life, 6, 60
emotional, 59
memories, 59–60
past, 76
scenes, 110, 114
sexuality, 3, 37
situations, 110
traumata, 28
vicissitudes, 71
wishes, 101
internal, 122, 127, 138
contradictions, 29, 39
discrepancies, 29, 39
evaluation, 74
events, 134, 175, 180
experience, 42, 128, 132–133
factors, 74
imagery, 168
objects, 75, 181
perceptions, 10
perspective, 43
process, 119
psychic state, 167,
psychological state, 169
reality, 78
interpretation, 14, 21–22, 35, 72, 93, 95, 97–98, 102–103, 116, 122, 140, 158, 162–163, 165–166, 187–188
authoritative, 168
correct, 28
genetic, 163–164
psychoanalytic, 124
reconstructive, 167
significant, 168
transference, 39, 75
intervention, 48, 110, 141–142, 151
clinical, 35, 135
effective, 140, 165
semiotic, 138
special technical, 29, 39
Isaacs, S., 61

Jaffe, J., 69
James, H., 44–48, 55
Joseph, B., 75
Joseph, E., 164–165
Joseph, R., 63–64
Jurist, E., 43

Index

Kanner, L., 114–115, 117
Klar, H., 125
Klein, M., 27, 61, 105, 176, 179
Kris, E., 38, 65, 152, 158–159, 161, 165, 170
   Study Group, 164–165
Kulish, N., 54

Lachmann, F., 69
LaFarge, L., 27–29, 34, 40, 43, 48, 106–107
language, 69, 77, 132, 142–143, 146, 148, 162, 175, 178
   centrality of, 148
   conceptual, 188
   evolution, 77
   -specific, 142
   symbolic, 17, 70, 142
   verbal, 70, 162
      pre-, 167
Laplanche, J., 176
Laub, D., 43
Lear, J., 103
Levine, H. B., 176, 188, 191
Lewin, B. D., 42, 154–155
life, 7, 17–19, 24, 51, 55, 71, 74, 78, 83–85, 88, 93, 97–99, 103, 107, 113, 125, 128, 130, 142, 160, 166, 179–181, 184, 188
   comfortable, 17, 142, 144
   conflictual, 168
   -cycle, 36, 38, 106
   daily, 113
   -drive, 183
   early, 45, 80, 82, 94, 102, 155
   emotional, 40, 56, 59
   entire, 156
   epochs of, 61
   exigencies of, 16
   experiences, 101, 182
   family, 30
   first years of, 63, 69
   future, 72
   history, 129, 140
   infantile, 6, 60
   inner, 137
   later, 22, 43, 56
   mental, 10, 24, 40, 78, 123, 133, 139
   -partner, 99
   past, 78, 101
   personal, 63, 122
   phase of, 164
   private, 53
   psychical, 139, 183
   real, 109
   social, 74, 112
   span, 179
   time of, 5
   transience of, 84
   uterine, 177
   whole, 49
Loftus, E., 125

Mahon, E., 56, 106
Mahony, P., 137
Malcolm, R., 43
Mancia, M., 174–176
Mandler, J. M., 186
Margolis, N., 164–166
Masson, J. M., 83–85, 90, 94–96, 99–100, 135–136
McDermott, K. B., 68
McLuhan, M., 116
Meltzer, D., 66, 105, 175
Molnar, M., 147
Mom, J. M., 41
Moore, B., 38, 106, 163–164, 171
Moskowitz, M., 63
Muller, J., 142

Nadel, L., 63
Nissen, B., 113
Novick, S. M., 45–46, 48

object, 23, 47, 50, 61, 65, 68, 75–76, 83, 129, 131–132, 142, 177, 180, 187
   absent, 47
   basic, 174
   beloved, 182
   concrete, 132
   good enough, 73
   human, 73
   impressions of, 148
   internalised, 74, 181
   lost, 71, 182–183
   love, 89, 98, 180, 183
   maternal, 132
   mechanical, 111
   mental functioning, 56
   new, 75
   original, 71
   past, 73
   primal, 73, 76, 174
   primary, 73–74
   relations, 55, 162, 183
   supporting, 78
objective/objectivity, 121, 140
   dimension, 130
   historical/history, 120
      truth, 124
   perceptual material, 61
   radically, 147
   reality, 120, 122
   referents, 138
   shared, 73
   standards, 133
   truths, 35
   veridical, 28
   world, 47
oedipal, 54
   child, 111
   conflict, 53
   desires, 174
   drama, 52

material, 53, 173
mother, 53
phase, 153, 175
pre-, 54, 98, 151
resonance, 143
rivalries, 55, 114, 143
situation, 174
triumph, 54
wishes, 54, 173
Oedipus, 73
complex, 73
myth, 73
Ogden, T., 175

Pally, R., 68, 79, 125
Parmat, S., 116
Peirce, C. S., 142
perception, 178, 185
first, 46
immutable, 28
internal, 10
of reality, 61, 66
original, 63
real, 182
self-, 155
sense-, 11
perceptual
material, 61
origins, 154
similarity, 141
Peskin, H., 43
phantasy, 3, 17–21, 89, 145
conscious, 19, 148
dandelion, 20
image, 186
screen-, 61
suppressed, 20
unconscious, 176, 187
projection/projective, 70–71, 75, 131
identification, 132, 179
of responsibility, 76
primitive, 162
psychic
act of repression, 149
activity, 148
blow, 151
comfort, 180
conflict, 111, 182
contents, 175, 183
development, 75, 176
distress, 125
dynamics, 110, 116
elaboration, 182
events, 70, 119
experience, 132
formations, 55
functioning, 109, 174–175
life, 183
material, 137
mechanism, 136
movements, 182

organisations, 179
phenomena, 175, 186
processes, 105, 122, 137
reality, 28, 38–40, 74, 77–78, 106
receptor, 69, 187
resources, 111
retreat, 74
state, 115, 167
structure, 77, 186–187
traumata, 153
truth, 121, 124
work, 182

Racker, H., 40, 105
Raphael-Leff, J., 98, 103
reality, 61, 65–66, 68, 71–72, 78, 124, 130,
    152, 159, 182–183
alternate, 54
experience of, 43
external, 36, 43, 55, 78, 133–134
falsifications of, 65, 78
field of, 182
figures of, 71
historical, 28, 39, 44, 106
internal, 78
objective, 120, 122
of death, 97
perception of, 61, 66
personal, 102
principle, 173, 178, 183
psychic, 38–40, 74, 77–78, 106, 187
sense of, 110, 153
Reed, G. S., 33–34, 176, 188
Reichbart, R., 55–56
Reiman, E., 68
Renik, O., 40
representation(al), 41, 43, 45, 47, 55–56, 62,
    69, 75, 84, 119, 143, 147–148,
    180–181, 186
capacity, 188
coherent, 188
dream, 158
dynamic, 181
human, 181
nodal, 170
of love, 18, 143, 147
pre-, 77
symbolic, 102
system, 69
theory of, 188
visual, 19, 145
repression, 10, 24, 32, 34, 58, 59, 62, 64,
    68–69, 71, 108–110, 119–120, 123–124,
    136–137, 139, 165, 172, 174–176,
    178–179, 181–183, 187, 189
childhood memory, 189
events, 110
instinctual derivatives, 178
material, 109
memories, 72, 92, 158
normal, 178

Index

primal, 179
product of, 59
psychic act of, 149
thoughts, 19
unconscious, 68, 178
wishes, 64
Roediger III, H. D., 68
Rowell, E., 65

Samberg, E., 171
Sandler, J., 65, 125, 180
Scarfone, D., 176, 188
Scarry, E., 69
Schacter, D. L., 64, 68–69, 125, 133, 186
Schafer, R., 40, 72
Schimek, J. G., 87, 101
self, 42–43, 47, 51, 73, 95, 133–134, 162, 187
   -analysis, 3, 83–84, 87, 94, 97–98, 100, 122, 135, 168
   -awareness, 155, 169
   -castration, 88
   -consciousness, 146
   -evident, 6, 124
   experiencing, 43, 47, 56, 61, 132
   -exposure, 87
   -hate, 30
   healthy, 182
   idealisation of, 76
   inner, 99
   narration of, 72, 138
   omnipotent, 173
   organising, 43
   -perception, 155
   -portrait, 146
   -reflection, 47
   -report, 140
   sense of, 43, 47, 50, 56, 121, 134
sexual, 61, 66, 99
   abuse, 65, 67
   act, 143
   aggression, 19
   congress, 45
   curiosity, 89
   desires, 119
   disposition, 19
   enlightenment, 152
   evocation, 95
   excesses, 95
   excitement, 156, 158
   fantasies, 86
   feelings, 152
   impulse, 90
   intercourse, 97
   matters, 85
   meaning, 85
   picture, 148
   psycho-, 154, 169
   relationship, 173
   secrets, 50
   seduction, 100

   symbolism, 92, 103
   theories, 90
   trauma, 153, 161
   verbal expressions, 85
sexualisation, 66
   mental, 66
sexuality, 50, 53, 89, 102, 113
   budding, 90
   infantile, 3, 37
   latent, 88
   themes of, 96
Shapiro, T., 38–39
Shengold, L., 132
Sherry, F., 186
Shevrin, H., 125
Siegel, D. J., 63
Simon, B., 100
Spector Person, E., 125
Spence, D. P., 72
Spero, M. H., 57, 61, 65
splitting, 42–43, 76, 112, 179
Squire, L. R., 186
Steiner, J., 74
Stern, D. B., 40
Strachey, J., 92, 102, 122, 135, 137, 139, 141, 144, 148
subjective
   experience, 133
   feeling, 20
   interaction, 81
   nature, 102
   psychic reality, 28
   sense of pastness, 133
   significance, 98
subjectivity, 40, 46, 102, 133, 138
   fragmentary, 138
   inter-, 190
   sensations, 155
symbol(-ic), 18, 59, 69, 82, 87, 92, 103, 137, 142, 144, 154, 166, 175–176, 178, 182
   a-, 114
   affects, 71
   connections, 80
   events, 174
   expression, 174
   formula, 142, 147
   language, 17, 70, 142
   links, 143
   masturbation, 87
   non-, 174
   representation, 102
   sexual, 92, 103
   shape, 177
   terms, 82
   verbal, 142–143, 145–146
   wishes, 174

Target, M., 43, 65, 125
Thompson, N., 28, 161, 170
transference, 36–40, 50–51, 54–56, 71–72, 75, 105, 109–110, 133–134, 167

analysis (of), 75, 105, 111
authoritative, 163
developments, 37, 39
dynamics, 74
enactment, 111
hostile, 109
interpretation, 39, 75
manifestation, 74
maternal, 53
obstructed, 114
persecutory, 70
positive, 30
psychotic, 70
relationship, 114
situation, 49, 53
themes, 53
unobjectionable, 76
trauma(tic), 28, 38–39, 42–44, 47, 49, 55, 64, 67–68, 70, 73, 75–78, 106–107, 114, 161, 163, 165, 171–172, 178, 182, 187, 190
   character, 73
   childhood, 42, 47
   content of, 56
   early, 28, 107, 178
   emotional, 66, 70, 73, 78
   events, 59, 64, 154, 164, 178, 183, 190
   experience, 43, 130, 132, 153, 165
   form, 73
   impressions, 128
   infantile, 28
   interest in, 39
   meaning, 178
   memories, 37, 42, 64, 118, 129–130, 132–133
   non-visual, 42
   origins, 42
   post, 128, 132–133
   psychic, 153
   real, 42, 165
   relationship, 70
   scenes, 110
   separations, 127
   sexual, 153, 161
   significance, 61
   situation, 182–183
   theory, 161
   understanding of, 43
   unspeakable, 181
   world, 54
Tulving, E., 186
Tustin, F., 114

unconscious(ness), 17–19, 35, 59, 61, 69–70, 76–77, 79, 83, 87, 91, 136–137, 143–149, 174, 176–177, 181–182, 185, 190
   articulation, 149
   awareness, 76
   composition, 143
   conflict, 109
   connections, 119

construction, 35, 136, 179
content, 34
dynamics, 35, 58, 61, 65, 69, 71, 81
   psychic, 110
elements, 38
emotional, 71, 78
fantasy, 32, 72, 86–87, 92–93, 149
functions, 71, 77, 136, 174, 176
infantile
   scenes, 110, 114
   situations, 110
   wishes, 101
layer, 119
linguistic activity, 145
manipulation, 64
material, 182
mechanisms, 119
memories, 18, 164, 175
organisational structures, 69
phantasies, 114, 176, 187
processes, 108, 119–120, 142, 145
   mental, 121
psychodynamic, 72
reading, 145
receptive, 71, 76–78
repressed, 177
second, 176
stage directions, 146
stratum, 119
terror, 112
thoughts, 18, 64, 143–144, 148
translation, 147
unrepressed, 177
visual form, 146
working-over, 136
writing, 145
United Nations, 115

Verene, D., 137

Waldhorn, H., 164–165
Winnicott, D. W., 111, 115
working through, 30, 41, 111, 119, 132, 165, 178, 181, 183, 190
   psychoanalytic, 176
world, 54, 56, 58, 91, 132, 183
   Autism Awareness Day, 115
   external, 23, 54, 132
   grandiose, 77
   imagined, 42
   object, 47
   of adults, 112
   of fantasy, 54
   private, 54, 56
   psychological, 151
   traumatic, 54

Yovell, Y., 65, 67, 75
Yun, L. S., 68

Zola-Morgan, S., 186